Overcoming
Life's Challenges

MOYA MULVAY

Copyright © 2016 by Moya Mulvay

Dedication

I would like to dedicate this book to my husband Rob, my children Sharon, Ryan, and Kane and my grandchildren Caitlyn, Hannah, Devon and Ava.

Thank you for your love and support, which have absolutely inspired me, and for the wonderful journey we have been on all these years, the one called life, the one made worthwhile by a very strong and beautiful love.

You have just taken the first step of the rest of your journey...

Congratulations on purchasing my book and I hope you enjoy reading it as much as I enjoyed writing it. I truly hope I can inspire you to move forward and break free from the things that are holding you back.

Please feel free to go to my website, www.inspirational-quotes-and-thoughts.com and browse through the articles and download these books for free as a bonus:

- Alcoholics Anonymous: The story of how many thousands of men and women have recovered from alcoholism.
- Patrick Meninga, *Overcome addiction*
- A list of questions for working the 12 Step program for recovery from addictive behaviour.
- 18 Steps to Create Change in Your Life.
- The *Think and Grow Rich* workbook.
- Outstanding Money Savings Tips.
- Believe it and you will Achieve it.

And, of course, there are many other books on my website http://www.inspirational-quotes-and-thoughts.com/ that you can download either for free or for a nominal fee. Some have been around for over a hundred years, yet they are so inspirational that we can still use the advice they contain in this day and age.

Contents

Acknowledgements 11
Introduction 15
The Beginning–Daughter
  of a Millionaire 18
Sent off to Boarding School 23
Growing Up with Parents Who Were Never There 31
Making My Own Fun 38
My First Marriage 44
Pregnant with Sharon 47
Pregnant with Ryan 49
The Writing's On the Wall 52
Moving Up North 53
The Demon Drink 59
A Single Mum: On My Own 63
Running Away to Perth 67
Break ups, Alcohol, Drugs, a Suicide Attempt and Marriage
  Number 2 73
  - Alcohol and Drugs 73

Pregnant with Kane: Here for a Reason 78
What No One Tells You When You're Pregnant 82
Marrying Rob 87
Drinking Stories: the Bad Old Days 88
- Attempting Suicide 90
Why and When I Gave Up Drinking and Drugs 96
Are You An Alcoholic? 99
My Father's Legacy 101
Out of the Blue: Bankruptcy 104
Another Business Down 108
- Whatever it takes 110
- Breaking Free 112
Getting Out of the Hole 114
Nutrimetics: Opportunity Knocks 118
- Journey to Success 119
- My First Nutrimetics Car 123
- A Big Day 124
- Speaking in Hawaii 126
- Tasmania, Here I Come 129
- The Power of a Positive Environment 132
Real Estate: A New Direction 135
- New Goals, New Purpose 136
- Never Too Old 136
- The Pursuit of Knowledge 139
- You Reap What You Sow 141
- Mission: Create Wealth 143
Losing Mum 146
Trashed! 149

My Daughter Becomes a Mother	154
The Fall: 2008	159
Bankruptcy No. 2	170
It's All Connected	175
Bankruptcy: the Full Story	181
- What to consider before declaring bankruptcy	183
- If You Can, Avoid Bankruptcy	183
- Protect Yourself	187
- You're Not the Only One Who Has Faced This Situation	188
- After Bankruptcy: Take Responsibility and Prepare For the Future	189
Educate Yourself and Your Children	194
- Change Those Voices in Your Head	196
- Believe In Yourself	198
- Challenges: Embrace Them	201
Just Do It	205
Getting Real: My Website and Books	209
Weight Issues and Bulimia	219
- An Overweight Child	219
- Bulimia Begins	220
- What is Bulimia?	221
- Are you bulimic? Is someone you love bulimic? Here are some signs:	222
- How Socialising Contributed To My Bulimia	223
Slimming Pills: An Addiction	226
- Effects of Slimming Pills	226
The Anthony Robbins Seminar That Changed my Life	229
- Hypnosis and Visualisation	232
Life as An Overweight Adult	235

The Journey to Better Health 238
   - Getting to the Root of the Problem 240
   - Diet is a Four-Letter Word 241
   - Excuses, Excuses 242
   - What is Your Passion and Your Goal? 243
   - The Benefits of Regular Exercise 246
   - The Difference Between Strength and Cardiovascular Training 247

My Diet and Exercise Routine 249
   - Moya's and Rob's Breakfast 250
   - Other Breakfast Options 251
   - Snack Options 251
   - Lunch Options 251
   - Dinner Options 252
   - Dessert Options 252
   - My Routine at the Gym: 252

Falling off the Rails: Don't Belt Yourself Up 255

Stories of My Family 258
   - Kane's Story 258
   - Kane's Story 264
   - Where Kane is Now 267
   - Ryan's Story 270
   - Sharon's story 271
   - My Daughter's Stroke 272

Living the Dream: Backpacking through Egypt 278

Back to Daily Life: More Health Issues 293
   - The Nail Biter 293
   - Tips to Stop Biting Your Nails 296
   - Panic Attacks 298
   - Melanoma: A Health Scare 298
   - Gallstones: A Pain in the Back 300
   - What is the Gallbladder, and What Are the Symptoms of Gallstones? 300

www.inspirational-quotes-and-thoughts.com.

- Diagnosed with Hypothyroidism 301
- What the Thyroid Does.. 302

Finding Your Purpose 307
- How do you think?.. 308
- How does a purpose make you feel? 310
- The process 312

Ingredients for Success 316
- Goals, resilience, sense of humour 317
- Motivation, determination, energy 318
- Belief in yourself, enthusiasm and self respect 318
- Commitment and persistence....................................... 319
- Initiative and risk taking ability.................................... 319
- Planning and preparation 320
- Resourcefulness and discipline 322
- Creativity, a desire to learn and knowledge.................. 322
- Self-made "Luck" and integrity 323
- Ingredients For Success 323

Taking Stock.. 325

Epilogue 333

Appendix I... 336

Appendix II 341

Appendix III.. 343

www.inspirational-quotes-and-thoughts.com.

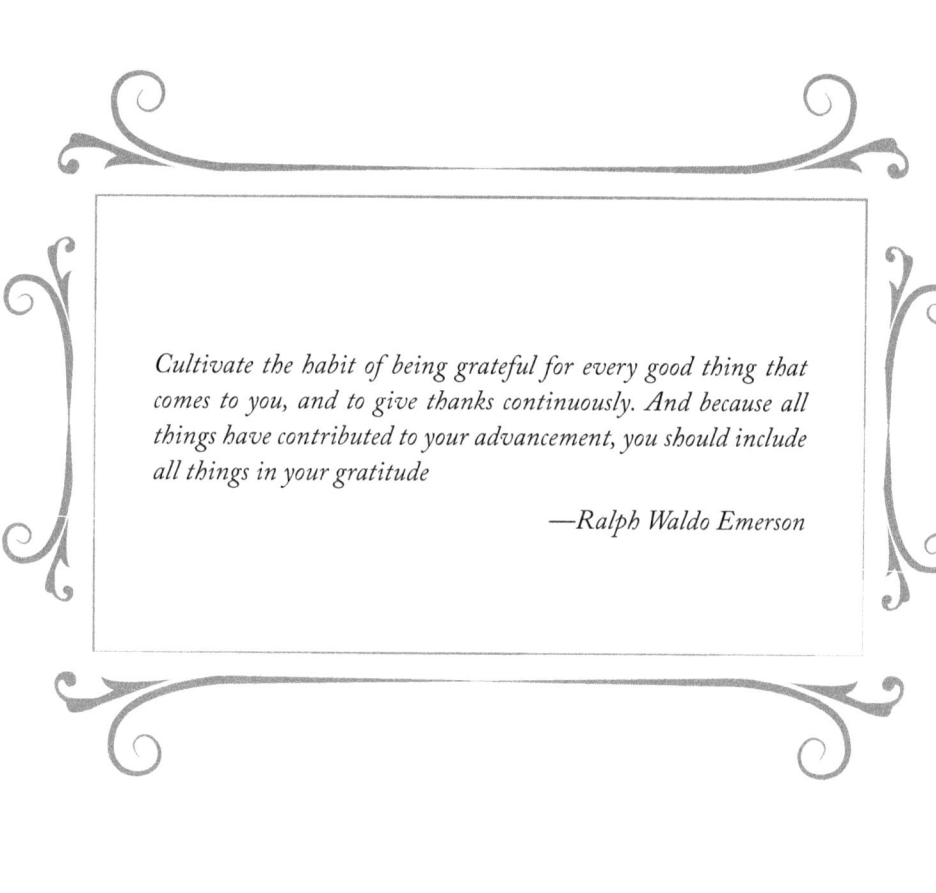

Cultivate the habit of being grateful for every good thing that comes to you, and to give thanks continuously. And because all things have contributed to your advancement, you should include all things in your gratitude

—*Ralph Waldo Emerson*

Acknowledgements

The path to overcoming many challenges and addictions is not a smooth and easy journey—not for me and not for my loved ones during my journey of self-discovery.

I knew I was here for a reason and I just had to find out what it was. I now believe paying it forward is my path. By sharing what I have been through, I truly hope that it will help whoever reads my story find that needed support and push to conquer the challenges they may have in their life. I hope my story serves as a torchlight that helps readers find their own way to healing and happiness, one step at a time.

Big love and gratitude to Amy, Michelle, Faisal, Leila, Ian, Rutchel, Shelley, Richell, and last but by no where least, my sister Cheryl.

Thank you to Margot for giving me the confidence to write from the heart, for nudging me to get more and more down on the page and then making sure my book makes sense. I wouldn't have had the courage to keep peeling back the layers until I dug deep enough to bring them all to the surface.

To Andrew and Julie Matthews who published part of my story in their book "Happiness in Hard Times."

I would like to express my gratitude to you all and to the many people who saw me through this book; to all those who provided support, talked things over, read, wrote, offered comments, and assisted in the editing, proofreading and design and helped me make sense of my words.

And finally, to my husband, Rob. This was a long haul for you, too, and there's so much to thank you for. Thank you for being such a smart, insightful first editor. Thank you for the times you've offered me the hug I needed at the end of the day. I would never have come so far without you by my side. You are and will always be my rock.

To my wonderful children Sharon, Ryan and Kane who have cried as I shared my story with them. While writing this book, I also gained valuable insights from my children.

And to you my reader—this book is for you. I wrote it to help you realize that you are never alone in your challenges. That you can overcome anything, if you work hard to make the right decisions every day. I am offering you my story as a source of encouragement and inspiration.

To my family and friends, you are what matters most of all. I know that without you I am nothing.

Wishing you the best of success, love and laughter,

—Moya

"Difficult times have helped me to understand, better than before, how infinitely rich and beautiful life is in every way, and that so many things that one goes worrying about are of no importance whatsoever."

—Isak Dinesen

Introduction

You picked up this book because you were curious about a real life story of someone who has repeatedly succumbed to alcoholism, despair, bankruptcy and being overweight, but has found an effective way to move past it…and flourish.

You want to know what leads people to do this and what goes on inside the mind of people struggling with addiction. (In my case, the main addiction was alcohol).

You want to know how people like me have found the solution and the courage to give it up for good, maybe in order to help yourself or a loved one. Or you simply want to educate yourself about this very real substance abuse disorder by hearing the facts straight from the mouth and mind of a person who was once an alcoholic.

No matter how this book landed in your hands, my hope is that my life story will be a source of inspiration for you, and that you may find the courage and the strength to overcome bad habits that may be preventing you from living the life you are meant to live.

It is also my hope that you will recognize that there is a real person behind every story of addiction. This person, like you, also experiences sadness, joy, and the inner struggles that he or she has failed to conquer at one point in their life—struggles that sometimes became stronger than their will to fight, because the inner self has long been consumed by unresolved battles.

I am no writer, but I have a huge passion for helping people. I do not have traditional qualifications or credentials, but one thing I do have is experience. I have been there and done that, and I am now able to share my first hand experiences and what I have learned along the way.

This book covers my experiences both as a child and as an adult, the challenges I faced, and how I moved forward in the face of daunting odds. It is my hope that you will find my story inspiring and helpful as you continue your own journey. By sharing my past, I want to give you a shortcut to health, wealth (and I don't mean in the monetary way) and personal fulfilment.

I hope that my story touches you in some way, and that you, too, may discover how life gives us unlimited chances to heal, change, and grow, for as long as we breathe.

*"Everything that has a beginning has an ending.
Make your peace with that and all will be well."*

— *Jack Kornfield, Buddha's Little Instruction Book.*

The Beginning – Daughter of a Millionaire

In preparation for writing this book, and this chapter in particular, I sat down with my sister, Cheryl. There were certain things that I wanted to double-check with her, including whether my memories were accurate. When I looked back on my childhood, I thought to myself, *it couldn't have been that bad!* But after talking to Cheryl, it turns out that it was. I realize now that when I was growing up, Cheryl was really my 'mother'. She was the person who looked out for me and kept me safe, even though she was so young, just a kid, just four years older than myself. Cheryl was even the one who told me about sex, as Mum was too embarrassed to even mention it to me.

Writing this has been difficult, as it has stirred up a lot of buried feelings for me, but it has also helped me to understand and accept the truth of what happened.

Let me begin by telling you about my childhood.

My name is Moya. In Irish, *Moya* means 'bitter,' but in Spanish, it means 'greatness.' My parents weren't aware of these meanings, but perhaps my name foretold my future…that I'd have a bitter experience with alcoholism, but I would also discover my inner greatness and conquer this addiction and all the issues that led to it.

I was born in Pinjarra, a small town in Western Australia and a 20-minute drive from where I live now, in a city called Mandurah. I have lived most of my life in Mandurah and the only reason I wasn't born here is because our town didn't yet have its own hospital.

From the time I was born until I was four years old, we lived between the Peninsula Hotel in Mandurah, which my father owned and worked in (there was a little shack at the back where we stayed), and a place called Subiaco. Subiaco is a suburb an hour's drive away, in Metropolitan Perth.

I have one sister, Cheryl and one brother, Harold, both older than me. My brother and I were sickly as children. My brother suffered from bronchitis and I laboured from whooping cough, so Mum stayed at home with us in Subiaco, while my Dad worked at the hotel, coming to visit us on weekends.

Living in Subiaco, with Dad working in Mandurah, was a lonely life for Mum, being without her husband and stuck with us kids, and it was around this time that she started to drink.

One shocking experience for Mum was when I was about 18 months old. On this particular night, I had a coughing fit and swallowed my tongue. As you can imagine, Mum panicked! Not knowing what to do, she finally put her finger in my mouth to pull out my tongue. Alas, I clamped down on her finger with my teeth and wouldn't let go! Then I had a seizure. At the same time, Mum was screaming out to my siblings to run next door and get the neighbours.

Mum's actions saved me. It must have given her a real fright, as she was all on her own, something I would also go through when I became a mother.

My father spent decades building up the family business that would make him a millionaire.

In 1899, the future Lord Mayor of Perth, W.G. Brookman, built an eleven-room, weatherboard holiday home on 3.5 acres of prime land. It changed hands a few times until in the late 1920's my paternal grandfather bought it with my father's money, because Dad was too young, at the time, to hold a licence. My father then transformed the house into what was to become the Hotel Peninsula.

Over the years, Dad built the hotel up from nothing into a multimillion-dollar business. It became a landmark in Mandurah, the primest bit of real estate in the whole of Australia. It was magnificent!

The Hotel Peninsula

The hotel was built on a point right on the water. It had water views all around it, overlooking the whole of Mandurah, and it was located right in the middle of town.

My father created the hotel in stages, bit by bit, piece by piece.

When he first bought the property, there was no drinking water on that side of the river, so he built a bridge from the hotel to the town site and ran a pipe along the bridge to the other side to service not just the hotel, but nearby properties, too.

Dad worked long and hard to make the Peninsula Hotel as spectacular as it was. He came up with the idea of building a retaining wall around the property, since it was surrounded on three sides by water. Eventually, one side was filled in to create a caravan park and later, a marina.

My father had a vision, which he realised. As the hotel was by water, he had a boatshed, jetty, petrol bowsers and hire boats. Over on the other point, he built a jetty where people could pull up in the boats and come in for a drink.

Mandurah had never seen anything like this. Dad made the Peninsula into a family hotel where the locals could go. It even had a playground and TV room for the kids. The playground was situated in a place that you had a full view of when sitting in the front bar or the beer garden. The TV room was in the boatshed. Dad had a black and white TV put in there, and the kids loved it.

In addition to being a hotel, this was also our home. It was a big wonderland with room to play, make cubbies, go out in the boats, swim off the jetty, and catch prawns, crabs and fish.

What an amazing environment for my siblings and me to grow up in!

When I was about four years old, the house we had been building in Mandurah was completed, so we left Subiaco and moved back to Mandurah and into our new home. It was a lovely home with stairs that led up to a great big balcony around the top of the house, on a huge block that went from the main street right through to the street at the back.

Even to this day, I remember my dad and brother climbing up the ladder (eventually replaced by stairs) and me at the bottom of the ladder asking Dad if I could come up too, to which he replied, "You're too little to climb up here!" I was already an adventurer. I wanted to get into everything.

"Your children need your presence more than your presents."
—Jesse Jackson

Sent off to Boarding School

People might jump to the conclusion that growing up in a hotel and seeing my parents drink all the time was the source of my problem. But, no, that didn't start my alcoholism. It probably started with the profound loneliness and isolation I felt in my younger years.

I attended the only primary school in town for two years. When I was five years old, Cheryl and Harold went off to boarding school, so they were hardly ever around. It was like being an only child.

When I was eight years old, it was my turn, so just like my sister, I was packed off to Methodist Ladies College, a very strict boarding school. The school had been built by convicts, and it felt just like a jail. We were extremely restricted as to what we could and couldn't do.

When I arrived, I was the youngest student at the school and I remained there until I was 15 years old. There, I completed my junior year, before leaving to work at our hotel.

During my boarding school years, every three weeks I would come home for the weekend. Because it was a weekend, Dad would be working at the hotel. Mum was sometimes home on Saturdays, but on Sundays, she would leave us at home and catch up with her friends at the hotel, drinking, so there wasn't much time left to spend with me.

At school there was no TV or radio, and we had to ask permission to use the phone.

The bedrooms were actually dormitories, the smallest having four beds and the largest having about 25. The beds were those wire-based beds with a kapok mattress, not at all comfortable. You had a small wardrobe and locker next to your bed, and that was it. The beds weren't blocked off, so there was no privacy. If you were a bit shy about getting undressed in front of everyone, too bad! There was nowhere else to go.

The bathrooms were shared and had about 10 showers each and there would be a roster to say who could use them and when.

My sister Cheryl was still a student at the school for the first couple of years I was there. However, she was in a different building to me, so I never got to see much of her.

I remember meal times being difficult. At first, Cheryl and I were at the same table and Cheryl had to show me how to use a knife and fork so I could eat properly. I used to get teased by the older girls because I had no table manners. I don't remember this part, but Cheryl told me they would give me a hard time, and I would get so upset that I'd cry.

Because Cheryl is four years older than me and the older girls were separated from the younger ones, the two of us were soon separated and had to sit at different tables for meals.

Even though the school was strict and "proper," I definitely didn't learn any good food habits at school. Our meals were what most people were eating in the 50s. We would get a basic main course, followed by sweets. There was also a tuckshop full of lollies, where we would purchase our "stash" to snack on in the afternoon.

One ritual we had at break-up time was midnight feasts. At this time, everyone would sneak food in (once again, lollies), and once the lights went out, we would make pigs of ourselves. Already, I can see an addictive behaviour pattern starting.

Morning tea, which we called "scrap," consisted of either bread and jam or ginger nut biscuits, which we referred to as "dog biscuits". They would come out on big silver trays and we would line up to get our ration.

I was just eight years old, but all of us girls had to strip our own bed every week, wash our sheets, polish our shoes, tidy up, and make the bed with hospital corners. I also had to wash my clothes and then iron them. I look at my grandchildren now and no way in the world would I expect them to do the things I used to do at that age!

But habits are catching, and because school insisted we do hospital corners when making the bed, I later taught my children to do the same. When my son Ryan joined the Army Reserves, he thanked me for teaching him because he'd been doing hospital corners for so long, he had them down pat. He was the only one in the Reserves who knew how to do them and he felt pretty proud of himself!

When I look back, I remember incidents like the night I got into trouble for talking after the lights went out and I was forced to stand in the passage. Well, they forgot about me, and I ended up falling asleep on the floor, huddled up in a ball, freezing, as I only had my nightie on. I was miserable, but I thought I'd better not move or go back to bed, because I would get into even more trouble. Eventually, someone came out, saw me and put me back to bed.

Up until I was 12, I was boarded at Langsford House, a house totally separate from the main school, where the young girls went to classes and lived.

I loved exploring, and around the side of the building was a big room the school used for storing all our sports gear. One day when I was in there, I discovered a hole at the back of the room, and on closer inspection, realized it was a tunnel. Being inquisitive, I decided to crawl in there. It was very tight and I felt a little scared because I didn't know what could happen. At the same time, I felt excited about what I might find.

The tunnel was long, and went into a room, with another opening going into another room. In addition, there was a tunnel coming off the original room, but there had been a landslide in there. A group of us thought of digging it out, but wisely decided against it in case we got trapped. So it could be interesting at times, and yes, fun going there, as the convicts had built it, but it was a bit spooky. One of the girls decided to go through the tunnel, but as she was crawling through, she became stuck. She couldn't breathe and started to panic. None of us knew that she was claustrophobic! Luckily, I was still at the entrance of the tunnel, so I crawled in there, tried to calm her down and then dragged her out. She never went back again.

You would think that once you had done this, because there was nothing to see, why go back? But something kept drawing me back there. Maybe it was because there had been convicts crawling through the tunnels at one stage. Did they escape? Did they hide? Yes, it was a mystery, and that part of it I loved.

Sitting on my bed one day, I dropped my doll on the floor. I jumped off the bed to pick her up, but when I looked under the bed, I saw a trapdoor. With the excitement of the unknown, I very quietly dragged my bed to one side and, careful not to make a noise, I lifted up the trapdoor.

Looking in, I could see some steps going down. We always had torches, so I grabbed one and climbed down the wooden steps to a room about the size of a small bedroom. This tiny room became my sanctuary. I used to spend a lot of time down there, making it my own little home. I took some chalk from the classroom and drew pictures and my name in code on the walls of my new home. It was my special little hideaway where I could be on my own. I would love to go back there one day, go down there and see if my name is still on the wall, see if anyone else found it and put their mark on it as well. Maybe one day.

As I grew a little older, we had a choice of doing extra sports or other activities in the afternoon, and since I had a passion for dressmaking, I chose to do that. I always wore Cheryl's hand-me-downs, which is why I was probably so interested in sewing. At last I could get creative, making my own clothes and not only mine, but eventually my children's and my husband's. In the future, this would become my means of living.

When I was married, as a dressmaker, I did a lot of weddings. One was for a friend, and it was wonderful to see her walk down the aisle with her three bridesmaids, all in dresses I had made. At the reception, her husband got up and thanked me for making the dresses, praising me for the wonderful job I had done. This was the first bit of recognition I'd had and it felt good. I can see now that it was the beginning of me wanting to achieve so that people would notice and praise me. It's an eye opener when you think back on your life and realize, "Ah, so that's why."

When I was in high school, there was a room at the side of one of the buildings where we could keep mice. I started raising mice – both white and brown "house mice" – in cages I had set up and every day, I would go and feed them. They were a bit smelly, but I loved them.

I now realize why I had them. The mice were something to love and, in a funny way, I felt that they loved me. Because I was feeding and looking after them, they depended on me. I even watched as they gave birth and I suppose, in my own way, I felt like their mother. I felt wanted and it was a nice feeling.

Mum had some cages made up for me, but the guy who made them didn't put the right wire on them. You can imagine what happened. I came home and put the mice in their shiny new cages and shortly after, they chewed through the wire and escaped. I had lost my babies, and I was devastated! And Mum was not happy.

At school, we had to study for an hour in the morning, and at night we had another couple of hours of study time, so it was pretty full on. I wasn't an "A" student–far from it! I was in a class that taught typing and office work, and I didn't really try that hard, as I knew I would be working at the hotel for the rest of my life. I had no way of knowing that we would eventually lose it.

Every Sunday morning, we students would get dressed up in our white dresses, hats and gloves, line up and then walk down to the Church for Sunday school. The highlight was communion and I always looked forward to the wine…a sign of things to come.

On Sunday afternoons, we would get dressed up in our party frocks and wait for visitors, but very few people came to see me. My aunt and uncle came a few times. A couple of times, Harold and his mates came over from Scotch College, where he went to school; once, he even roller-skated over and it wasn't a short distance!

Mum and Dad never came to visit. Not once. I suppose Mum's way of compensating was writing letters, and each time she wrote, she would put in 10 shillings as pocket money which, of course, I always spent on lollies at the tuck shop. But money does not buy love. Mum's letters were always lovely, telling me how much she missed me and loved me, but they were just words. In the real world, she would never show those feelings to me.

When we were older, we were allowed out for one hour on Saturdays to go down to the shops and this was the highlight of the week. We would get all dressed up and walk there, not to buy anything, but just to get out of school and be free. It was wonderful! Such a small thing, but such a highlight.

One thing used to annoy me. As I mentioned, I used to make my own clothes. The girls liked them and we used to share each other's clothes, but sometimes I would go to put on a dress and it wouldn't be there, and when I went down to tea, another girl would have it on. At school there was no privacy or respect for other people's possessions.

Our school was right on the river, high up on a cliff. Next door was a school for boys, Christ Church, and when I was 14, half dozen of us decided to go down the cliff to look around, exploring, but with no intention of going to the boy's school.

We scrambled up the cliff with our heads down so we could see where we were going. Just as we got to the fence and looked up, there was a teacher, standing with her hands on her hips. We were in trouble! The teacher accused us of sneaking over to the boys' school, and we were marched straight into the principal's office.

We were grounded for a whole term! Half of us had to wash dishes at lunchtime, and the other half had to wash them at teatime. We had to clean up the yards for rubbish and report in every day.

On top of that, we weren't allowed home, or anywhere else, for the whole term. Everything was so strict, but we knew no different.

School was an hour's drive away from home and one day Mum drove over to pick us up. On the way home, there was some traffic congestion. Mum became so overwhelmed that she pulled the car over and cried her eyes out. After a bit, she pulled herself together and made it home. But in the end, the drive had been too much for her and she never picked us up again. So, to get back and forth between school and home, our aunt and uncle, or friends of the family, or even the odd barman, had to drive us.

When we rode with our aunt and uncle, we weren't exactly in good hands. Once when they came to get us, Uncle parked behind another car, but didn't notice that his car was in drive and just sat there as he drove straight into the car in front. He hadn't realized we were moving; he thought the car in front of us was backing into him. It wasn't. We would often drive with him, on the road, with other cars…

My education was good, I suppose, although I have nothing to compare it with, but I do remember that we were doing home economics one day when the teacher said, "On Mondays, you do the washing and on Tuesdays, you do the ironing." She was teaching us how to be housewives and even back then, I thought to myself, *what if you want a career?*

Because I didn't live at home, I missed out on so much – simple but special things like bedtime stories, a kiss goodnight, a hug when I was hurt or upset. There was so much missing, but back then, I didn't realize it was missing, because I'd never had it. And frankly, even if I'd lived at home, I wouldn't have gotten it either!

I'm just so glad I was able to break the cycle of neglect with my own children. Even though my life has sometimes been hell, there have always been love and cuddles for my children who were, and are, everything to me.

"No child, no matter what path they may have chosen, should be abandoned by the people who should love them the most. When two people come together and make the conscious decision to create a life, they have an obligation to protect and love that child until death."

—S.L. Jennings

Growing Up with Parents Who Were Never There

Mum wasn't all bad. One incident that I remember quite clearly, took my breath away. I was six or seven. I came home from school and saw that Mum had built me a cubby out of leftover bricks at the side of a shed. (She knew I loved my cubbies.) I remember crying because I was so happy that she had done this for me.

Contrast this with when I was 10 and ready to get braces. I had way too many teeth, so I had to have a few taken out, and stitches. Cheryl, who would have been just 14 at the time, and I caught a taxi from school into the centre of Perth to the dentist's, about half an hour's drive. As I walked in, I was shaking. I was terrified, as I didn't know what they were going to do to me, and whether it would hurt. They called me into the room and I was ushered into the dentist's chair. There was a strong light above me and the smell was terrible. I was put under using a local anaesthetic and had three teeth pulled, and my gums stitched up. When I came to, there was blood everywhere, and I felt groggy and sick and left the room crying. They called a taxi for us and Cheryl helped me to walk, as I was very wobbly. I was so out of it that I slept on Cheryl's lap.

I was put into sick bay at school. Since I was really not well and very sore, Cheryl wanted to stay with me, but they wouldn't let her. At a time like this, a child needs a bit of TLC from their mum or dad, and a loved one to look after them and hug and comfort them. What a child doesn't need is to be thrown into a cold sick bay, all alone, getting checked every now and then by an even colder nurse. There is no way in this world I would ever put my children through this. I still can't understand how Mum, or any mother, could do this.

Today, when I get sick, I want loving and comfort and I now understand why; it's because I rarely had it when I was young. Just recently my daughter, aged 42, had to have a small operation, and yes, I was there the whole time for her. That's what mothers do.

On our birthdays, neither Cheryl nor I ever had a party and neither one of us remembers our parents ever being there on our birthdays. Instead, we would get a birthday cake from Mum and Dad delivered from the local department store, and we shared the cake with our friends. Once again, I didn't know any different. I thought this was just how it was. To make up for it, as my children were growing up, every single birthday, I would give my children a birthday party.

School sports were a big event at the school, but again, Mum and Dad never came. One year I was asked to carry the flag out onto the field. It was such an honour and I felt so proud, walking in front, holding the flag with the whole team behind me. I felt like I was standing 10 feet tall. I looked out into the crowd, hoping to see Mum or Dad, but they hadn't turned up. I could feel myself drop. My shoulders drooped, my body drooped, and I just wanted to cry right there. How could I feel proud and excited when there was no one I loved to share it with?

One of the weekends that I came home from school–it was a Sunday and I was about 10–Mum and Dad were over at the hotel drinking with their friends, while I was home alone. It was becoming dark outside and I was getting really scared. I rang the hotel to see when Mum and Dad were going to come home. They had friends down from Perth and were still having a few drinks, and although they said they wouldn't be long, they were.

For me, that was one of the longest nights ever. I was so scared that I went around and turned every light in the house on, locking every door. We had a German Shepherd, so I got him to jump up on Mum's bed with me and the two of us cuddled up and waited. Around 11 p.m. they eventually got home.

That night I felt abandoned. Unloved and alone.

I remember feeling this way a lot.

I could see what my parents were doing: Dad was always at the hotel working and every night, my mum would sit down and drink a bottle of sherry. Every night. She was a nasty drunk and the nastiness got to me, because I couldn't understand why she was so mean. When she drank, she didn't treat me like her daughter, so much so that I began to think I was adopted. I felt like an outcast.

I wanted someone to take notice of me, and I decided I might get some attention if I ran away, so I went to my room, packed my bags and stole away from home. I didn't have anywhere to go, so I hid in the public toilets. Before long, I was bored, cold and uncomfortable, as I only had a hard bench to sit or lie on and the smell wasn't exactly comforting. You'd think I would have had a better place to stay, but at least I had a shower and toilet. I thought I was going to be staying for a while.

As the day wore on, it grew late and I got scared, so I decided to walk home. Dad wasn't there; he was at work, as usual. Mum was drunk and hadn't even realized I was gone. I'd run away and no one had missed me. Once again, I felt alone and deserted.

Mum had her moments. One particular evening, she had a bit too much to drink and went into my sister's room, telling her how much she loved her. I was lying in bed listening to all this dribble. Back then, I didn't think it was dribble; it hurt, it really hurt, and I got up and went into my sister's room, hoping Mum would say the same to me. But no, it was all about my sister.

I was so upset that I walked down to the end of the backyard where I'd made a cubbyhouse for myself. We had a massive backyard and down the back was a stable for my sister's horse. Next to the stable was a room that contained all her riding and grooming gear, but I'd made it my personal hideaway, with a table, chairs and a bed.

I used to spend a lot of time down there in my cubbyhouse; it was my retreat, my own little home. I had lots of these.

My sister knew I was upset and came down and cuddled me until I fell asleep. But when I woke up in the morning, she was gone. In her defence, it wasn't a really comfortable bed; it didn't have a mattress, only boards. But again, I felt so alone. The next morning Mum said nothing to me about what had happened.

What could I do to be noticed?

I'd never had anything to do with the horse. I didn't know how to ride or put a bridle on it and even to this day, I don't know how I managed it: I put the bridle on, then the saddle, opened the back gate and went for a ride. When I came back, everyone was there waiting. Boy, did I get a telling off! I was starting to get used to this attention, but it was the wrong way for a child to go about it.

While I was a lonely child, I seemed to find things to occupy myself. Some nights, I used to go out and break into houses (just two that I can think of). They were holiday homes that were easy to get into, and I never damaged anything or stole anything. Once inside, I would just walk around, sit in the lounge and look at the photos on the mantelpiece. Our family didn't have any photos up, except a gigantic one of Harold. These holiday houses, with all their photographs, truly felt like a "home," so I kept going back to re-live that feeling.

I remember one incident when I was 11 years old; I went to the "shack" where we lived on and off on weekends before our house was built. In there, I played around with the old treadle sewing machine, the place where my love for dressmaking began. I must have gotten a bit bored, so I went into the bedroom. On the bed was an old kapok mattress. The mattresses were held together, from top to bottom, with string and fluffy balls on top. I sat on the bed and with some matches, tried to light those little balls, but they wouldn't light. I got frustrated and just threw the matches under the bed and left.

Later that day, Dad came home and asked if I'd been in the shack and I said yes. Little did I know why he was asking. It turns out that I nearly burned the whole place down! Dad actually thought I'd been smoking. After I'd left, the little balls had kept smouldering and eventually ignited into a fire. Luckily, someone saw it, got help, and put out the fire.

Dad was very upset with me. He got the strap out, put me over his knee and belted the hell out of me. My reaction was mixed. Yes it hurt, but I was finally being noticed; I was finally getting some attention. Sure, it wasn't the attention I would have liked, but it was still attention.

I didn't have much interaction with my family. My siblings were older and they were off doing their own thing. Dad was at the hotel every day working, and when I came home on the weekends, I was really there on my own. Mum would mostly go to the hotel to drink and socialise with her friends.

Meals were a solitary affair. As a child, I can never remember going on a family holiday, sitting down with the family and having a meal. Instead, what I remember is sitting in the dining room of the hotel, eating alone. Sometimes my paternal grandfather would be there, but that was it. At home, no one sat together to have a meal and a laugh. Everyone ate at different times. I never had a birthday party or a Christmas meal with my family.

Cheryl confirmed my memories.

One enjoyment was that every Christmas we'd have this big, blue Christmas tree and would receive a huge number of presents. Maybe Mum and Dad were trying to compensate for their shortcomings with gifts, instead of love. Or maybe my parents just didn't know how to express love.

My father had been abandoned by his mother when he was just two years old, and there was also no love shared between him and his father. My mother, well…her mother had pushed her to live with my father when she was just 16. It was 1931 and he was a good catch and of means. Born in 1907 and 1915, my father and mother were from the old school.

As my parents grew older, my father slept in a separate bedroom from my mother. It had an extra mattress on the floor and a TV. Dad and I would watch TV in his room and sometimes I would sleep in there. Mum watched TV in the lounge and I really didn't like going in there to watch TV, as she was always drinking.

Even though I didn't see a lot of Dad, I was closer to him. I looked up to him. He worked so hard and had achieved so much; I just wish we'd had more time to talk to one another. I really would have liked to know more about him and what he had been through. I suppose it's one reason why the writing of this book is so important to me, so my children better understand me, even though they already know me well.

Last year, my daughter and her family, Rob and myself spent 10 days in Bali together. I took a copy of this book and my daughter read it. She is an emotional darling, just like her mum; she cried just about the whole way through the book, later coming up to me to say, "I didn't know that." That's what I wanted to share with her and the rest of my family.

Don't get me wrong; I loved my parents. They did the best they could and they didn't know any different. Back then, was "good parenting" an issue that people talked about? And more than that, I didn't know any better; I thought this was how every family was.

As a mother, I now know that things should be different.

Because it was a lonely existence at home, I was glad to return to boarding school. Once I completed school, I didn't have a place to hide, so all I wanted to do was get married and get out of the house for good. My brother and sister had already left, Dad was still working and Mum was still drinking. Mum would get so drunk, she'd pray to the huge photo of my brother that hung on the wall.

Mum was obsessed with my brother. One particular night she wanted to see him, so decided to walk over to the hotel where he was living. She walked straight into his room and caught him in bed with a woman. Being drunk, she stormed off and acted like a maniac. What was her son doing?

My brother rang home to tell Dad what had happened and Dad got me out of bed to drive the streets to try to find her. She wasn't too hard to find, but then I had to get her in the car and listen to her crying and ranting about what Harold did. He was an adult by then, in his twenties, but to Mum, he would always be the "son," the "baby", even though he was the oldest. All she could talk about was Harold, and I got sick of hearing about him all the time.

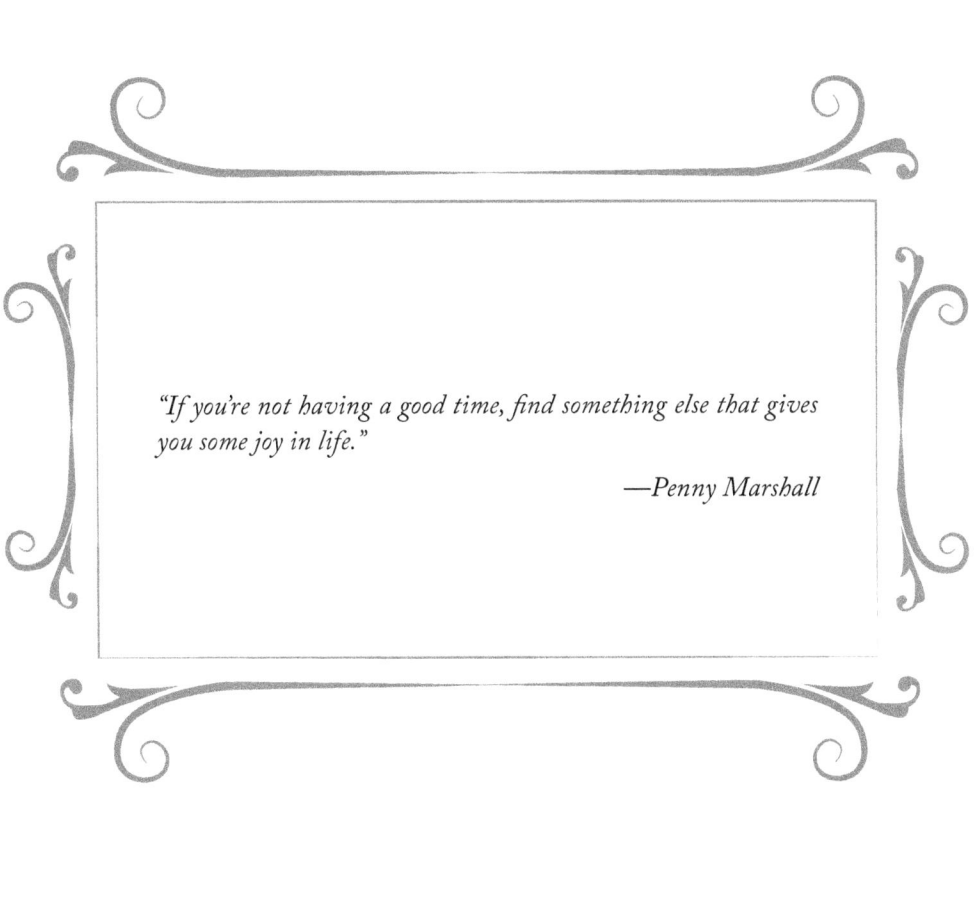

"If you're not having a good time, find something else that gives you some joy in life."

—*Penny Marshall*

Making My Own Fun

I really wanted to share in all the fun things you do as a family: holidays, birthdays and the like. Alas, there wasn't much of that at all, but what I do remember are the adventures I had by myself or with the select friends that I had–something the kids these days no longer seem to do. Yes, I had a fun childhood, but mostly by myself. That's probably why, to this day, I enjoy my own company.

When I was really little, about four, I loved the boat shed we used to have at the hotel on the water's edge. This is where we rented out the hire boats and sold petrol from the petrol bowsers. (There used to be a bridge from the hotel to the other side of town, but it was being pulled down.) Harold had collected some wood and built a cubby house under the boat shed, but I couldn't always get into it as when it was high tide, the water would come under the boatshed and flood the cubby. However, it was the start of my cubby-building days.

One of my fondest memories, when I was nine, concerned an abandoned caravan park on the way to the hotel. All of the caravans were gone except for one little, funny-shaped round one. I have never before or since seen a caravan so small! It was very cute. The door was broken, so I didn't have to break in.

Every couple of days, I would take a bucket and cloth and clean up the inside of the van. When I was satisfied, I would put a vase on the table with flowers I had picked from outside. I used to just sit inside and think and dream, and enjoy the peace and quiet of my own little domain.

Another place near the hotel was the King Carnival. It had everything–games, go-carts, a merry-go-round, a Ferris wheel, and then there was the fairy floss and toffee apples. From the age of eight, I virtually lived there. I got on so well with the operators that every Christmas, they would receive a hankie and a card from me, and every Easter I would give them an Easter egg. They would give me reams of free passes to all the rides and they even let me operate the merry-go-round. As I grew older, I was able to drive the go-carts like a maniac. It was awesome!

Looking back, really, anything could have happened to me, something I really don't want to think about, and back then I never thought of it. The men may have been undesirables and even a bit strange, but I knew them as brothers, and they were lovely to me.

From the hotel to our house, you would walk along the water's edge, over a little bridge, then to the main road to home. If I ever found a dead seagull or other creature as I was walking, I would pick it up and take it home. I would find a box and make it nice and comfortable for the creature, even though it was dead. I would bury the small coffin in the backyard with its own cross. I would even say a few words. Eventually, there was a nice little graveyard at the back of house.

On this same route home, there was a small lake that would dry up and turn to mud. I used to love the feeling of walking through here with no shoes on and have the mud squish between my toes. Luckily, I never stepped on broken glass. It's the small pleasures in life that can make it such fun!

When my friends came down from Perth between lunch and dinner time, as the kitchen was closed, we used to go to the hotel, get the key to the big pantry and take out jelly crystals (in a packet) and condensed milk, open these and eat them just as they were. I am sure this is where my sweet tooth came in.

We had no idea how to make a cake, other than to use flour and eggs. We would make the cake in the kitchen, and just outside the kitchen, there was a woodshed with a boiler room where we put the cake on top of the boiler until it was cooked. I don't know why we kept making these cakes, as they were horrible. But it was fun.

Another weird thing we did was to eat a plant that here in Australia we call "sour grass." It has a long stem with a yellow flower on the top. It grew everywhere and was very pretty. We used to pick these and eat them, just the stem. They tasted sour, but were still yummy. We never washed them, and now I wonder how many dogs weed on them!

Some friends of the family used to have a house that sat on the Estuary and my brother owned a huge white wooden ski that he left there, as it was near the water. The ski needed two people to carry it. We would drag or carry it down to the water's edge and jump on it and just float around on the water. It was so nice lying there in the sun with the water washing around you–until one of your friends came and tipped you up.

A couple of friends who lived in Perth had their caravan set up at the hotel. On school holidays and some weekends, they would travel down to Mandurah. I was so jealous of them living in a caravan, which was weird, but I think the adventurer part of me liked that it was something different.

One particular weekend, I travelled up to their place in Perth. We were going to go to the zoo the next day, but before we were allowed to go, we had to water the front lawns and make banana sandwiches to take with us. That was going to take some time, so I got up early. Nobody heard me and by the time they'd got up, I had watered the lawns and made all the sandwiches, so we could leave straight away. I was so excited about going to the zoo; I just wanted to get there. How small things like the zoo used to excite me!

When I was around 13 years old, I found another sanctuary. My brother had a big wooden boat with a cabin underneath. It was either parked in our back yard or tied up to the jetty at the hotel. It was a great little cabin with curtains on the window, matching cushions on the benches and a door that you could lock once you were inside. When I needed time to myself, which was often, I would get my pillow and blanket and some food and sleep there. I made it my little home. Even when the boat was tied up to the jetty, I slept on it. I wasn't scared. I loved it.

One particular day, some friends and I decided to go swimming at another friend's beach house in Mandurah. I can't forget that day because it was the first time I got dumped by a wave. I felt like I was choking on water, going round and round like a washing machine. I couldn't get back to the surface to breathe, and I thought I was going to die. Then a sharp pain jolted me back to reality as my right knee landed on my left foot. Once I got out of the water and looked at my foot, I saw it had a huge lump on it, like a big black ball.

My friend and I hobbled home. Then Mum came to the door and screamed and yelled at my friend, which was very embarrassing. That was the last time my friend wanted to come to my place. I didn't go to the doctor. Mum just bandaged my foot up, and it wasn't until I went back to school that the nurse told me I had fractured my foot. No wonder it was so sore.

When I was 14, Sue, my girlfriend from school, and I were over at the hotel and Harold's scooter was in the shed, so I jumped on it and started it up. Off it shot like a bullet, straight into the tank stand! I got off, shaking. What was I going to do? Harold was going to kill me.

One of our workers, who'd heard the bang, came out, saw the bike and me and thought that he'd better fix the problem. Thankfully, he pulled the front mudguard away from the tyre.

I must have been obsessed with the bike as a couple of days later, Sue and I decided to take it for a ride. I really don't know how we got away with it. You just turned a key and put your foot on the pedal; so easy. We didn't have helmets back then and I would drive, with Sue on the back. One day, when we were driving down the main street, a police car approached and both of us sat up tall, trying to look older–as if that would make any difference! We had so much fun on that bike until Harold found out. Then, boy, did I get into trouble.

Once I left school, my next "cubby" on wheels was my little blue Mini. Dad paid for it and I paid him $20.00 a week out of my wage until it was paid off. I was 18 and I loved this car, which had a rug and matching pillows in the back seat. I had so much fun in it.

I still had this car when I dated my first husband, Bruce. Well… have you ever had sex in a Mini? I can tell you, it's not easy and it's very uncomfortable. But it was the adventure of it all.

One night we received a phone call from Harold. He had hit a kangaroo about five kilometres out from Mandurah and wanted me to come out and swap cars with him.

When I got there, he was trying to ease the front of the car away from the front wheel so I could drive it. Once that was done, he started the car, gave me the keys, got into my Mini and took off. I climbed into his car and found there were no lights; they had been smashed in the crash, so I had to drive back home in the pitch black. On this stretch of main road there were no street lights; nothing. It was the middle of nowhere and of course, back then, there were no mobile phones. What was I going to do?

What could I do, but drive home.

It was the scariest, most harrowing drive of my life. Cars were coming the other way. They would be about to overtake another car, then would see me at the last moment and quickly drop back. I was lucky I wasn't killed.

I held it together, but once home, I collapsed, sobbing, and shaking. It was a terrible night.

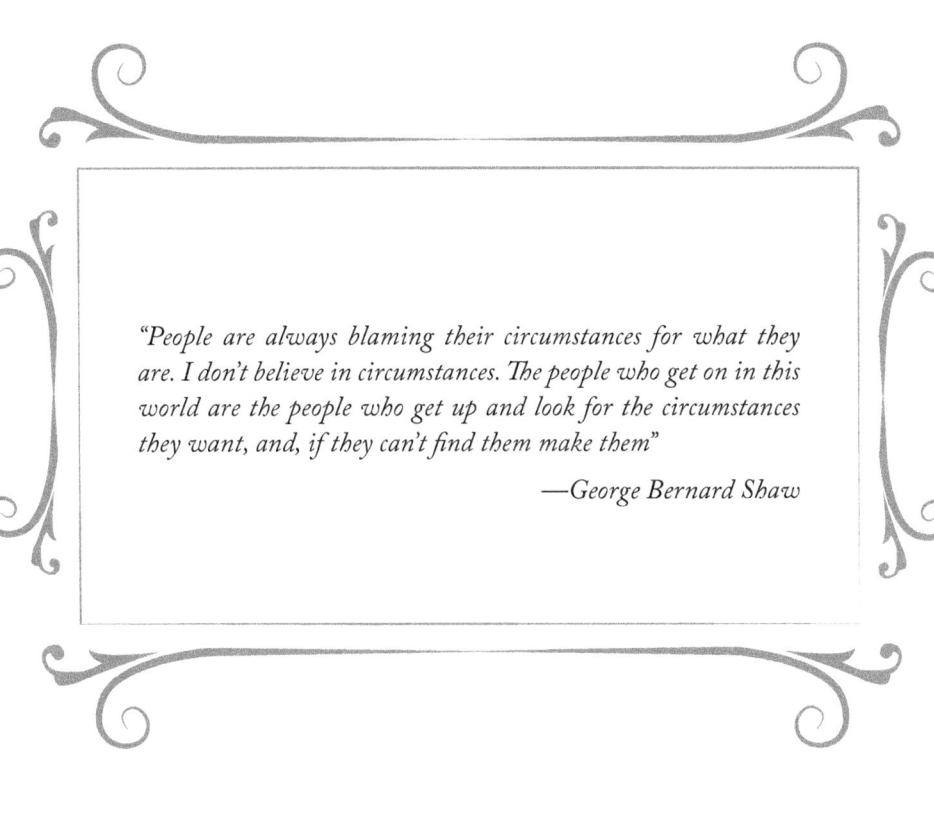

"People are always blaming their circumstances for what they are. I don't believe in circumstances. The people who get on in this world are the people who get up and look for the circumstances they want, and, if they can't find them make them"

—*George Bernard Shaw*

My First Marriage

The day Bruce and I got married, my brother Harold had borrowed my Mini, which he brought back later the same day. It never occurred to us to check it. Just as we were about to leave on our honeymoon, we discovered there was only a drop of petrol in the tank. It was 11 o'clock at night and we were heading out of town, so we got on the phone and started ringing petrol stations to see if they were open. We finally found one about 5 kilometres out of Mandurah. We only just made it. The guy in charge told us we were lucky, as we wouldn't have got much further before running out of petrol. As it was our wedding night, we were not too happy with Harold.

Once I was married, all I wanted was to have children. This way, I knew that I would always be loved. This was important to me, as I had never felt love at home.

I started going out with my first husband, Bruce, when I was just 16. Before we got married, he was called up by the Army and was sent to Vietnam. I waited for him and wrote to him every day. I was very much in love.

We got married when I was 19. We had our first child, Sharon, when I was 21, and the second, Ryan, at 23—which was also the year I got divorced.

Before I married, I had only dated one other person, and that was for just one night. Bruce was my first and only love when we got married.

I had really wanted children, but looking back, I realize Bruce wasn't ready.

When we decided to try to get pregnant, I had no idea it was going to take a while. I now know that many women have to try for years and even use fertility treatments to get pregnant, and I can't imagine how difficult that must be. When you want to be a mum, each month that you find out you're not pregnant is a crushing disappointment.

The first month went by, and nothing, then the next month, and again, nothing. I was beginning to worry that I couldn't have children, so I started to do all the silly things you read about to improve your chances of conception, like standing on your head after sex and closing your legs tight to prevent leakage.

Worse still, my girlfriend was pregnant. So on the seventh month of trying, I gave up. I figured I just couldn't have children and that was that. I decided to forget the whole thing and move on. I was disappointed and miserable, but I thought, what can I do? I considered adoption.

When in the eight month I missed a period, I was so excited I could barely contain myself!

I went to the doctor to confirm my suspicions. I was sitting in his exam room when he came in and told me to get undressed and get up on the table. He left the room, and when he returned, there I was, still dressed, sitting on the table… I was so young and shy that I couldn't imagine being undressed in front of a stranger, even if he was a doctor.

After a little bit of encouragement, I got up on the table and found out that yes, indeed, I was pregnant.

I had been waiting my whole life for this.

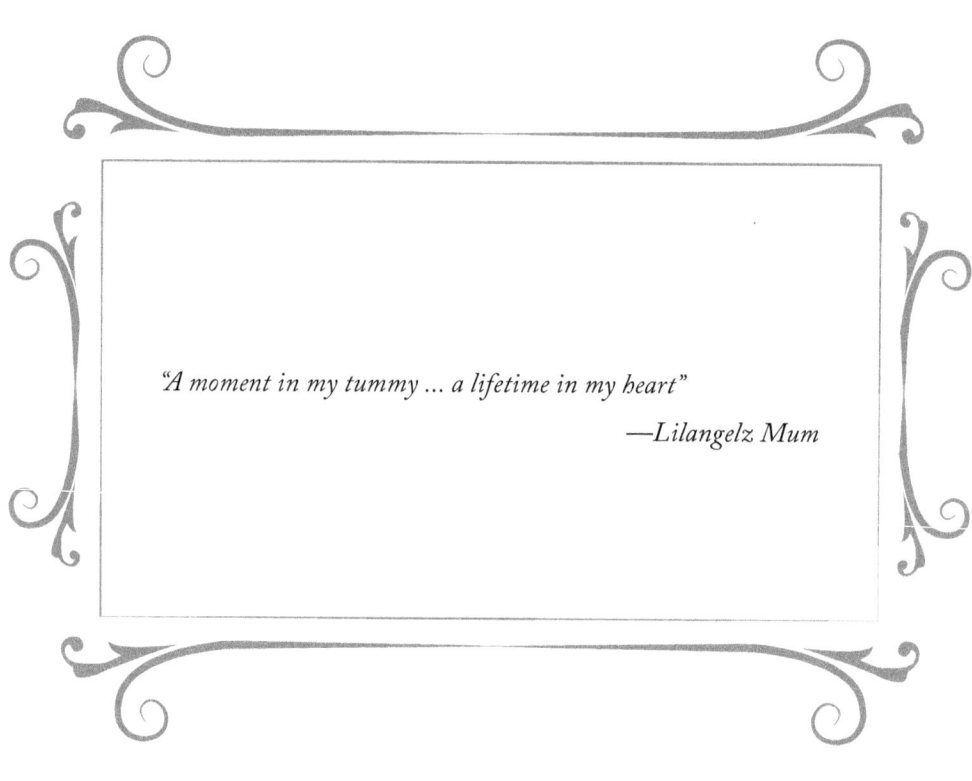

"A moment in my tummy ... a lifetime in my heart"
—*Lilangelz Mum*

Pregnant with Sharon

I was over the moon at being pregnant! And then came the morning sickness.

Every morning, I would get up feeling nauseous and desperately wanting to be sick, but I just couldn't bring myself to vomit. However, Bruce could. He would wake up feeling sick; then off he would go to the toilet and throw up. I got him to stop drinking to see if this might have been causing the problem, but to no effect. It was comical, really. They call this phenomenon 'sympathy morning sickness'. Luckily for Bruce, it didn't last long.

Mum never told me anything about anything, so I consulted my sister, Cheryl, because things were starting to happen to me that I just didn't understand. For example, I would forget where I put things and was continually finding the car keys in the fridge. On top of this, I felt dizzy, and was forced to take it easy.

My breasts were swollen and painful. I wanted to breastfeed, so Cheryl told me to massage my nipples to get ready for it. Bruce was as green as I was, and he asked me when I was going to get my nipples pierced so I could breastfeed. What a pair we were!

Bruce was a carpet layer. He had lost his driver's licence and as he had to go to work on his own, he needed me to drive the truck. Here we were, jumping into the truck, me with my 9-month pregnant belly just squeezing in behind the wheel. Once, when we got to work, we found the owners waiting for us, and there Bruce and I were, walking up the driveway (well it was more of a waddle for me), carrying the carpet into the house. What was I thinking?

The next morning I started to get pains, so I rang Cheryl to find out what was wrong. I wasn't due yet, but Cheryl said I was probably in labour.

I wasn't supposed to go that soon! I had planned on doing a whole list of things before I had the baby, like cooking a pile of food and freezing it, and giving the house a good clean. I panicked and rushed around trying to finish cooking a stew and cleaning before I went into hospital. But the baby wasn't going to wait.

I rang the doctor, who was an hour away in Perth, and he told me I had better get there quickly.

I had no idea it would be so painful and take so long to give birth. We had been at the hospital since before lunch, but the pains had started at 5 a.m. that morning.

Dinnertime came and I was starving. I would eat a little bit, then grab Bruce's hand and squeeze it to help me through the contractions, and then eat some more. It must have been quite comical to the people around us.

It was getting close to midnight on the 8th of August when Bruce said to me, "You have to have this baby today! I can't remember the dates of anything, but today is easy: the 8th day of the 8th month."

So I pushed and pushed, and had my beautiful baby daughter, Sharon, at 11:50 p.m. on the 8th of the 8th, 1974.

Later, after Bruce left, I remember the quiet time I had in my room, looking down at my little daughter. I felt so much love. My dream had come true.

Pregnant with Ryan

Bruce and I decided we wanted another baby and since Sharon had taken so long, we started trying right away. However, it didn't take as long as it had with Sharon, not at all.

When I got back from the doctor's with the news I was pregnant and went into the pub to tell Bruce, he just wasn't as excited as I'd thought he would be. I now realize why. When I was just three months pregnant with my second baby, Bruce started having an affair.

As a result, he wasn't around much, and I also didn't get much support from him in caring for Sharon.

You Chose

You chose.
You chose.
You chose.

You chose to give away your love.
You chose to have a broken heart.
You chose to give up.
You chose to hang on.

You chose to react.
You chose to feel insecure.
You chose to feel anger.
You chose to fight back.
You chose to have hope.

Overcoming Life's Challenges by Moya Mulvay

You chose to be naïve.
You chose to ignore your intuition.
You chose to ignore advice.
You chose to look the other way.
You chose to not listen.
You chose to be stuck in the past.

You chose your perspective.
You chose to blame.
You chose to be right.
You chose your pride.
You chose your games.
You chose your ego.
You chose your paranoia.
You chose to compete.
You chose your enemies.
You chose your consequences.

You chose.
You chose.
You chose.
You chose.

However, you are not alone. Generations of women in your family have chosen. Women around the world have chosen. We all have chosen at one time in our lives. We stand behind you now screaming:

Choose to let go.
Choose dignity.
Choose to forgive yourself.
Choose to forgive others.
Choose to see your value.
Choose to show the world you're not a victim.
Choose to make us proud."

—Shannon L. Alder

A person who is in love can see no faults or imperfections in the person who is loved.

—*Unknown*

The Writing's On the Wall

When love is blind, you tend to have blinkers on and not see or read between the lines.

One night, Bruce was late getting home from work. Sharon was 16 months old and I was six months pregnant with Ryan. I was beside myself, not knowing where Bruce was. (Remember, there were no mobile phones back then). I rang the hospitals and the police station to find out if there had been any accidents. Then, after what seemed like forever, Bruce walked in, all happy. He told me he'd been in his mate's car when they'd hit a kangaroo and had to be towed back to work to get another car to come back home. I grabbed him and hugged him with relief, crying my eyes out.

A week later, we went to have dinner with this "mate" and I brought up the subject of the kangaroo. The mate looked at Bruce, then went along with what I was saying. I had an inkling he had no idea what I was talking about, but I pushed it aside, because love is blind. It turned out that yes, that night he had been with Anne, the other woman.

Every Friday night, Bruce used to go out with the boys and it wasn't until our marriage was over that I found out that this wasn't true. Instead, he would pick Anne up and go to Perth. I now know for what.

There were so many incidents that I remember, but I won't go into them. It just shows that when you love someone so much, you don't think for a minute that he or she can do any wrong.

Moving Up North

When I was pregnant with my son Ryan, I found out we were having financial problems. I hadn't known, because Bruce took care of the finances, giving me a household allowance. Sue, my girlfriend from school and her husband, Ron, lived in Kununurra, where Ron had a plumbing business. So Bruce decided that he was going to pack us all up and travel to the top of Western Australia, thousands of kilometres away, to work for Ron.

I found out later that he also wanted to try and sort out our marriage. Naive Moya hadn't even known that there was a problem!

We rented our house to my sister and Bruce took off, driving all the way up there with what little stuff he could fit in the car.

A few weeks later, we decided to join him. I was seven months pregnant when I arrived at the airport, and Sharon was 17 months old. I was already so big that they weren't going to let me on the plane, as they thought I was ready to have the baby then and there. Luckily, I'd thought to get a letter from my doctor, so all was good. I had booked one seat and the plan was to have Sharon on my lap. Big mistake. Do you think that worked with a huge stomach? Luckily, the plane wasn't full and the man who was sitting next to me gave up his seat, so I was able to lie Sharon down.

Bruce used to play tricks on me all the time, and when he picked us up from the airport, he drove to a caravan park. Pointing to a beaten-up vintage caravan, he announced, "This is where we'll all be living." I didn't mind; I was with him and my family. But he was just joking.

Moving to Kununurra was a whole new adventure. Sue and Ron were the only people I knew up there, so we set up a small duplex house opposite them. It was basic, no air-conditioning, just fans (and it was hot!). There were no curtains, so I made some. There was also no furniture, although Ron and Sue gave us a few bits and pieces. We didn't need much and it was home; it was all part of the adventure. You do this kind of thing when you're young and, for me, in love.

One night, coming back from Ron and Sue's place, Bruce had a few drinks. We were mucking about and I asked Bruce if he had ever played up on me. He said no at first, and then he admitted he had, but that it had only happened once. I believed him.

I must have got myself into a bit of a state though, as not long after, I went into labour. I was a month early! I was rushed to the hospital, where they prepped me and put me in the labour room all by myself. To this day, I still remember feeling utterly alone as I lay there having labour pains, watching a gecko crawling up the wall.

If you have ever experienced labour, you'll know what it's like. I was in extreme pain and I was also getting nervous. Bruce wasn't there and no one was coming to see how I was doing. I rang the bell for the nurse again and again, but no one responded.

I was starting to get really worried, so I crawled off the table and waddled down the corridor looking for someone. I eventually found a nurse—the only one in the hospital—who took me back to the room and tested the bell. It wasn't working, so too bad if I'd really needed someone! I had strong contractions for hours and then, just like that, they went away.

Eventually, the doctor came to say I wasn't ready to give birth, as I was too early. Why couldn't he have come in sooner and told me this? I had just endured hours of pain, thinking I was going to have my baby.

The doctor gave me pills to stop the false labour pains and I was sent home.

Sunday came. It was a big cricket day for the boys. Up we all got, packed a lunch and off we went.

I had taken my pills for the labour pains. I was starting to get a few pains, but pushed them aside, thinking they were not real, and *was I ever going to have this baby?*

Lunch ended and the pains were getting strong, so I mentioned to Bruce that we'd better go home. He wasn't happy; he was playing cricket, after all.

Once home, I put Sharon to bed. Bruce had a sleep–so supportive!–as I walked around the unit, the pains getting stronger and stronger. I guessed I was in labour for real this time.

As Sharon's labour had taken so long, I didn't go to the hospital right away, but when Bruce eventually woke up, I told him I felt it was time. It was around 6.30 p.m. and I went over to my girlfriend's house and asked her to watch Sharon while I went to the hospital.

By 7:30 p.m. I was settled into the labour ward. There were a couple of nurses on, but no doctor. He was at the movies, so they had to go and fetch him. As it was a small town, it wasn't far away.

Once I had given birth to Ryan, I had a strange premonition; I had given Bruce a son, but I didn't know whether we would eventually be a whole family. Little did I suspect that our marriage was going to be over before I knew it.

I'd given birth to Sharon in a modern hospital in Perth, but we now lived out in the middle of nowhere, so I gave birth to Ryan in a real country hospital. There was only one labour ward, so you had to be in and out quickly in case someone else came in. The baby was never in the nursery as this was too small, and the hospital didn't have a lot of staff. So Ryan was always with me, which was fine, because this was what I wanted. I needed him with me.

There was only one other patient in the maternity section, a young girl, and one nurse. You could lock your hospital room from the inside, which was fortunate, since this poor young girl's grandfather came to the hospital one night, drunk out of his mind. He was ranting and raving up and down the corridor. I was so scared that I locked myself in my room. Something like this would never have been allowed in Perth.

Straight after I had Ryan, a friend, Paul, came and stayed with us. One day he went out and left all of his paperwork on the kitchen table. As I was tidying up, I came across a card from a girl that my husband was friendly with and reading between the lines, I realised something was going on between my husband and her.

I approached Bruce and eventually he admitted that "it" hadn't happened once, but a couple of times. But he said he loved me, and wanted to try to make our marriage work. Again, I believed him, so I tried to push the affair out of my mind and work on building our marriage. But being up north with almost no friends or family grew to be too much. I had no one to talk to except Sue across the road, and she was at work all day. The days were so lonely. I couldn't ring home because what was I going to say? And who was I going to say it to?

I had only been out of hospital for a week when I did one of the stupidest things I have ever done in my life: I went water skiing. Yes, I had just given birth to a baby, and I went water skiing! I had stitches that I should have been taking care of, but instead, I fell off the skis. A rush of water came up into me and made a hell of a mess. You have to be young to do such foolish things.

I was trying to get my marriage back together, but I was having a huge problem breastfeeding. I couldn't feed Ryan as my nipples were so sore. In the hospital, they gave me a solution to put on them, which burnt them, and I was in so much pain feeding Ryan that I stopped and put him on a bottle. As I totally believe in breastfeeding, I put a heat lamp on my breasts to try to heal them; they were so engorged that it even hurt to wear clothes. When my nipples finally healed, I went to see the nurse, and she told me it was no use trying to breastfeed as all my milk had dried up.

I am not one to give up, so before I gave him the bottle, I would put Ryan on each of my breasts so that his sucking would stimulate the milk supply. Eventually, I was able to throw away the bottles and fully breastfeed Ryan, but by this time, I had been through so much that I decided to go back home for a while.

I rang Mum and Dad, who sent me the money to get home. My main reason for returning was to show off my new son, get back to my breastfeeding, and to see my regular doctor for a routine exam. You can imagine what the doctor had to say when he saw my condition. He gave me cream to put on my wounds and my sister was the one who had to apply it, because I couldn't see where to put it, down there. That's what sisters are for.

It didn't occur to me that I would never be returning, so when I left, I took only the essentials. I would be going back home to my husband–or so I thought.

I never did, because I found out my husband had been seeing Anne from when I was three months pregnant. I started looking back at all the "incidents" and excuses he'd made to me and realized when the affair had started. I could even work out the times they must have been together. It tore my heart out and at the same time, made me sick to my stomach.

Ryan was only a couple of weeks old when I returned to Mandurah, and I was staying at the hotel when a phone call came from Bruce. We couldn't make sense of the phone call as the reception was bad and dropped out, but when he called back he was distraught. He had been in a car accident with his friend Paul, the one who'd been staying with us, and Paul had died in Bruce's arms.

Totally devastated, Bruce returned home to be with the kids and me. Or so I thought.

The first night Bruce was back home, I wanted to talk about our marriage, but that was the last thing Bruce wanted to talk about. He had just lost his mate and worse yet, Paul had died in his arms. As Bruce had been the one driving the car, the guilt was killing him. I look back and realize how self-centred I was that night. I didn't understand, and all I could think about was myself.

We tried to mend our marriage, but in the end, you can't put spoiled milk back in the refrigerator; all you get is cold, spoiled milk. You can't make it right again. We couldn't get it together and six weeks after I gave birth to Ryan, my husband left me for the woman he had been seeing all along.

Once again, I was abandoned.

"There are as many nights as days, and the one is just as long as the other in the year's course. Even a happy life cannot be without a measure of darkness, and the word "happy" would lose its meaning if it were not balanced by sadness."

—*Carl Jung*

The Demon Drink

I was devastated and I wasn't allowed to live at Mum and Dad's. I really don't think Mum liked children; only ever once did she look after mine. When she was a baby, I left my daughter Sharon with Mum one day so I could go downtown for some shopping. When I got back, Mum was a mess and in tears. Sharon had woken up. She wasn't crying, just whinging a little, but Mum hadn't picked her up to console her. She hadn't known what to do with Sharon and as she didn't know how long I was going to be out, she got herself into a real state. Never again did I ask her to look after any of my children, and she never asked if she could.

As I had no income or money, I started to live and work at the hotel. For some reason, I couldn't go on a pension and it had something to do with the hotel.

This was when the drinking started.

I began with either Green Ginger Wine or port. I eventually moved onto the "hard stuff," a liqueur, Tia Maria with ice every night. My drinking got so bad that Dad wouldn't get any more Tia Maria in and if we needed any for the clients, we had to buy some downtown. With only one bottle in the whole hotel and me not being allowed to drink it, I went back to drinking Green Ginger Wine and port. It wasn't long after this that I bought my own Tia Maria, and this was my preferred drink for many years.

I would put the kids to bed and, being in the hotel, I would drink. I was surrounded by people on holiday and workers after work, so why not join in? One night, when I was drunk, I went to bed just as Ryan woke up for a feed. It was bad. I was so drunk that at the same time as I was breastfeeding him, I was vomiting on the floor at the side of the bed. I shouldn't say this, but he slept really well that night.

When Ryan was about eight weeks old, everyone was nagging me to go out and have some fun. I thought, *why not?* So one night I went to the Brighton Hotel for drinks, where I met John. Our relationship lasted several months, and in those months I regained the confidence to go back out and face the world.

John was my first real relationship since Bruce. It was weird going into a new relationship with a baby and a toddler – and a breastfed baby, at that. Even though John and I broke up, we remained friends for years.

After Ryan was born, I had a loop fitted as a form of birth control. I was having trouble with it, so had x-rays taken to find out what was happening. The doctor found that it had moved and I had to have it removed.

In the meantime, I fell pregnant. I didn't have any tests; I just knew. I didn't tell anyone and when I went to hospital to have the loop taken out, I said to the doctor, "I think I'm pregnant. Can you please take that, as well?" And he did.

John and I had broken up by then and because I'd had x-rays, which you shouldn't have when you are pregnant, I just couldn't keep the baby.

When my son was seven months old and Sharon nearly two, I moved out of the hotel into a unit, and the drinking slowed down quite a bit. But then Bruce came back to town, and I went off the rails. Try as I might, I still loved him.

He was still with Anne and by then I was living with a wonderful man named Graeme, who my daughter called "Daddy," but the old memories and emotions came flooding back. I really don't know what happened or why I went off the deep end again, in every sense. It was just horrible; I was a train wreck.

As mentioned, I was still good friends with John, and in what can only be described as bad judgment, I decided to make Graeme jealous by playing John off against him. The strange thing is, in every relationship I have had—even with Rob, who has been my husband now for years—I really didn't realize what I was doing.

I felt compelled to tell Graeme about John; I wanted to hurt him like Bruce had hurt me. Graeme could only take so much pain and I hurt him a lot, and eventually, we broke up.

I now realize I was just feeling sorry for myself. *Poor me, nobody wants me.* If only I had realized that my children wanted and needed me.

After Graeme, not only did I hit the bottle really hard, but I also became promiscuous. Alcohol did this to me, and made me believe I wanted sex.

Back then, I equated sex with love. Now I know it wasn't sex I really wanted; it was love. It took me some time to find out that they are two different things.

I made another bad mistake of leaving the unit and moving into a house that Dad owned right next to the hotel—an extremely wrong move on my part.

I was still working at the hotel, mixing with a group of heavy drinkers, and I, too, started to drink heavily again. But the worst was yet to come.

"What lies behind us and what lies before us are tiny matters compared to what lies within us"

—*Ralph Waldo Emerson*

A Single Mum: On My Own

Being a single mother can be hard, especially when something happens to your child and you don't know what to do.

One night, I heard a funny noise coming from the kids' bedroom. Ryan and Sharon shared a room, with Ryan in a cot and Sharon in a bed.

I found Ryan on his stomach, foaming at the mouth and jerking back and forth. I didn't know what to do, so I just grabbed him, ran to my car and drove to the police station. Why the police station? Because it was always open and I knew several of the officers from the hotel. Plus, we didn't have a hospital in Mandurah back then.

I was so panicked that I didn't realize I was standing there in my nightgown. One of the policeman gave me his jacket to wear.

Ryan was okay that night, but they suggested we take him to hospital. I had left Sharon at home, so I rang my sister-in-law to go and pick her up, which she did straight away. When I'd left Sharon alone, I wasn't thinking. I believed Ryan was dying.

And this is what I mean about being on your own. Sometimes you don't think; you just go on instinct, which is what I did that night. I thought my son was dying and my daughter was safe in bed asleep, so I did what my gut was telling me: I went and got help for my son.

Once at the hospital, the doctor told me I had Ryan bundled up too tight in bed and he'd become overheated, which is why he had

had the fit. As the doctor was saying this, I knew I didn't have him rugged up too tight, but how do you argue with a doctor? He kept him in hospital for a little while just to make sure everything was fine and then sent us home.

Once home, I rang Carol to let her know what had happened and said that I would pick Sharon up the next day.

That night, Ryan slept with me. I didn't sleep much, as I kept watching him to see if he was okay.

The next day, on my way to pick up Sharon, I was driving past the police station when I glanced in the back and there was Ryan, having another fit in the back seat! And this time he wasn't rugged up too tight.

With my heart pounding, I looked for somewhere to park. I couldn't find a place, so I left my car outside the police station, grabbed Ryan and ran in. I must have looked like some hysterical madwoman, but as it turns out, John was there and he and his partner bundled me into the police car and took me to the hospital. By the time we got there, Ryan was okay and was acting like his normal happy self again. I could have come back home, but being concerned as to why this had happened again, I stayed to have him checked out.

The hospital kept Ryan overnight and of course, I stayed with him, just to make sure everything was okay. In the morning, they checked him out, saying everything was fine and that we could go home, but they couldn't offer an explanation for what had happened. Their advice was just to keep an eye on him. This is where a parent becomes paranoid and doesn't let their child out of their sight. I never left Ryan's side, checking on him all through the night to make sure he was okay. Time passed and fortunately, to this day, he has never had another fit.

Ryan was a handful, a typical boy who got into everything. One day, I was driving back from Perth with Ryan in the back of the car. It seemed awfully quiet and I turned around to see that he had put a plastic bag over his head! He had already sucked all the air out. I screamed and pulled over to the side of the road, ripping the bag off his head. He just looked at me and smiled. We sat in the car for a bit while I hugged him—one, to make sure he was fine and two, for me to take a deep breath and calm down. Thank heavens he was unharmed! I'd turned around to look at just at the right time. If it had been any longer, I really don't think I would have him now.

I hadn't even known there was a plastic bag in the car, but it made me aware never to leave bags in the car, or anywhere else.

I have had so many mishaps with the kids, but that's what happens. Here are a few of the other events that have happened throughout their lives…

When we lived near the hotel, the laundry was down the backyard. My washing machine consisted of one tub with a ringer on the top. One day, I was hanging the washing out to dry and the kids were playing around the yard. All of a sudden, I heard a scream. I looked over to the laundry and there was Sharon with her arm in the ringer of the washing machine! I raced over to her, but at the time, I didn't know that in such an event, there is a release handle that you push to make the top ringer pop up. I watched Sharon's arm go through the ringer, up past her elbow. As I didn't know about the release switch, I reversed the switch and had to watch as her arm came back out, while she screamed. I think it was more frighting watching her arm go through the ringer a second time.

She was only about three, so her arm was tiny and I thank my lucky stars no damage was done, but I did take her to the doctor to have it checked. It was fine. To this day – and she's now an adult– Sharon laughs about the incident and keeps reminding me about it.

The Sunday session at the hotel usually finished up just after lunch. One day when Ryan was ten months old and Sharon was 19 months, we were invited onto a cray fishing boat. We were going to travel to the Ravenswood Hotel, a few hours away, for the next session. If you drive, it is only about 15 minutes, but by boat, it can take a couple of hours. You have to travel over a huge expanse of water to get there and it can get quite rough.

There were about 15 adults, plus the kids and me. It was a great, leisurely trip down and when we got to the hotel, the kids had a ball running around, playing. The hotel scene was different back then, much more family oriented than now.

When we started the trip home, it was getting dark. We got about halfway across this expanse of water when we ran out of petrol. It was pitch black and we had no lights, food or water, so to try to attract attention, we took Ryan's nappies out of the bag and lit them and waved them around.

It started getting cold and the only cover was a small section by the anchor at the bow of the boat. The kids and I huddled in there to keep out of the cold and as I was sitting in there with a child on each side, I thought, *if I have to go, at least I have my kids with me.* It was so scary out there in the dark, not being able to see land, and with no food or water.

We just drifted, and my mind began to race. I thought about the boat sinking and how in the past, so many people had died in this area. How could I save two children if the boat sank? This was a time when I wished I had a partner. My children were so good; they hadn't eaten, but not once did they cry. I had finished breastfeeding Ryan, so I couldn't help him out there, but they didn't cry or whine.

Finally, someone spotted us. As we were towed back into Mandurah, arriving at around one in the morning, the relief was unbelievable. We stepped off the boat and I have never welcomed dry land so much in all my life. I packed my kids into the car and went home. And that night, we all slept together, cuddled up

It's at times like this that you realize just how special your little ones are and how much they depend on you.

Running Away to Perth

I lived in a house right next to the hotel and since I didn't have a garage, every car that drove by could see who was parked at my place. For a while I was dating a policeman (John) and I became friendly with many of the guys on the police force.

While they were on duty, they would sometimes drop by for a "cuppa" and a chat, so often, if you went past my house, you would see a police car, van or motorbike parked outside. My friends would visit frequently, too, so there were always a lot of cars coming and going.

It got back to my father that I had a lot of different cars at my place, especially the police cars, and he wasn't too impressed. I was starting to get a reputation, but things weren't as bad as people were making them out to be and I didn't think I deserved all the gossip. Even so, the talk eventually got the better of me, so I decided to leave town and live in Perth, about an hour's drive away. At the time, Sharon was four years old and Ryan, just over two.

In Perth, I rented an absent friend's house and stayed there until they came back and needed the house back. I wasn't ready to return to Mandurah, so I moved to a house in a different suburb.

At this point, I was becoming very independent and self-sufficient. When I moved, I hired a trailer and shifted all my furniture myself. And I mean by myself! At one point, I was trying to move some furniture into the house and the guy who lived next door came over and asked me if I needed a hand. He was just being friendly, but I said no. I had no desire to get to know my neighbours. It may sound silly, but I had just left my home town because of stupid gossip, so there was no way I was going to give someone anything to talk about, especially when it involved me!

I soon joined a gym. One day, when I was in the sauna, some of the women there asked about me and found out I was a single mother. Their whole attitude towards me changed. Suddenly, it seemed, I was there for their entertainment. How insecure was that?

Overall, I found Perth to be not as friendly as Mandurah. I suppose part of it was living in a big city, whereas I had grown up in a small country town where everyone knew each other. However, even though I was alone, I wasn't really lonely, because I had my kids and I loved just being with them. But yes, it did get a bit lonely when they went to bed and I was sitting there on my own, watching TV. I missed having another adult to talk to. I had a phone, but I didn't use it much, as it wasn't the same.

In the end, though, I think being alone was good for me. It made me stronger.

I'd never had Christmas lunch with my family, and Christmas day in Perth was a mixture of loneliness and joy.

The kids jumped out of bed and opened presents and we had so much fun! I made Christmas lunch for us all. Sharon and Ryan were only five and three years old, but I always tried to make it special for them. We sat down and ate, and the rest of the day took naps and just enjoyed each other. I did feel a little sad because I had no adult to share this special day with. But sometimes it is just nice to celebrate as a family.

Sharon started preschool when I was in Perth, but I didn't want to know the other mums. I was a loner because of all I had been through.

I fell into a routine. Monday to Friday I would be at home with my children and I wouldn't drink at all. Then Bruce would pick the kids up on Friday. I would drive to Mandurah to work for the weekend and stay at the hotel, and then I'd let loose, some weekends more than others. But I would always pick up my kids and drive home.

One day during the week when I was home with the kids, one of the policemen I knew rang and asked if he could come around for a cuppa at 6 p.m. He didn't turn up, so I put the kids to bed and went to bed myself.

At 9 p.m. there was a knock on the door and it was the policeman. I thought maybe I should ignore it. I was a bit annoyed that he would have the gumption to call on someone at that time of night and I didn't realize until I had let him in that he had had a few too many drinks. That's probably why he had the courage to show up. I let him in and gave him a cuppa. We sat and talked for a bit, but it was getting late, so I asked him to leave. I could tell he didn't want to and it was the first time in my life that I was petrified. I just didn't know what to do; he was a big guy, and a policeman!

I started to walk to the door, trying to edge him out, but when we reached the door, he wanted a kiss. I told him no, and he said, "Well, I'm not going to go until you give me a kiss." He towered over me, so I gave him a quick–and I mean quick–kiss, opened the door and I don't know how, but I gently pushed him out.

I quickly locked the door and turned off the lights. I checked on the kids to make sure they were okay, and then just sat in the lounge in the dark, crying my eyes out. My heart was pumping out of my chest and I felt sick, thinking of what could have happened.

He was a policeman, for goodness sake! Why should I feel like this? But I'd honestly thought he was going to rape me.

When I first moved into this particular house, I called a man to mow the lawn and we started chatting. My kids were there and he said he was married with two kids, as well. Since we were talking, I mentioned that I was divorced, and I couldn't believe what happened next. He hit on me!

Of course, I told him where to go. I never called another lawn man again. I bought my own lawnmower and from then on, did the lawns myself.

When the lease was up on the house, the kids and I moved into another one, but it wasn't long before I decided to move back home to Mandurah. I can remember the incident that made up my mind.

When I cooked, I always kept a bowl of cooking oil next to the stove, and when I needed oil, I would use it. Then, when I was finished cooking, I would drain the oil back into the bowl.

I was in the lounge one day when I heard a scream and went racing into the kitchen. The kids had turned on the stove and moved the oil onto the hot plate. I went in to take the oil off the stove, but it was so hot that I spilled some oil onto the hot plate and it suddenly went up in flames.

I stood there in shock as flames went shooting up the wall. The kids were screaming and I was simultaneously trying to keep them out of the kitchen.

I didn't know what to do, so I called my mother. She didn't know what to do, either! I dropped the phone, soaked a towel in water, and hit at the flames enough so that I could at least turn off the hotplate. I was crying and screaming, yelling at the kids to get out of the kitchen, and they were crying because flames were shooting up the wall. They were scared because I was yelling at them, and they didn't realize the seriousness of what was happening.

I kept wetting the towel and hitting the fire and eventually got the fire out. Picking up the phone, I told Mum it was all okay and hung up. I didn't want to talk to anyone. All I wanted was to be with my kids. I grabbed them and went into the lounge and sat on the floor. We were all crying and hugging each other.

In the end, I just couldn't cope on my own. Not knowing anyone and being so far away from everyone was getting to be too much for me.

I rang Bruce and told him what I was going to do, and let him know, too, that I couldn't get Sharon into preschool in Mandurah. Luckily, he pulled a few strings and we got her into school. I couldn't wait to get back home to Mandurah! Yes, being away was great for a while, but it is so hard if something goes wrong and there is no one close by who can be there for you. Living alone so far away was something I had to do, though, and I did learn from it.

We moved into the same little house we'd lived in before, next to the hotel.

Bad move.

Meanwhile, Bruce's sister-in-law kept saying that she would watch the kids for me. What I didn't realize until later was that she wanted my kids for herself.

When we were living in Perth, Ryan developed a sore on his leg. One day, I ironed his pants and put them on him when they were still warm, and he knew this was because of the iron.

I came down to Mandurah and my sister-in-law was looking after the kids. When she was changing Ryan, she noticed the sore on his leg and asked him how he got it. Because I had just ironed his pants and put them on him, and because he was too little to speak in full sentences, he said "iron." Carol took this to mean that I had burned his leg with an iron.

She turned me into child welfare.

I found out about this later from Bruce. He'd stuck up for me. He told the authorities that I was a great mother and that there was no way I would ever have done something like that.

The whole thing died down, thanks to Bruce, but I never spoke to Carol again.

So what is this chapter about?

No matter how independent or tough you think you are, you have to have some support around you to call on when you are in trouble. You can't do it all by yourself, especially if you are a single mum.

It's also a lesson about not running away from your problems. If you try to run away from them, most of the time they follow you.

Do not let people you hardly know into your home at night, or any other time for that matter!

And, lastly, be good to the people who are there for you. By being civil to Bruce, the problem with child welfare was solved, whereas if we'd been nasty to each other, it could have turned ugly and he could have taken custody of the kids himself.

"Character cannot be developed in peace and quiet. Only through experiences of trial and suffering can the soul be strengthened, vision be cleared, ambition insured and success achieved"

—Helen Keller

Break ups, Alcohol, Drugs, a Suicide Attempt and Marriage Number 2

Alcohol and Drugs

I have done the same thing in every relationship I've had, even to my wonderful second husband, Rob. Even though I know what it feels like to be betrayed, I had two affairs during our marriage–although they happened while we were separated.

I had to hurt Rob, push him away, and have him abandon me like everyone has done to me, because I deserved it–or so I thought.

It took me ten years of being sober to realize what I had been doing.

I also didn't think I was an alcoholic. I thought an alcoholic was the kind of person I saw in the hotel, someone who would arrive in the morning and be there drinking all night, or someone who would come in after work and stay until last call.

Bruce would take the kids on weekends and this was when I really hit the booze. Looking back, my life from the age of 23 to 30 was a roller coaster. Parts of it weren't so bad, but at other times, I would totally go off the rails.

When I was 29, I found "drugs." Thank heavens this was only marijuana and slimming tablets, which give you a high. But there I was, on a mixture of drugs, tablets, and alcohol at the age of 29, when I was old enough to know better. What was I thinking?

Well, that was the point; I wasn't thinking. I thought I was having a ball. I can't remember most of it, as I was so out of it. It was all one big blur.

And speaking of blurs, on Friday nights, the kids would go with their father and I would go out until the early hours of the morning, work the next day, drink all night, work the next day, and then drink that night until the kids came home the next morning.

Being in the party scene, you want to look good, so I had to keep my weight down. One way of doing this is bringing all your food back up. Yes, I was bulimic from the age of 15, but it became worse as I hit the party scene. And I lived on slimming pills.

The pills, drugs and alcohol were not a good mix on many different levels. I tried to kill myself a few times with sleeping pills mixed with alcohol, and I'm amazed that I am still here with a functioning brain.

I had known Rob for quite a while through the hotel. At the time, he had a girlfriend and I was also going out with someone, but both Rob and I would only see our partners on weekends. My girlfriends had been trying long and hard to push Rob and me together, so we started to see each other during the week and our "others" on the weekend.

One particular weekend, it was the opening of the new downstairs bar at the hotel. Ross, my boyfriend, was coming down to accompany me to the opening and stay the night. I knew Rob was going to be there without his girlfriend, and I was to see him there.

When Ross arrived, I told him about Rob and while we were at the hotel, Ross went up to Rob and asked what his intentions were. What a joke! I ended up breaking up with Ross that night and went home with Rob. He broke up with his girlfriend, and we have been together ever since.

Rob came into my life when I had two children and later, we had a son together. He was in the building trade, and as tradies tend to "live" at the hotel, right from the start, we were as good as doomed.

When Rob and I drank, we would fight like cats and dogs. When we went out, we would rarely come home together, as we would always have a fight.

When we drank, the violence between the two of us escalated. Not only was Rob violent towards me, I was also violent towards him. And jealous! I was the worst. If Rob and I went to a party, I had better not catch him talking to another female!

This had a lot to do with my own insecurity.

One night at a party, I was drunk and had also just had a joint. Rob was going to get me another drink, when I saw him talking to a woman.

I thought my head was going to explode. I was furious! I ploughed through that crowd and I threw in his face whatever was left of my drink. He was stunned. I turned around to leave, fell down, and heard a crack. I didn't realise that "crack" was my arm.

I really don't know what happened next. When I arrived home, apparently I went to the medicine cabinet and took a handful of tablets. Next door to our house was an old, unoccupied building full of bits and pieces from the hotel. I took the key, went in there and fell asleep. Upon waking, I didn't know where I was, since it was pitch black. And every time I tried to walk out, I would hit something and fall back down.

What a sight I must have been! Looking back, it was like I was trapped in a giant pinball machine, and I was the ball. Eventually, in the early morning as it grew light, I found my way out. I came through the back gate just as Rob was walking through the front gate. When we met, he went ballistic, thinking I had been at the hotel this entire time and was only just getting home. But he, too, was only just getting home!

I ignored him and went to bed, but I was having trouble breathing and my arm was black and blue. Rob rang the doctor, who came and examined me. He said I was lucky to be alive.

The combination of alcohol and pills had tightened my windpipe, so air couldn't get through; that is why I was having trouble breathing. I'd also fractured my arm. I was in so much pain and was so tired that it took the whole day and night to sleep it off.

When I was drunk, I didn't care about anyone. I would work myself into such a state that I just didn't want to be here anymore.

When I was like this, I didn't even think about my children. It was horrible! I was ready to leave my kids, yet that is the last thing I really wanted, I loved them so much. But that is what alcohol does to you. It messes with your mind and just takes over.

I fell into a drinking routine. When I came home from work, I would have a drink to relax, because that's what most people do, right? After that first drink, I couldn't be bothered getting up to cook dinner. I actually couldn't be bothered to do much of anything. Alcohol makes you lazy. I would eventually get up because my children and husband had to eat, but I had to push myself.

I was very involved in working, and of course my work was the hotel, so we just about lived there. We would meet up with friends at the hotel. Our house was next to the hotel, so our kids would also come and go to the hotel as they pleased. They grew up there, and it was a second home for them as it had been for me, all those years ago.

In writing this, I have just seen the pattern, the same pattern my mother and father had. I was doing exactly the same thing. The only difference was that I loved my kids with all my heart and soul and was there for them. I felt the hotel was their playground, as much as mine.

Rob's and my relationship consisted of six months on, six months off. Even so, there was chemistry between us that we couldn't ignore. Even when we were separated, we would still sleep together.

As I grew older, I realized that the more I drank, the more I was forgetting things. And the hangovers weren't lasting just one day; they were lasting two. I began to think, *what a waste of time.*

I normally never drank beer, but when I woke up during the night with the dry horrors, I would go to the fridge and down a can, as this was the only thing that would quench my thirst. Also, when I thought about taking a pill, my mouth would water. Boy, did I have a problem.

Since I've stopped drinking, I love Rob more and more every day. I can't imagine my life without him. But it wasn't always like that…

"Before you were conceived…
I wanted you.
Before you were born…
I loved you.
Before you were here an hour…
I would die for you.
This is the miracle of life."

— Maureen Hawkins

Pregnant with Kane: Here for a Reason

I am going to share with you the story of how Kane came to be, and throughout the book, you will hear my mantra, "Things happen for a reason." The first time I started to believe this was when my youngest son was born.

I had just gone into hospital to have a laparoscope, and the doctor told me there was no point in taking birth control pills at that time, as the other medication I was taking would counteract it and cancel it out.

A month or so later, Rob had to go away for work, which was fine with me because we were in one of our fighting phases. While he was gone, I began to think I might be pregnant, but I couldn't call him as this was before mobile phones.

I got checked out and sure enough, I was pregnant, but I was very nervous about letting Rob know, not knowing what he would say or do. I went to visit his mate's girlfriend and asked her to tell Rob (once he got back from working down south) to contact me straight away. When Rob eventually walked in, my darling daughter Sharon blurted out, "Mum's pregnant!" As we had been fighting, Rob's face wore a look of shock, but it all worked out as we soon made up.

This was an extremely stressful time for me, but I won't make excuses, I'll just say that even though I knew I was pregnant, I drank anyway. I wasn't coping well with being unmarried and pregnant, and I had two other young children to care for. I was working full-time to support my family, and at the time, my relationship with Rob was rocky, at best.

I worked at the hotel until the very last day of my pregnancy. We decided that I would get induced a couple of weeks early as the doctor was going on holidays, and the night before I was scheduled to be induced, I went to work and did the books for that week. The next morning, I went into hospital and was induced at around 10 a.m.

I had dropped the kids off at Bruce's the day before. I still carried Bruce's last name and I wasn't yet married to Rob, but the nurses knew that the baby was Rob's and going to have Rob's name. However, when I was going through labour, the nurses kept coming in and asking, "Who's Bruce?" I explained that he was my ex husband. Apparently, he'd been calling the hospital repeatedly to see how I was.

Bruce and Anne had, after all, been a love match, and in an extraordinary coincidence, Anne had given birth to their son just that morning. Rob and I had our son that night, which means that my children, Sharon and Ryan, have two brothers (Kane and Chad) who were born on the same day.

Years later, when Kane's and Chad's wives became pregnant, both were due to give birth at the same time. They both had girls, though Kane's wife had Ava 3 weeks early; otherwise they could have been born at the same time. How uncanny is that?

I remember thinking to myself when I went into heavy labour with Kane, *what am I doing?* Sharon and Ryan were seven and nine, and you definitely forget the pain of giving birth. They say we forget it because if we remembered, we wouldn't have a large population; no one would ever have a second child!

I had Kane on a Friday and on Sunday, some of the staff from the hotel brought the wage rosters in so I could work out the pays and pay the hotel staff. The doctor walked in and when he saw what I was doing, nearly had a fit. But that is how it was back then: work, work, and more work. Even when I came home, I went straight back to work, and I was breastfeeding.

When Kane was born, the doctor asked me if I'd been spotting or bleeding through the pregnancy. I told him no, and questioned why he was asking. He replied that my placenta had deteriorated. He told me all placentas naturally start to deteriorate between 40 -42 weeks (sometimes earlier). The main thing that happens is that calcium deposits develop, making the placenta less efficient and causing reduced nutrients and blood flow to baby. It is just part of the natural cycle of the organ.

I asked myself if Kane was conceived to keep Rob and I together. Getting pregnant was the furthest thing from my mind, and I'd definitely not tried. We've never said Kane was a mistake. He was a pleasant surprise!

"In giving birth to our babies, we may find that we give birth to new possibilities within ourselves."

—*Myla and Jon Kabat-Zinn*

What No One Tells You When You're Pregnant

I will share with you the absolute joys of being a mother and nanna.

There are a lot things I wish I had known when I fell pregnant with my first child. Sure, you know certain things, and you know your life will change once the baby arrives. Friends, relatives and books on the topic tell you to prepare for sleepless nights and 3 a.m. feedings. But there are other things that no one tells you, not even your best friend or mother.

These little titbits are kept quiet and secret, as if passing the information on will stop every woman in the human race from having babies. However, I believe that applied knowledge is power and that all pregnant women should be given the full story *before* the baby comes into the world. That way, you'll have time to get used to certain ideas and concepts—and adapt to the end of life as you know it.

You will never go to the bathroom the same way again.

You will never again take a trip to the bathroom when you and your little one are alone in the house. Why, you ask? You will be gripped with fear that the baby will choke or fall out of her crib, or sustain some other horrible injury if you close the door. Trust me, it becomes second nature and you won't think twice about it in a couple of weeks. The only issue that arises is when you have guests over and you have to remember to close the door when you go.

To this day, my children and grandchildren love to stand at the toilet door when it is open and talk to me while I'm going. They even say, "Nanna, you smell!" I tell them to go away at that point, but no, they don't. They just stand there and keep talking.

You will never be alone again.

Even though you'll always leave the door open, going to the bathroom is about the only time that you'll get to yourself. But don't get used to it; that will only last until baby starts walking and can follow you in there. Whenever you are at home, you will be constantly checking on what the baby is doing, and getting out of the house won't happen for quite a while, unless you have a very good support team ready to step in. When you do go out to enjoy yourself, you'll feel so guilty about leaving your innocent babe behind that you'll be back home in no time.

Everything will become a "fitness challenge."

If you're not in shape yet, don't worry – you will be soon! Shopping trips will become a workout session. Oh, I know you're breast-feeding and don't need to buy boxes of formula–but have you actually picked up a bag of diapers? Packages of 24 aren't too bad, but unless you want to have to take a trip to the grocery store every other day, you're going to need the packs with 72 diapers. Try picking one up next time you go to the store. Wait – I take that back, don't! You're pregnant and it's probably not a good idea to lift that kind of weight. Baby wipes and other baby bath products also need to be added to the weight of your weekly shop. A baby is only a few pounds, but none of this baby stuff is light!

You will become a certified project manager.

Taking your new baby out of the house sounds simple enough – but it's not. It becomes a voyage requiring great organisational skills. You wouldn't climb Mt. Everest unprepared, would you?

Nor will you take a trip with the baby unprepared. Your baby-bag should be well stocked with supplies that are only used when you are out and about, and you can buy small-sized products for this purpose. That way, you will not have to check the bag every time you go out. Just remember that you'll need spare diapers, because you'll be astonished at how fast your baby-bag supply is wiped out. And remember to replace the baby-bag diapers when your baby grows into the next size up; there's nothing like trying to stuff a 14 lb. baby into a 12 lb. diaper! I'm sure it can be done, but your baby isn't going to be happy. Pack spare baby clothes if you are going out for the day. You may like to consider two spare sets–especially if your baby is male. One tip is to plan your outing to begin just after baby has eaten, otherwise you won't get very far before you hear the distinctive howl of a starved baby. If your baby isn't happy, be prepared to go home before your outing's purpose is achieved.

Babies cry.

I know that you're thinking, "Please, I know babies cry!" But, unless you are already a mum, you won't be prepared for how much this will affect you. Each heartbreaking sob will tear at your heart and cause you physical pain. You will find yourself at a loss sometimes as to how to comfort this sad little being, and wonder, from time-to-time, if you were really cut out for motherhood. You'll think, "This isn't for me. Maybe I can find a good mum to take this baby off my hands." Try to remember, it's just what babies do. Go with the flow, remind yourself that all babies cry and that yours is no different. It isn't a noisy reflection of your parenting skills at all. Soon, every time you hear a baby—any baby—cry, you will feel the urge to go over and try to comfort it.

From day one, babies have personalities and ideas all their own.

This idea may come as a surprise and take a little getting used to. You've probably read all the books by now, or have a list of those you intend to read, but once you've read them, just put the concepts in the back of your mind. After your baby has arrived, you can sort through them and use the appropriate ones, since not all of them will work for your baby. "Why? A baby is a baby," you say. Not so fast. Some books say that babies sleep for around 20 hours a day, but I know parents who tell me that they were lucky if their baby slept more than eight hours for the first two months. Some babies will eat a lot one day, and then next to nothing the next. Some babies will never conform to "normal" baby behaviour. Doctors will tell you that this is normal—so why don't they say that in the books? Not all babies crawl; some skip that step and go right to walking. You can try explaining to your baby that this isn't what it says in the book, but your baby will ignore you. Babies are born with their own ideas, and yours will be no exception. So, go ahead, read the books, but remember: your baby will do exactly what he or she wants.

A mother's love is very special.

The last thing I want to explain to you is this concept known as "mother's love". You already know you're going to love your baby. You probably already talk to it, sing to it, and gently stroke your growing bump, just waiting for the time that your arms can finally hold your bundle of joy. Even so, nothing will prepare you for the moment you first look down and make eye contact with your newborn child. From that second on, you will cease to be a person in your own right. You will become a willing slave to everything pertaining to your little baby's happiness. You will want to protect him/her from all the evils of the world and surround her/him with a wall of love that no hurt can pass through. Even if your baby is the most fussy and colicky baby in the Western World, screaming 20 hours, your love won't fade. And that first smile? Well, nothing can prepare you for the way that will make you melt inside. There will be many "almost" smiles before it, but you'll know the real thing when you see it, and by that time, you know you will gladly give up your life for this tiny being.

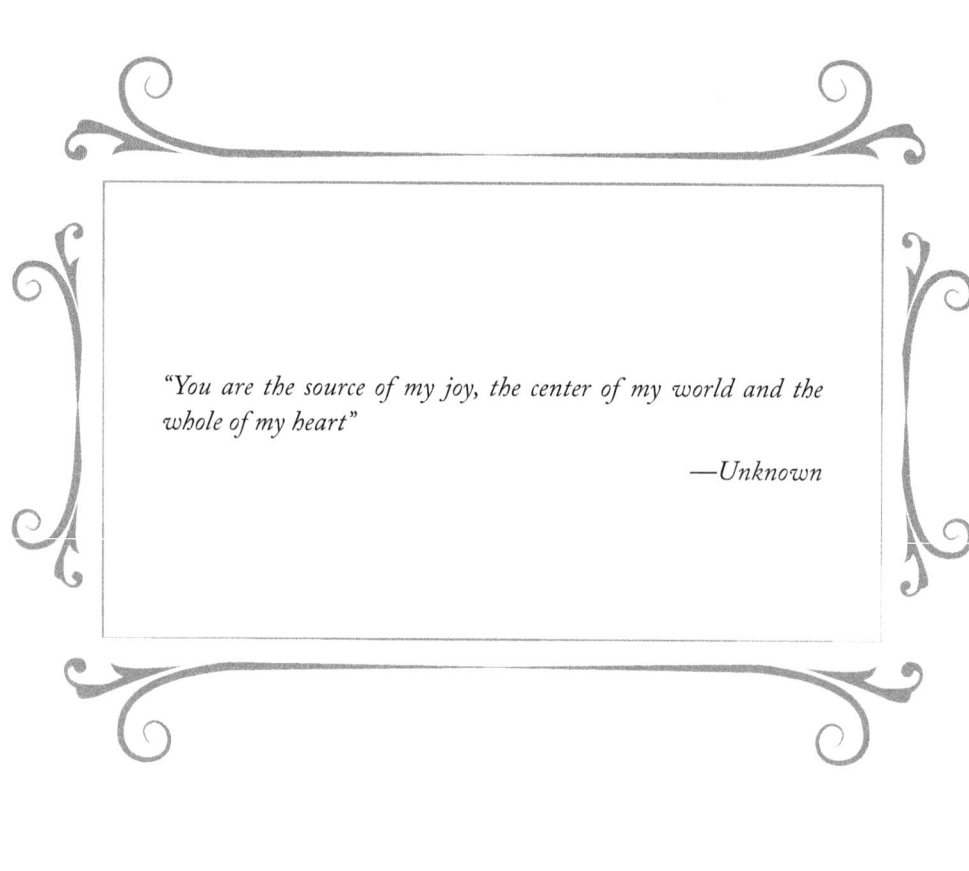

"You are the source of my joy, the center of my world and the whole of my heart"

—*Unknown*

Marrying Rob

When Rob and I got married, it was beautiful and I didn't indulge in alcohol too much.

Sharon, Ryan, and Kane were eleven, nine, and two, respectively, and of course, they were part of the wedding. We got married in the back yard of our home, the home we had near the hotel. We then had our reception at the hotel. It was a lovely day, although it rained a bit at the ceremony.

We stayed at the hotel that night and the kids had a room next door with the babysitter (who did have a few too many drinks!)

We all went to bed at the same time, but all I could hear from Sharon, who was eleven at the time, was, "Mummy! I want my mummy!" Really, you don't want to hear this on your wedding night.

Our babysitter eventually quieted her down. And the next morning, Rob, the kids and I all went out to breakfast to celebrate.

And here we are, married now for 33 years. Despite masses of ups and downs, we beat them all and are still very much in love.

> "Alcohol ruined me financially and morally, broke my heart and the hearts of too many others. Even though it did this to me and it almost killed me and I haven't touched a drop of it in seventeen years, sometimes I wonder if I could get away with drinking some now. I totally subscribe to the notion that alcoholism is a mental illness because thinking like that is clearly insane."
>
> —*Craig Ferguson, American on Purpose*

Drinking Stories: the Bad Old Days

The stories I am going to share with you are embarrassing. I'm not proud of them.

So…why write them?

To let you know that no matter how far you fall, you can still get up. If you fall and hit bottom, you can either lie there and wait for them to bury you, or you can get up. The choice is yours. Me? I chose to get up, and these stories are living proof.

Where do I start?

Before I met Rob, I was seeing a guy called Ross, who got on really well with the kids. He asked me out for dinner after we had been drinking at the hotel all day. I said yes, but there was a party I wanted to check out before dinner. We went to the party and I made the mistake of parking my car in the driveway of the party house.

As we were leaving, Dave, the village idiot—who is also a thug—started to urinate on the bonnet of my car. When he was finished, he reached through the window of the car and tried to grab the keys out of the ignition. Ross was behind the wheel and I leaned over to stop Dave from taking the keys.

Dave grabbed my hair and called me a slut. I'd had a bit to drink and that made me wild. I got out, walked around the back of the car, and slapped him across the back of the head. I said, "Dave, don't you ever say that to me again!"

With that, he lined me up and punched me right in the face. I didn't know, then, that he used to be a boxer.

I saw stars, and fell backwards. When I straightened myself up, I had blood gushing out of my mouth, so I took a handful of it and wiped it down Dave's t-shirt. Crying my eyes out, I climbed back into the car. As we were backing out, Ross looked at me in shock.

Ross went back inside and approached Dave as I sat in the car, blood pouring out of my mouth and my mind going around in circles. *What am I going to tell the kids? I have to work tomorrow, what am I going to do?* And that's when I realized one of my teeth had broken in half.

Ross got back in the car and took me straight to the doctor, who cleaned me up as much as he could and told me I had to see the dentist. I rang my local dentist, who I have been seeing all my life.

My appearance shocked him. My lip had split where my teeth had gone in; one tooth was snapped off and another was cracked. Keep in mind that these were my front teeth!

When he found out who had done this to me, the dentist said enough was enough; he was going to call the police. He told me that all he did was fix up people's teeth after this particular guy punched them out.

When the police came, it was humiliating. I had blood all down my white dress and they had me stand up against a wall to have my photo taken–smiling, to show what a mess my assailant had made of my teeth and mouth.

After the police left, my dentist pulled out the snapped off tooth and took an impression of my teeth for the false ones I now needed.

I rang Coral at the hotel, telling her what had happened and that I couldn't come to work. I couldn't believe it when she said, "That's okay, come to work, but just don't open your mouth." I was a barmaid at the hotel, so how could I not open my mouth? It was embarrassing. In the meantime, I had to put up with a temporary tooth, which was yellow compared to my other teeth.

In the end, the dentist pulled my right tooth, and I received a bridge of three teeth, two front and one on the side. This was fine for 10 years until my gums started to recede and the bone in the gums got infected. Then I had to have the bridge out and the other front tooth pulled. I now have a plate containing three front teeth. I hate them, they don't sit right and I can't bite into anything.

I ended up taking Dave to court, where he was ordered to pay over $5000, which he paid at a rate of $2.50 a week. (Actually, it was his mum who paid it.) He did this for a couple of months, then stopped, so I went to the police to see what I could do. They said that even with a summons against him, he still probably wouldn't pay. Where is the justice? So I had no choice; I just let it be.

Attempting Suicide

When I drank, I would get depressed. Back then it was so easy for me just to grab a handful of pills. By doing this, I didn't have to think about whether I was doing the right or wrong thing. I didn't have to think about anything; as soon as I swallowed the pills, that was it. It was over and I slept my worries away, finally at peace.

One particular night when I'd been drinking, my kids were home and I'd taken a handful of pills. All I remember is my brother Harold walking me around the room, trying to keep me awake. Harry, the guy I was dating at that time, had rung him. I hadn't taken enough pills to kill myself, just enough to make me sleep. When pills put me in this state, nothing mattered, not even my kids. All I wanted was peace. I would wake up in the morning and go through the day as though nothing had happened. I didn't think about the stress and worry that I had just put my family through. That's just it; you don't think of anyone else but yourself when you are in this state.

I remember a time when I was still going out with Graeme, I was drunk and we were fighting, and I locked him out of the house. I remember as clear as day that I went to the bathroom and got a razor (a modern one, not a razor blade) and sat down in the lounge room trying to pull the blade out so I could cut my wrists. All this time, I knew Graeme was looking through the window, watching.

He eventually broke back in and stopped me. While I was sitting there doing this, I was thinking, *please stop me; I don't want to do this*.

I have heard people say to me over the years that they could never understand why people commit suicide, that they are selfish because they don't think of the people they leave behind.

I found the answer to these questions each time I was in that dark place. When you consider taking your own life, you don't worry about what other people think. Suicide is all about you, and you honestly believe the world would be better off without you. You are in a place where you just can't live any more. It is just too hard; life and surviving hurts. Even if you have money, love, everything, it doesn't matter to you, because you just can't cope with "life" any more. It has gotten just too hard to be happy.

I had now broken up with Ross and was with Rob,

One day, Rob and I went out on our friends' boat with the kids. Drinking in the sun didn't help. After a full day on the water and having had a great time, we decided to pull up to the hotel.

Once again, I had an episode of memory loss. One minute I was sitting in the disabled toilet, looking in the corner and thinking how comfortable it looked, and the next thing I remember is that the bouncers somehow opened the door and got me out. I couldn't remember what happened after that. All I knew was my kids were little and a friend, who also drank, was looking after them. The next morning, I woke up in my bed and the kids were home with me. My friend had taken us all home and put us to bed. That is what friends are for. Right?

Rob and I broke up, and I had been drinking when I drove to his place, knocked on the door and asked him for some maintenance money for Kane. I don't know what happened next. Rob said he went back inside. He had one of those windows that pull out to open and apparently, I went over to it and banged my arms on it, slicing open my right arm.

I remember going to the car, blood everywhere, and I was crying. A couple of guys came out, looked at me, then left. I drove home and then walked to where my girlfriend was staying in the caravan park next door, and she took me to the hospital. I don't know how many stitches I had, but there was a big slice right around the arm; you could see all the fat cells, it was so deep. In the morning, the police came around and said that Rob wasn't going to lay charges, but to keep away from him. How embarrassing!

I used to breastfed Kane, and I had an aunt who lived in one of the units who would buzz me when Kane was awake. When the bar closed, I would wait for the band to pack up and leave. I used to have Kane with me in his bassinet, either on the bar or on the pool table.

On this particular night, Auntie had Kane, and when I finished work, she told me to take him. I hadn't been drinking, I had just been working, but I didn't want to go home, so I wrapped Kane up and took him to the nightclub with me. With all the smoke and idiots there, it was not a good environment for my child, but that was how I was brought up. I didn't stay long. I got my fix (not drugs) and went home.

Rob and I went to a party one night. We dropped Kane off at the babysitter's before we left. Once there, I got heavily into the drugs and alcohol and was soon off my face. Once again, I became jealous, grabbed my keys, got in the car and left. I remember going to pick Kane up and driving home with him on my lap. I was terribly out of it, and I had my little baby on my lap and was driving. Seriously, what was I thinking? Well I wasn't. I never did when I drank; I never thought of the consequences

I was out of my mind. Looking back, I am totally ashamed of myself. What if I'd had a car accident? My son was on my lap, for God's sake! I am in tears as I write this, imagining what might have happened.

I arrived home and Kane and I slept in the same bed that night. Rob was home in the morning, and both of us felt sore and sorry for ourselves. We did stupid things when we drank, but we didn't think we were doing anything wrong. We just went with it.

Another of those times when Rob and I were separated, he was living with one of his mates and the mate's girlfriend.

I went to the hotel and Rob was there with his mate, so I got really drunk and, as I mentioned, I generally get to a stage where I want sex. Well, Rob didn't; he was with his mate, and it wasn't the "done" thing to leave your mate.

I got in my car, drove down to the river and jumped in. I then made a show of trying to drown myself. I was stupid, sitting in shallow water, trying to keep my head underwater, and eventually I gave up. I got back into the car and decided to drive to where Rob was living. Unbeknownst to me, I'd passed him and his mate walking home.

I arrived at his place and saw his sporty little Mazda in the garage. I was in my Tarago van, and I put my foot on the accelerator and smashed into Rob's car, reversed back, accelerated and smashed into it again, until his car went through the back of the garage wall.

Reversing out the last time, I flipped the car and ended up on the neighbour's front lawn with the car on its side. I actually flipped a van! I must have passed out for a while, and when I came to, I had no idea what had happened.

By now you can see how terrible it was. I had a drinking problem, and tried to kill myself many times by taking pills, cutting myself, smashing cars, and trying to drown myself.

Rob's mate's girlfriend came out, got me out of the car, took me inside, and put me in some dry clothes. I don't remember much from that point, only that I walked home and I don't know how I managed; it was a long way. When I woke up in the morning, I was sore and covered in bruises, and boy, did I have a headache. The night was a blur.

I rang a friend of mine to organise getting the car towed away so that it could be fixed. I was so ashamed and embarrassed. I couldn't go around there and face them, and Rob was ropeable. He didn't want anything to do with me, and I didn't blame him. I suppose this was when I thought our marriage was really over; not only had I smashed up his car, but I had totally embarrassed him in front of his mate.

The next story is the one that really put me over the edge. It was the point when I realized I had a problem and absolutely had to stop drinking.

As far as I was concerned, Rob and I were finally over, so I started to go out with a guy who had been trying to get me into bed for ages. I wasn't interested. Even so, we went on a wine cruise and I got totally hammered. I even kept drinking on the drive home.

I don't remember much of what happened when we got to his place, except spewing in the toilet. I know I had sex with him, but I couldn't remember it at all. He then took me home.

The next day, I felt cheap and dirty. This was a big wakeup call for me about my drinking.

Rob knew I was going out with this guy, and he realized he was going to lose me. Isn't it funny how your ex will want you back as soon as they see you with someone else? What Rob didn't know was that I was dating this man in the hope of making him jealous.

Our son Kane kept mentioning the man I was dating, so Rob rang me. We talked and decided to try to make our marriage work. All along, we wanted to be together, but our relationship was just too volatile.

I broke off with the guy and got back with Rob. We then decided to buy a house and start all over again.

"Take the first step in faith. You don't have to see the whole staircase, just take the first step."

— Dr Martin Luther King Jr.

Why and When I Gave Up Drinking and Drugs

The following part of the journey brought me to my destination today, which is being alcohol-free for 25 years.

I was back with Rob and we had bought a house. Then the girlfriend I went to school with, Sue, decided we should go to a health farm. It was a farm on acreage, nothing flashy, and there was a three-day cleansing retreat, walking up and down hills, listening to talks, doing yoga and having massages, with no tea, coffee or alcohol.

What those three days did for me was cleanse my brain. For the first time in years, I could actually think. My mind was not in a fog any more. It is quite hard to explain, but there was no numbness; I could feel and "be" again. It was a wonderful feeling! And another thing, which I hadn't felt for a while, was being "me".

It is so hard to explain, but it felt like a light had turned on, that I had learnt the lesson. I could now see what I was like when I drank, and how I was hurting people, and I knew it had to end. And I realized I had the same addiction to alcohol as I did to food.

I realised it didn't matter if I felt depressed, happy, sad, overwhelmed, in control, on my own, with people or without (and the list goes on), I found every excuse to drink or to take some type of drug.

The hangovers always took a couple of days to get over, and I wasn't much good to myself, let alone anyone else, at those times.

I had started to become forgetful. I was doing things when I was drinking that I couldn't remember when I was sober.

I was also becoming more jealous and violent. When Rob and I drank, the verbal abuse and violent tempers we shared between us were not healthy for the children to see, nor were they healthy for Rob and me.

I'd gone to Al-Anon, partners of alcoholics, thinking my husband was the one with the problem. I'd heard some terrible and sad stories, husbands and partners drinking all day long, spending all the money. Yes, I could relate to that. Rob and I didn't drink all day, just at night and on weekends, but still we had a problem.

My mind was always in a fog.

I never had enough money, because I was spending so much on alcohol and drugs.

I thought I was enjoying life, but I wasn't.

By drinking, I was getting more depressed, which gave me suicidal tendencies. And I never wanted my family to go through that again.

I wasn't myself when I drank. I became someone else and that person was not a nice person. But I never saw that at the time.

When I was in the hotel game, my whole life had been a bad cocktail mix of so many things, but now I had made up my mind (through a lot of hard work) that I wasn't going down that road any more. I wanted to become healthy and more alert. I wanted a future with my family, a strong healthy future. I could finally see what I was doing to them and I didn't want them to be hurt any more. They could see what I was doing to myself and I didn't want the environment for my children to continue to be centred around alcohol and drugs.

What helped, too, was that Rob and I were out of the hotel by then, so of course, the huge temptation wasn't there any more.

When I returned home from the health farm, I stopped drinking straight away. I also no longer drank coffee.

I have had neither coffee nor alcohol since 1991, the year I turned 38. 25 years of sobriety.

THE SERENITY PRAYER

God grant me the Serenity,
To accept
the things I cannot change,
The Courage
to change the things I can and
The Wisdom
to know the difference.

— Reinhold Niebuhr (1892-1971)

Are You An Alcoholic?

I never thought I was an alcoholic. Please, feel free to answer the questions below and if you answer yes to any of them, it may be time to get some professional help.

Ask yourself:

Do you drink by yourself?

Does your personality change when you drink?

Do you have memory lapses after drinking?

Do you find other people slow to finish their drinks?

Do you take a drink before you have to face a problem?

Do you drink because you like the taste?

Do you drink for the effect it will have on you?

When you are at work, do you sneak away for a quick drink?

Does alcohol give you courage?

When you drink, do you become loud, abusive, slow and sluggish, or depressed?

Does alcohol take up a significant portion of your finances?

If you have decided to quit the drinking habit for good, never question why you are giving up drinking. If you do that, you are setting yourself up for failure.

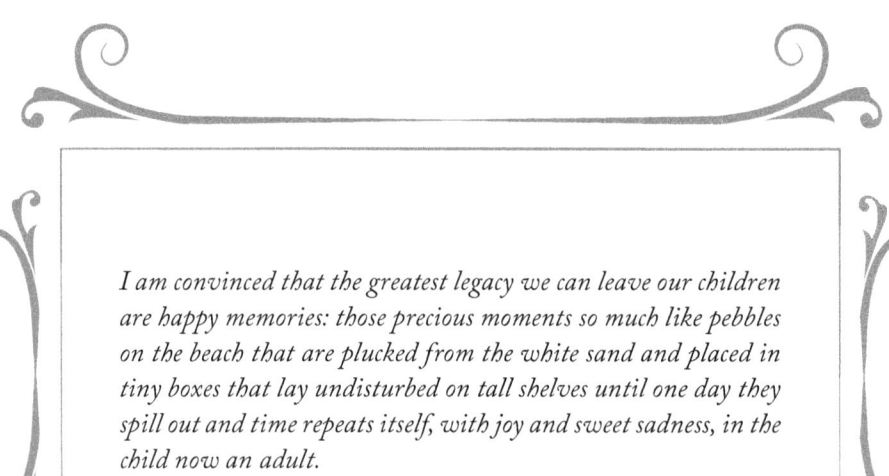

I am convinced that the greatest legacy we can leave our children are happy memories: those precious moments so much like pebbles on the beach that are plucked from the white sand and placed in tiny boxes that lay undisturbed on tall shelves until one day they spill out and time repeats itself, with joy and sweet sadness, in the child now an adult.

—Og Mandino

My Father's Legacy

My father was a pioneer in the town of Mandurah, where we lived. I had always wanted to sit down with him and hear his life story.

Rob and I owned a children's wear shop and I told Dad that when the shop closed, I would have the time to come and sit down with him and learn his history, as well as our family history. Dad was still as sharp as a tack and had all his wits about him. We were both really looking forward to talking.

Then my sister called to say that Dad was in hospital.

I think most people believe that their parents are going to be here forever. I know I did. I didn't think too much of Dad going into the hospital, since I didn't think anything major was wrong. I went up to see him that night and he asked to see my children. I told him I would bring them the following night, as I didn't have room in the car that night because I'd brought my sister, brother, and mum with me.

As I write this, I am crying, because I wasn't really "with" him that night. My mind was on other things. *Besides*, I thought to myself, *I'll be back tomorrow*. I didn't think he was going anywhere.

That night Dad didn't want us to leave, but visiting hours were over, so I told him I would see him tomorrow.

"Tomorrow" never came. Early in the morning we received a phone call telling us that Dad had lapsed into a coma. My mum, who had Alzheimer's, my sister and my brother went straight to the hospital and stayed with him. We followed him as he was transported by ambulance to a hospital in Perth to have a scan. He died on the table.

At the hospital, it seemed like everyone was rushing around and looking at us. I just knew he had gone, but nobody told us for about 20 minutes. Eventually, someone came out and said that he had died. Mum didn't really understand what was happening because of her Alzheimer's, but my brother, sister and I were in shock and shattered.

The doctor asked if we wanted to see him one last time, so Harold and I went in to say our goodbyes. I couldn't believe it. He was gone.

The saddest part was, Dad died when there were only 10 days left before Rob and I were going to close the shop doors for good, when I could walk away and finally catch up with him.

But it never happened. Life gets too busy and before you know it, it's over. When we lost Dad, it devastated me. And I don't know a great deal about our family history. I never had the time to sit down with Dad, as we were both so busy, and now all that time that I wanted with him, and all that history, have gone with him.

What I do know is what he did with his life, and that he was my motivational force to succeed.

It took me a long time to get over Dad's death, and I would wake up every morning and cry.

When I started selling products for the skin care and make up company, Nutrimetics, I gave a demonstration in a house that was on a street named after Dad. As I was doing the demo, I started crying. I felt like an idiot, but I missed him so much.

What I've learned from my father's death is that you must take time to smell the roses and spend time with your family, because you never know when the people you love might be snatched from you. It can happen sooner than you think.

I am still a workaholic, but it's a different type of work. I absolutely love what I do, so to me it isn't work; it is helping other people. Most people spend most of their lives earning a living, rather than designing a lifestyle. My work is my passion, but having work/life balance is very important.

"You cannot control what happens to you, but you can control your attitude toward what happens to you, and in that, you will be mastering change rather than allowing it to master you."

—Brian Tracy

Out of the Blue: Bankruptcy

From the age of 13, I'd worked in our hotel, doing anything that needed to be done, which included pouring jug after jug of beer for the customers with a Pluto (a handheld hose) until my hand was frozen. After closing time, bags of money, wet with beer, would be brought to the office, and I would sort it and count it. I loved every aspect of my work.

When I left school to work at the hotel, I did every job imaginable.

I lived for that hotel. It was my past, present and future, my world, my life, and my security.

Later, it was also home to my children and me, even though technically, we lived in a house over the road. As I was always working, all of our time was spent at the hotel. My kids all grew up there, so it was a real family affair.

But this kind of life wasn't perfect. The downfall of being involved in a hotel is that Mandurah is a tourist resort and I always worked longer and harder on holidays like Christmas, summer and long weekends. As a result, there wasn't a lot of time left for my children, but being a family business, the children could come and go as they pleased. You could do this back then, as it was safe, not like now.

I was brought up with a very secure feeling knowing that thanks to the hotel, there was always going to be an income there. Why wouldn't there be?

Of the three of us, my brother Harold was the major shareholder, while my sister Cheryl and I were minor shareholders. Dad eventually turned the hotel over to my siblings and myself.

Even though I was always working at the hotel, doing anything and everything that needed to be done, I wasn't aware of all that was going on. A business as large as a hotel can be very difficult to manage and I'll be the first to admit that mistakes were made. The hotel, like any company, had its ups and downs. Business was a little shaky, but I wasn't worried, as we had gone through rough patches before.

Then, it was suddenly taken away from us: the hotel, the income, the feeling of security—all of it. Gone!

It was a Friday and I was working at the hotel as usual, when our bar manager came in and said she'd heard through the grapevine that receivers were on their way down to seize the property. I could barely believe my ears!

"What? Receivers! What are you talking about?"

My sister and I looked at each other and prepared to face the music. We rang our brother and told him, but he wouldn't come over. He couldn't face it.

The worst part was the waiting. We didn't know what to do. Should we take some of the memorabilia around the place as a memento of our time there? What things had sentimental value to me? I couldn't even think straight.

When the receivers finally did arrive, there were eight of them in total. They walked in, introduced themselves, and then dispersed through the hotel, the bars, the kitchen, the restaurant, the storerooms, and the units. They had walkie-talkies and the sound of them talking to each other completely filled the place.

Two of them stayed behind with my sister and me and asked us for our keys. From that point on, we were never to be alone in the hotel; we always had to have one of the receivers with us.

It's a horrible feeling when a stranger walks up to you and asks you for the keys to your life, and there is nothing you can do about it but hand them over. To me, they weren't just keys; they were a symbol of stability, and not just my stability, but my family's.

My sister and I sat down with the receivers as they explained the receivership process and went through what was going to happen next. We then left the hotel. We went to see our brother and told him what happened.

What a horrible feeling that was, climbing into our car, crying as we drove away. The hotel wasn't ours anymore.

The feeling is indescribable; in one hour, our future had turned to ashes. It couldn't have been any worse if the hotel had burned to the ground.

It wasn't just the material things or losing our heritage that was devastating to me; it was what I lost of myself. Wrapped up in that hotel was my self-esteem, my confidence, my identity, and my security for myself and my family.

These values were all replaced with a feeling of failure and an uncertain future. And not being able to go to the hotel anymore, except as a paying customer, was just heartbreaking.

I felt lost.

"It's these turnaround or these pivotal moments that introduce you to yourself, these small or these huge catastrophic events in your life. I do think that, that's where you really meet yourself."

—*Sheryl Crow*

Another Business Down

Rob and I had a children's wear shop, so it was natural that when we lost the hotel, we would lose our other business as well. We held our own for a while but eventually, it got to be too much. It was going to happen, so we just bit the bullet.

The night we were closing, everyone in the complex came and had a goodbye drink with us. There were so many tears; we had been there for seven years and met some wonderful people.

When everyone left, Rob, the kids and I packed everything up, stacked it high on the Ute, and closed the doors. Again, that horrible feeling came back.

After we closed the door of the shop, I made a few phone calls to friends down south to see if I could bring the items that were left and sell them. I hired a small moving van and my daughter Sharon and I packed it up and off we went.

We travelled south, living in hotel rooms, going from house to house, unpacking, selling, packing up and taking off. We sold a bit, but not enough. When we got back, we had to take all the clothing into the bank, where they took possession of it. It wouldn't have been so bad if it had been witnessed only by the bank manager, but all the staff were there, so it was very humiliating.

The worst part was that my husband, Rob, who'd had nothing to do with the hotel, had to declare bankruptcy as well, just because he was married to me; everything we owned, we owned together.

So at the age of 40, I went bankrupt. My family lost our hotel, Rob and I lost our business, and we all lost our homes. Even my car was towed away!

We heard the bailiff was coming around to create an inventory of the contents of our home to see what could be sold to raise cash. I didn't care that much about the furniture, but when he asked if I had any jewellery to declare, I quickly turned my engagement ring around.

After everything else, how dare they try to take my rings? They were a symbol of the love, connection, and commitment I have with my husband. It tore my heart out. We were about to lose our home and cars, and they wanted to take the only thing we had left—the representation of our love for one another.

The gut-wrenching nausea and embarrassment Rob felt when he had to walk into the bank and hand over the keys to our home was distressing. Worse yet, he had to hand them to the woman who had helped us get our mortgage just a couple of years earlier, and had become our friend. Our dreams were shattered.

But that wasn't the worst part of bankruptcy. It was losing the hotel, our "real" home. Wrapped up in the hotel was who we were as a family.

In the end, we were left with some basic furniture, Rob's work car, his tools, my sewing machines, and, yes, my wedding and engagement rings.

We had worked all those years and we weren't young any more. Having to start from scratch, and the feelings of worthlessness and loss that this creates, consumes your very soul.

To me, bankruptcy is a dirty word. It can be degrading and demoralizing. It's a traumatic event and having friends who are supportive goes a long way in helping you keep your sanity and sense of self worth. Once you are bankrupt, you soon find out who your real friends are. It's not what people say to you; it's what they don't say to you. Even with family, I still felt a sense of failure. We felt like outcasts.

My children were totally bewildered. All their lives their family had owned the landmark of Mandurah, the Hotel Peninsula. We were a well-known and respected family who identified ourselves by the hotel; it was who we were.

Emotions erupted all over the place. We were stunned, angry, shocked, scared, and anxious. As you can guess, there were family disputes and also a lot of finger pointing about what went wrong. Luckily, these squabbles did not include my husband and children, but the stress from such fights was absolutely draining. My greatest fear was the unknown. How was I going to support my family?

Whatever it takes

I had a huge fear of what people would say to me or about me, so it was very hard for me to get out of my comfort zone. Besides dressmaking and working in the hotel, I didn't know how to do anything else. In addition, I had never worked for anyone, so I really didn't know where to start. I was used to being my own boss.

When you have had your own business, suddenly working for and answering to someone else can be a shock. And when you are bankrupt, you can't get credit or own a car worth more than $2,500, and this restricts you. It's a form of punishment that you have to endure. Rob worked as a bricklayer, so with three children, it wasn't easy to make ends meet.

We sold some of our furniture to cover living expenses and had garage sales to earn some money. We sold anything that we weren't using and didn't need. At one point, we didn't even have a dining room set, so we sat on the floor to eat our meals.

The kids and I delivered papers. And we all went without takeaway meals. I had already stopped drinking alcohol, and we stopped going out to restaurants and to the cinema, basically anything that cost money.

I'm a dressmaker, so I started sewing at home. It was great for a while, because I could hide from the world, but something inside of me was dying. I needed something to fulfil me again, but the time wasn't right. I was terribly confused and just didn't know what to do.

With the dressmaking business, I took every job that was brought to me, no matter how distasteful. Old men would bring me their pants to have new zippers put in. The zips would be corroded with urine and the pants so smelly, I would nearly vomit. At first I started to unpick the old zips, and put the new zips in. Eventually, I couldn't take it any more as it made me so sick, so I ended up washing all the pants and then I'd put the zips in. At least this way the guys were getting their pants back not only with a new zip, but freshly laundered and ironed as well.

I thought to myself, *what has my life come to?*

I was approached by the local drycleaners to do dressmaking from the back of their shop, and agreed. This was a mistake. Because I was desperate, it was easy for them to use and exploit me, but as we needed the money, I stayed there. I felt useless and I didn't think I could do anything else.

I picked up and delivered dry cleaning all over Mandurah and the surrounding areas for $5 an hour, in addition to serving customers in the shop and cleaning the Laundromat at least four times a day. It wasn't the work that worried me—I was used to that—but I wasn't getting paid for a lot of those bits and pieces I was doing for the shop owners. I was doing all of this extra work for them and that left very little time for my real bread and butter: sewing.

It was starting to get me down. I was even taking my sewing home, as I didn't have time to do it at work. Something was wrong here.

The final straw was when the owners disapproved of my children coming to the shop to visit me, and told them not to come any more. Keep in mind that I was paying the shop owners rent for my little space in their shop!

Rob and I talked about me leaving and just sewing from home. I was worried I wouldn't get the work, but I had to take the chance. I decided to leave the shop and work from home.

It was the best move I could have made. Not only was I home for the kids, but I was well known in the area. People knew my work and were glad I could take more jobs. I now had time to do the work I wanted to do and I got very busy, very quickly. And I could sew at night if I wanted to.

Breaking Free

I have always believed that things happen for a reason. While it was devastating at the time, losing the hotel was the best thing that could have happened to me because of the following:

I broke free from the hotel and from all the restrictions it imposed on me, including being under the control of my brother.

Being apart from the hotel also reinforced my decision to give up drinking, which I believed saved not only my life, but my future with my husband and children.

And I could look at my husband and know he really did love me for me, and not just for what the hotel had offered in terms of money and lifestyle. When we were about to lose everything, he was still there for me 100%.

"Faith can giveus courage to face the uncertainties of the future"
—*Martin Luther King Jr*

Getting Out of the Hole

It took years, which seemed like forever, before we were formally discharged from bankruptcy. Rob was out of bankruptcy before me. When we were both out, we wanted to move forward. It was exciting and we felt free at last.

We were renting a house, and down the road was a block that Rob wanted, so we thought we would try to buy it, even though we never imagined we could afford it.

To our surprise, we could.

We organised a house and land package, and started to build. Once we'd built the house, the developer said we had to have the front landscaping finished within three months. This was a pretty big obstacle, as we didn't have any more money. But our friends, who had stuck by us, had some big conifers and other plants, which they gave us. It was a start and we were so thankful.

Another friend, who was a plumber, came down and did the reticulation for us for free, just charging us the cost of the equipment.

The council decided to put a path on the other side of the road, which meant the pavers and grass of nearby properties had to be dug up. Seeing an opportunity, we approached all the property owners and asked if we could have the pavers and grass, and they said yes. Once again, things happen for a reason.

We then asked the bobcat driver if, when he dug up the grass, he would mind putting it on the empty block next to us. He did this, but didn't want any payment, so we thanked him with a carton of beer; in Australia, that's like money! We now had a lovely mixture of different grass. It was a little mismatched, but so what? It was still grass and it was free. Rob would come home every day after a full day of bricklaying, and he would use a tomahawk to chop the grass up and put it in the front of the house. Our front lawn soon looked absolutely beautiful.

To get the pavers, I would drive my car over to the property owner's driveway, put all the pavers in the boot, and stack them behind our house. Once again, just by asking, we got what we needed for free.

As we lived on a corner lot, the developers told us we had to have a brick wall up around the property. Since Rob is a bricklayer, he was able get the bricks cheap and of course, he lay them himself. I still remember the day he built the wall; it was Father's Day. The kids were away, so he thought he would just do it and get it over with.

One day I went to a friend's house as she had two big steel gates for sale, which she sold to me for a fraction of what they would have cost new. Then she told me where I could go to buy some cheap, smaller side gates, which we needed for the side of the house. We asked a friend if he could put them up for us. All you need to do, sometimes, is ask.

I had started in real estate and it had taken off. More money was coming in now, so we were able to put up a beautiful triple patio, barbeque area, big shed, paving and herb garden. All of this work was done by Rob and me and our mates. The patio was huge, comprised of three structures joined together. I would paint it whenever I could. It needed two coats and I thought I was never going to finish it. I was up there like a monkey, going from rafter to rafter, but when it was finished, I could look back with pride and say, "I did that!" That was how we felt about everything we did to our home; it was built out of love and a lot of hard work

We painted the inside of the house ourselves.

I went to garage sales and bought old furniture and painted it.

Being a dressmaker, I made all the curtains.

So we were pretty comfortable, although the back yard took two years to complete.

Nevertheless, the house hadn't been finished for long when we decided to put it on the market.

It was hard work, but we had obtained a loan, built a house, landscaped it so that it looked beautiful at very little cost, and sold it for a profit – all because we took a chance and asked for a little bit of help from other people. We could have rolled over and wallowed in self pity, played the "blame game," or spent all our time being bitter about what happened. But where would that have got us? We chose to move forward.

Next, we bought a canal block, which we were going to build on and then move to.

We were now out of the hotel business as well as our clothing business, and a new journey was about to unfold.

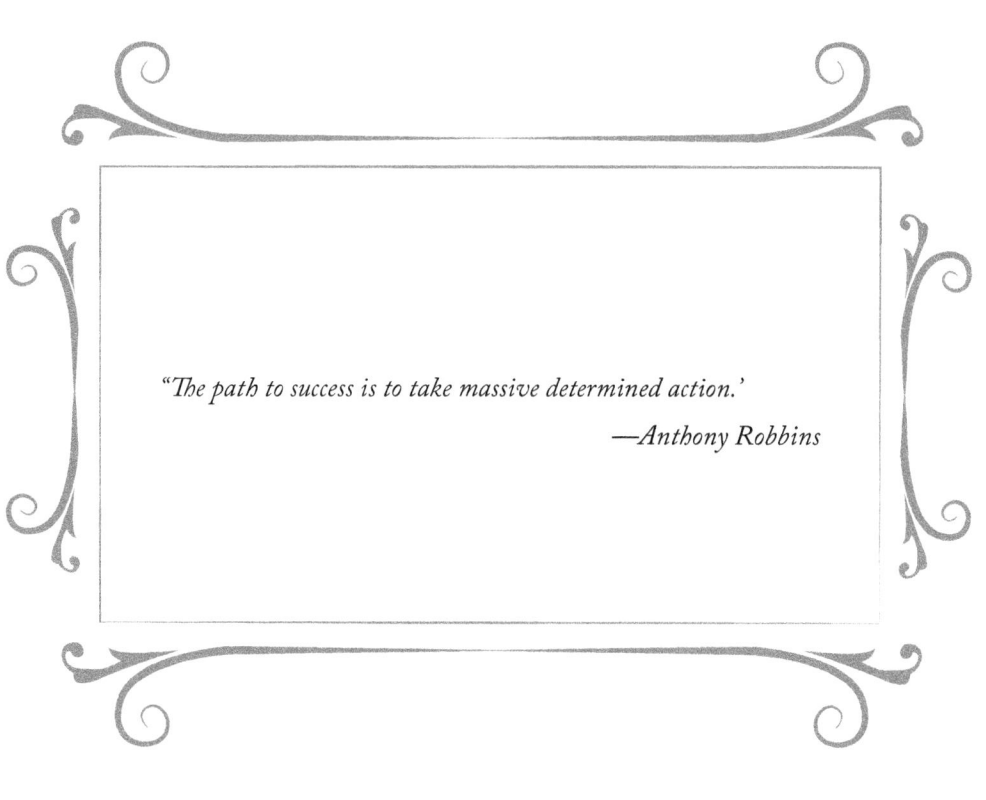

"The path to success is to take massive determined action."
—*Anthony Robbins*

Nutrimetics: Opportunity Knocks

I had used Nutrimetics skin care and makeup products since I was 16 years old. In fact, I believed in the products so much that when my sister-in-law invited me to a business preview at Nutrimetics, a multi-level marketing company, I agreed to go. But when I arrived, the high flyers earning cars and conducting the seminars were just too much for me.

I was overwhelmed. It didn't seem achievable for someone like me. I really didn't think I was capable of succeeding in that type of environment. Yes, I would love the exotic trips that the salespeople earned, the extra income and the cars, but it was a dream that seemed out of my reach.

Then I thought to myself, *what have I got to lose?* If you truly want something, you'll make it happen.

At the time, I didn't have a car and I desperately needed one. I didn't just want a car; I needed one, as my own car had been towed away during the bankruptcy proceedings.

Then there were other obstacles, beginning with the fact that I didn't have the money for the Nutrimetics kit that I would need to get started.

As luck would have it, my sister-in-law, Dianne, was able to lend me the money for the kit.

Being in the position I was in, I couldn't get financing to buy a car, so we decided to buy Dianne's old car.

And then there was me. The bankruptcy had taken its toll and I was at rock bottom, full of nagging self doubt. *How will I do this? I have no chance at succeeding. What am I doing?*

I turned to family and friends and asked them to let me do a Nutrimetics show, but there were no takers. Now I knew that I had to push myself out of my comfort zone, get out there and just do it.

I was petrified.

I parked my car in downtown Mandurah and looked around. As there was nothing else I could do, I began by approaching strangers and asked nearly everyone who walked by to let me host a Nutrimetics show at their home. By the end of the day, I'd obtained permission to do 12 shows.

Okay, fine, the asking part was over. But now I had to actually *do* the shows.

I was sick with fear before each one. Yet I dragged myself out, forcing myself out of my comfort zone.

Oddly enough, after a couple of shows, I began to enjoy myself.

Journey to Success

While I was involved in running the hotel, I never had dreams or goals. The hotel was everything. It was always going to be there and I never thought about doing anything else.

Looking back from where I am now, I realize that the life I now lead could never have existed while I was in the hotel, because I'd never known anything else. And you don't know what you don't know. Since then, I've learned to write my dreams and goals down on paper and create a plan to achieve them. By writing down your dreams and goals, you make a commitment to yourself and you commit what you've written to your subconscious mind.

When I first made a commitment to my goals, I knew it would take a lot of time and hard work.

When I first decided that I wanted to earn a Nutrimetics car, I called a meeting with my family to discuss what was going to happen and to get their input. They all said, "Go for it Mum, and we will help however we can."

We worked together as a family. I delegated the jobs that needed to be done and they could see the rewards as we worked together as a team. We worked towards a common goal and we saw what the power of teamwork and helping each other could achieve, and this created an energy and passion that kept us going.

So, the first lesson is to get the support of those around you and then learn to delegate jobs to others. I am not a superhero; I can't do it all on my own, and neither can you.

Every night I would write a to-do list. Once it's written down, you know what you have to do. You don't get confused and the people helping you understand their role. It's such a great feeling when you start to cross things off the list. You feel fulfilled because you have achieved something, something that you wanted to do, or maybe even something you didn't want to do – but it's over, and you don't have it hanging over your head any more.

Joining Nutrimetics was the best thing for me. It changed my life, as I was taught, motivated, inspired, supported, and encouraged by everyone around me.

During my seven years at Nutrimetics, I had many months of achieving number one in Sales and Sponsoring. I became a Sales Director, had my name placed on the Honour Roll, and over the years, I earned not one, but three Nutrimetics cars!

Each year, a King and Queen for the whole of Nutrimetics is named, and one year, I was fifth in line. That year, when our region had a Queen, I was named number one (Queen) and received a magnificent trophy.

When you have setbacks–and I have had many–learn by them. Analyse the situation: What went wrong? Why? How can I do it differently next time?

Setbacks have made me more determined. I admit I used to hate challenges and setbacks, but I now welcome them. That feeling of achievement when the brick wall that was holding you back is smashed down, is fantastic. And when you smash it down, watch yourself and your business grow. Take time to think, change your attitude, refuel and put a plan into action.

After every achievement, our family had a little victory celebration, which is so important. Have milestones you can check off as you move closer to your goal, and celebrate every time you reach one.

To build my business, I decided to spread my wings a little, and by thinking outside the box, grew my business tenfold.

The company told me Albany (a four hour drive from where I lived) was crying out for someone from Nutrimetics to go down there, so a consultant and myself decided to do it. But where to start?

We got the phone book and rang everyone in Albany. Well, it felt like everyone! Soon, we were booking 3 shows a day for 7 days, and once we received those shows, we then had to find somewhere to stay that wasn't going to cost an arm and a leg. We found a caravan park.

We got down there a day earlier, and walked the streets and picked up even more future shows.

After that first week we had sponsored, we received orders that needed to be delivered. So we booked a venue for our new consultants to learn and bring their future consultants, and every week we would drive down to Albany and I would run the training of the consultants, do one-on-ones with them and then do the leadership meeting. It was full on, as it was a 2 day event, and I would then drive back and look after my team at home

But I built a huge business in Albany, turning over $40,000 in sales a month!

The following happened one time when I was out and about by myself during my Nutrimetics days.

I was driving back from Perth in my old bomb of a car when I noticed smoke coming out the back. I pulled over and realised that the smoke was actually coming from the engine and travelling under the car to the back. Back then, I didn't have a mobile phone, but just a short distance away, there was a car yard. I was about to walk over to it when a car stopped and a man got out and looked at my car.

He suggested going back to his place to ring someone, and not thinking too much of it, I said okay. He lived about 10 minutes away and he told me he was married with kids, so it all seemed on the up-and-up.

When we arrived at his place, the neighbour across the street waved to him, as we went inside. I made my phone calls, and he asked if I wanted a cuppa, which I declined. I was starting to feel a bit nervous about being in his house with him, so I suggested we go back to my car in case we missed the tow truck, and I headed out of the house. We got back into his car and he took me back to mine.

As far as I can tell, he was a Good Samaritan, but what if he hadn't been? I can't believe I just got into his car, but you see, I was in trouble, and he'd offered to help me, which I was thankful for.

But why didn't I just go to the car yard? Then again, why didn't he take me to the car yard? It was right there. What would have happened if his neighbour hadn't seen him come home and wave? What if no one had seen him? I will never know and I don't want to know. I was so stupid. Once again, I'd reacted before thinking about what I was doing.

The reason I have added this story is to let you know that even when we try to do the best we can, we aren't perfect, we are only human, and it can be especially hard when you are on your own. When you have someone else there, and there are two of you making a decision, it's one thing, but when it is only you and you have to make a decision all by yourself and make it quickly, it is much harder, and sometimes you just can't think straight.

Never, never get into someone's car if you don't know them! Even if you feel as though you're stuck, don't let someone take advantage of that.

I often found I was reacting to situations like this, instead of analysing them and thinking through my options. It is so easy to do this.

My First Nutrimetics Car

When I started with Nutrimetics, a new program had just been established that would make it easier for salespeople to earn their first car. You were able to achieve it a lot faster than before, so I decided to take full advantage of this. However, just before the program started, I had a major hiccup in my business plan—so much so I that was going to throw in the towel and walk away. You see, right at that time, the top sales people in my region, who I was depending on, decided to take a break from the business.

I was devastated.

People come and go and that's just a fact of life, but in the months that my business was falling apart, so was I. Somehow, I let those obstacles stand in the way of my goals and my commitment to myself. I felt I was falling out of love with my business. Then I realized I was falling out of love with Nutrimetics only because things weren't happening the way I wanted them to. So it was up to me to make them happen my way.

After many tears and talking with my up lines and my family, I decided to push on. I realize now it was one of those brick walls that sometimes come our way. If you can break down those brick walls—and you will keep getting them—you will come out a lot stronger in the end. That little hiccup was the best thing that could have happened to our group. It made my team and myself a lot stronger and more determined.

But don't think it was easy! I needed some self-motivation.

It's important to figure out techniques to motivate yourself. Certain people can inspire you, but you need to identify what works for you and keep yourself motivated with CDs and books, as well as any other tools.

As I didn't just want the car, but *needed* it, striving for the car was what motivated me and it changed how I thought and acted. I am not a quitter and I can see the big picture. I was going to go for it! Every minute was so important and I had to use that time wisely and not procrastinate.

The hardest part of any business is getting started, but with focus, belief and a little hard work, you can make it happen, just like I did.

I bought myself a little white Dinky toy car, attached a Nutrimetics emblem on the side and at every show I went to and everywhere at home, that little car was on display. I went down to the local car yard and had a photo of myself taken sitting in the same sort of car that I would be receiving. (That photo, too, I put up at home for me to see at every moment.) When I got into that car I was able to feel it and smell the leather, and really imagine myself driving my new car. So every time I was driving my old bomb and passed a glass window, I would look and see myself in my Nutrimetics car. And as I was driving my old bomb around, I could now smell the leather and feel the comfy seats of my new car. Visualization is a wonderful thing, and it works.

A Big Day

Finally, the day arrived. I was going to receive my car! The kids and I got up in the morning, climbed into our little bomb of a car and travelled up to Perth to the leadership meeting. On the way there, my son Ryan said, "Mum, give me a piece of paper and a pen." He then proceeded to write a poem for me, but he didn't read it to me in the car. Later on, I understood why.

That meeting was one of the most exciting days of my life–and one of my proudest. There were a lot of my team members there, along with flowers, champagne, presents and, of course, the car.

When John— the Manager who ran meetings for Nutrimetics all over Australia—called out my name, I walked up onstage with my three children. It was all very emotional and I was on the verge of tears. After I was presented with flowers and my sister-in-law Dianne spoke some wonderful words about me, Ryan asked if he could read his poem to the audience, the one he had written in the car. He called it, 'Resolved.'

RESOLVED

"Anticipated events that led to this moment
This moment is what brings us together,
Together to celebrate our mother's achievements
Achievements through pain, setbacks and tests
She followed through, though
Through her strength and determination
Strength that comes from within
Rather than from without
We were there through the moods [During this part, he laughed and said that there were a few of them!]
Through the success
Never stop believing in yourself Mum – we didn't."

I lost it and started crying my eyes out right there. I was crying because this was my son, and this was how he felt about me. Everyone stood up and clapped, and if you could have seen the looks on their faces…well, I don't think there was a dry eye in the house.

I love reading this poem and it's not just about Nutrimetics; it's about working hard with my family towards a common goal, something that has brought us so much closer. To have my son look at me that way filled my heart with love and pride.

John then took me by the arm and—I have never seen him do this with anyone—escorted me to my new car. Such an honour!

I had photos taken with John, my children, my team and my up lines. To share all of this with the most important people in my life was absolutely fantastic. It was a true team accomplishment. It was the goal we had been visualizing. And right there was my trophy on wheels.

The sweet smell of success stayed with me every time I got into that car. I was in a world of my own, with my CDs playing, knowing that I had earned this car with the help of my team. It was a warm, fuzzy, rewarding feeling. Success is wonderful!

Speaking in Hawaii

Once a year, Nutrimetics organized a seminar in some exotic place. We could earn a free trip to this seminar by making sales and building a team through sponsoring. Even though it's a seminar, you still had free time and you were spoiled rotten and pampered. At the seminars, you met the crème de la crème of the Nutrimetics business: the high flyers, including the owners and presidential directors of Nutrimetics.

One of those exotic places was Hawaii, and I'd earned a free trip for Rob and myself. Rob wasn't able to come along, but one of my sales leaders, Sue, had earned a trip for herself, so she would be coming with me.

However, there was one glitch: I didn't have a passport, as I was bankrupt at the time. I did some homework and quickly found out that if the trip was given to me as a gift, I could go. So I had Nutrimetics write a letter to the Trustee of my bankruptcy to see if I could get my passport from them in order to take the trip.

While I was waiting for the Trustee's response, I was asked by Nutrimetics to give a talk in Hawaii. What an honour! Not only had I achieved the trip, but I was going to give a talk, as well.

Inside me I felt a mix of happiness and exhilaration, but also dread. What if I couldn't go? The waiting was killing me. My tummy was turning inside out and I just wasn't functioning at all. I couldn't sleep; in fact, I could barely think about anything else. I was a real mess!

Then the waiting was over. I could have my passport, but had to return it as soon as I got back. I just cried and cried, all those emotions of the weeks of waiting released, and now I had to focus on the most daunting task: writing my talk. Nutrimetics wanted me to talk about "Being Strong," which was basically my life story.

This was harder than I had ever imagined. Going back to certain times of my life was awful. It brought back things I never wanted to think about again, things I wanted to forget. I didn't want to remember those thoughts or feelings and every sentence I wrote made me cry.

Was I ever going to finish writing this talk? And if I did finish it, how was I ever going to be able to present it? Every time I read what I'd written, I cried. So how was I going to go up onstage and read it to thousands of people? And all along, the thought kept haunting me: *What if they don't like it?*

I had the absolute pleasure of travelling with one of my consultants, Sue, who always made me laugh. She made it so much easier for me to cope with it all.

When I travel, especially over long distances, I have a little problem: I tend to pass a lot of wind. We were on the plane, dozing with rugs over us in a row of three, when I suddenly passed gas. Horrified, I kept the blanket as close to me as possible in an attempt to hide the odour and sat there wondering if the people around me could actually smell it. Then I looked over to Sue and could see her nose twitching (yes, she could smell it!). I started to smile, a huge grin on my face as she turned and looked at me, and we just lost it.

I tried to hold the gas in as much as possible, but that was clearly a losing strategy because as we got off the plane, there was a huge line of us wives with their husbands and we were laughing so much that I just couldn't help it; I just started farting again. This time, I passed gas loud enough to be heard. Worse, it was followed by another one, and them some more. I just couldn't stop it: the more I laughed, the more I did it. It was so embarrassing; I wanted the floor to just swallow me up. But no one cared. After all, we had landed in Hawaii and nothing could spoil it. I didn't care; I was happy and the place was beautiful!

Unfortunately, I couldn't take much in, as I was very nervous about the talk I was about to give.

Then the moment arrived.

When I walked into the room that day, I was incredibly nervous and thought to myself, *Well, at least I'll be standing up on the stage a little bit away from the audience, which is good.* If everyone had been sitting close to me, it would have been even more intimidating.

Then I saw it: a humongous television screen, so that during my talk everyone could see me close up. Not only that, the whole seminar was being videotaped. I felt sick. I wanted to throw up. I thought to myself, *I can't do this.*

As my name was called, I was shaking. I wanted to cry, but I was able to muster a little courage to walk up to the stage and calmly present my story. And guess what? I didn't cry, although I felt the classic lump in my throat a few times. When I was finished, everyone stood up and gave me a standing ovation, clapping and cheering. I later found out that of all the speakers who presented that day, only two received a standing ovation. And I was one of the two!

I was just so overwhelmed. I cried and smiled at the same time. I have never felt so tall; my heart was pounding and I just felt so proud. It was over! I had delivered what they wanted to hear and I was on top of the world. I had stepped out of my comfort zone once again and achieved something I thought was beyond my reach.

The Nutrimetics seminar included a big celebration night and we had to dress up as our favourite TV character. Sue and I decided to dress up as Edi and Patsy, the girls from 'Absolutely Fabulous'. I was Edi and Sue was Patsy. We had the wigs, outlandish clothes and a drink in one hand and in the other, I was able to find a cigarette in a holder that lit up so it looked like we were smoking.

Neither Sue nor I drank or smoked, but we had a ball, carrying on and talking like Edi and Patsy all evening. We must have pulled it off, as we won the competition for the best dressed.

When the trip was over, I was on an amazing high. Then I had to send my passport back to the Trustee. Putting it into that envelope sent me crashing back to earth. I was reminded again of how I was bankrupt, of how I'd failed.

My up line had videotaped my talk and gave it to me, so what I did over the next few months was watch the video over and over again. I had to get myself out of the whole I-am-a-failure mindset I had fallen back into. I had grown and come so far, and I knew I could grow a lot more. I couldn't go back—I could only go forward.

It was time to move on to the next challenge.

Each year there was a new exotic destination for the Nutrimetics Seminar and, yes, every year, I had to ask for my passport back. When Rob came with me, we had to ask for his passport, too.

Rob and I attended seminars–both awesome–that were held in Malaysia and the United States. We flew to Los Angeles and visited Disneyland, and I can't even put into words what a tremendous place it is. We then boarded a cruise ship and travelled down to Catalina. Rob also played golf in Mexico, which was a wonderful experience. All of this was paid for by Nutrimetics and I'd earned these trips by reaching my sales goals and building a Nutrimetics team.

Tasmania, Here I Come

During that first trip to Hawaii, we had to fill out a form asking where we would like to go for the seminar next year. One of my dreams was to go to Tasmania, so I put it at the top of my list.

Shortly after, I received a phone call from the State Manager, who said how impressed they were with my talk in Hawaii and as a result, they wanted me to do some talks in Hobart and Launceston. I was to speak at business meetings and, in addition, the leadership and car club meetings, so I was pretty busy getting all the talks organised. Once again, I felt honoured. And I was going to Tasmania!

Dreams do come true. The difference between ordinary and extraordinary is the "extra." Who wants that extra? I do! Try it. Once you do, you'll achieve great things.

Before I left for Tasmania, my son Ryan again handed me a poem. He asked me to read it at the Leadership meetings. This one was called 'Faith.'

"You have heard what life has dealt my Mum. This poem shows how Nutrimetics has affected her, through my eyes.

FAITH

> "Others believed in you
> Long before you believed in yourself
> Their belief gave you confidence
> Self esteem followed soon after
> This all stemmed from your friends' faith
> Their faith in bringing you into "the business"
> Your drive and determination gave you success
> Your friends, peers and family gave you pride
> We now look at you, proud of your achievements
> Those whom you have sponsored are inspired by your success
> To see someone like them rise through the ranks
> Achieve what you have
> Create what you have achieved
> You are an inspiration
> To your friends, team and family
> All because someone believed in you
> Thanks.
> Love Ryan xx"

Once again, I received standing ovations. It was wonderful. I can't begin to describe the buzz.

It was time to leave Tasmania. I had loved it; it reminded me of the kind of small English countryside that you only see in pictures.

There is really something about flying and me. On the flight back home, the flight attendants handed out icy poles after lunch. They looked delicious, so I decided to have one. Big mistake. Have you ever seen the movie *Dumb and Dumber* when he got his tongue stuck on the icy chair lift? Well that was me; the freezing cold icy pole got stuck on my bottom lip.

I tried licking it, thinking I could get it off that way. And when I got tired, I dropped my hands, hoping the icy pole would fall off my lip, but it just hung there, stuck fast. I kept licking and licking, but it was not budging and was starting to hurt. In the end, I had to rip it off. Yes, I ripped it off my lip, and boy, did it hurt! Looking back, I can imagine how funny I must have looked to the people who saw me struggle with that icy pole.

What is this chapter all about? It shows that when you pull together with your family, you can achieve anything. Don't try to take on the world by yourself. Be sure to include those around you, because not only will you be growing, your family will as well. You will then see, as the journey continues, how your children grow and learn. Because ours was a family journey, we became closer and stronger.

I realized that success is not something you pursue. It is something you become. My success has exceeded anything I have ever imagined. When I first joined Nutrimetics, I was shy, unsure of my identity or my potential. I had faced rejection and many setbacks. But I went back and tried and tried again.

Eventually, I tasted a small measure of success, and along with it came recognition, which I had never experienced before.

These small steps started to build a ladder of confidence and with each step up, something deep inside me began to crystallise: the magic quality of self confidence.

Then, I found my purpose. A true purpose is not something you accomplish, then you put aside to retire. A purpose is the driving force that fuels the passion; a purpose is bigger than life itself. It's not just about money, cars, and trips. It's about personal development and growth, and friendships that last a lifetime.

When times get tough, your purpose can pull you through. The power you will feel as you get in touch with your purpose is truly incredible.

And that power is your passion.

Think about your purpose and ask yourself these questions:

Why do you want it?

What will this purpose do for you and your family?

How different will it feel?

And along the way, who or what can give you recognition?

"You will find, as you look back upon your life, that the moments that stand out are the moments when you have done things for others."

—*Henry Drummond*

The Power of a Positive Environment

There is no way that immersing yourself in a positive environment won't change you—I can fully attest to it. Nutrimetics changed my life and changed my way of thinking.

After so many years, I was able to connect with my friend Sue, who became a consultant of mine. We had so much fun working together with Nutrimetics and we still do, to this day. The motto of Nutrimetics is: "Help People to Help People."

Even though I have used Nutrimetics for so long, it was only when working with the company that I learned how to look after my skin and apply makeup properly. I learned the correct way of caring for the skin and enhancing one's beauty through makeup, plus how this can benefit a person. I would never have learned or fully appreciated this if not for Nutrimetics.

Nutrimetics allowed me to acquire skills that would propel me to success. I learned how to set goals and communicate with people.

I understood what it was like to have a team and how to mobilise a team to achieve your goals.

I discovered success books that I needed to read for guidance and inspiration. I still read these to this day, and offer them on my website.

I realized just how much positive thinking and the power of visualization could make a difference to the way I worked, and how they accelerated my journey to success.

With little outlay, you can feel that success is attainable and actually grow a business. The best thing about it is, you can help other people grow their own business.

"Don't wish it was easier, wish you were better. Don't wish for less problems, wish for more skills. Don't wish for less challenges, wish for more wisdom."

— *Jim Rohn*

Real Estate: A New Direction

Working with Nutrimetics instilled in me many qualities, including the perseverance to move forward. I was now a self-confident person, full of passion for life, and I felt I could take on the world. Nothing could stop me. I was never going back to the old feelings that alcoholism and bankruptcy brought to me.

Little did I know that it was all going to come flooding back, tenfold!

I began to get bored with doing the Nutrimetics shows. Going out night after night to do them, I soon began to miss my family. Also, I was starting to grow in a different direction and I needed more than Nutrimetics to keep me excited. But what? What was it that I was missing?

I didn't know where to start. Then my sister-in-law, Dianne, told me about Robert Kiyosaki's book, *Rich Dad, Poor Dad*. I didn't think about it too much until one day when I was out shopping. I'd almost walked straight past the bookstore when it hit me: *I have to buy that book.*

I read the book and got hooked immediately. I decided to also buy a book on property and real estate, so I returned to the bookstore. When I walked in, I was drawn to a book by Jan Somers, bought it, went home and devoured it. This was when I realized that to get somewhere financially secure, we had to get into property and real estate.

Being the person I am—a person who never does things halfway—I decided I had to become a qualified real estate agent in order to understand more about the business and how it really worked. My husband and I had only bought one house—the one we lost in bankruptcy—and I needed to know more. I wanted to get inside the mind of a real estate agent.

New Goals, New Purpose

Around this time, I had a friend who owned a secretarial business and she kept telling me about a real estate company, Elders, that was looking for a full-time sales representative. I was still quite busy with Nutrimetics, so I told her that I could do part time, but not full time. As the company needed someone full time, this didn't suit them. But, as time went on, my friend Ruth kept pushing me and pushing me, telling me I would be good at it.

I thank her to this very day, because eventually, I decided to go for it. I thought, *maybe this is what I need; maybe this is just where I am meant to move forward.*

I told her I would do it, but when she contacted the company, they informed her that the job was already taken. However, as a courtesy, they still offered me an interview.

Never Too Old

There I was at 46 years old and I'd never had a job interview in my life!

I felt sick with fear. I knew the original job was taken and if I wanted a full-time position, I would really have to sell myself. But how was I going to do that?

I didn't know how to prepare, as I had never been in this situation before. So I decided I would just go in there and be "me."

When I arrived, I was directed to an office and asked to take a seat. Then all these people came in and introduced themselves and sat down with me. I wasn't only getting interviewed by the owners of the company, but by all the other sales representatives as well! They were asking me questions left, right, and centre, and I sat there, feeling overwhelmed. I hoped I was answering the questions correctly, but they came so fast and furious that I couldn't be sure. When finally it was over, they said that they would call me.

Patience is not one of my strong suits and I was not very good at waiting for the answer. That afternoon I tried to make myself busy, but my stomach was in knots.

Later that afternoon, Doug, who was one of the owners of the company, called me up. He said, "Guess what? You have the job!" So I must have sold myself pretty successfully!

As you can probably tell by now, I am a very emotional person, and I cried with relief when I got off the phone. I was both nervous and excited.

To begin the job, I had to take a four-week licensing course, but the time when Doug wanted me to take the course didn't work for me. I couldn't do it. I was facing serious dental surgery (thanks to when I'd had my teeth punched out) that couldn't be put off any longer and I didn't know how bad I was going to feel physically. Also, I wanted to be fully prepared when I was in class. As a result, I would have to wait a month until the next set of classes began.

In a way, this was fortunate, since it gave me a chance to meet with my Nutrimetics clients as well as other members of my team, to let them know what I was doing. Of course, no one was happy. I felt terribly guilty, but I knew I had to make a change or else I was going to fall into a rut.

And I knew working in real estate was meant to be.

Although I didn't have the money to pay for the licensing course, Doug offered to pay for the tuition for me up front, and I would reimburse him after my first sale.

I know I am not a rocket scientist, but I do have passion and tenacity, and one of my biggest passions is to help people achieve their goals. For many people, that includes buying their own home. I had no idea about, or experience in, real estate. I had only bought one house, and even then, hadn't taken much notice. In fact, at the time, I was so disconnected from the process that, looking back on it, when we did buy our first house, I now know we got a bad deal.

So, there I was, in my mid-40s and to top it off, going through menopause. At the time, I didn't know what was wrong with me. In addition, I hadn't studied since I was at school, which was 31 years earlier! I was finding it very hard to concentrate, and dealing with hot flushes, mood swings, and memory loss, all side effects of menopause.

The month I took the licensing course was hectic, to say the least. My youngest son Kane was working in Perth, an hour away, which is also where the course was. My day would start at 3 a.m., when I would get up to study, then drive to Perth, drop Kane off to work and then attend my course all day. Then I would pick Kane up, and I would get home at 8 p.m. On weekends, I took care of Nutrimetics deliveries. After four weeks, I was exhausted.

At the end of each week of the course, we would have an exam. For one of those weeks, you spent a week at the office where you were going to work. You also had a huge workbook that you were asked to complete in that time. But Elders wanted me to attend a week-long training session with them in Perth, which meant I had to do that week's coursework in my spare time. Can you imagine how tiring that all was? Especially while going through menopause.

The first two exams were rough and I barely scraped through. In the last week, there was a final exam. When they put the exam paper in front of me, I went blank, as in…blank! I could not think. I was hot and cold, sweating then freezing. My heart raced. I didn't know it then, but I was having a panic attack–right there, during my final exam!

After the exam, some classmates and I went out to lunch and talked about it. Everyone seemed happy, all except me. I knew I hadn't passed. How could I?

We had to wait for the results, and no, I didn't pass. I had failed and felt terribly embarrassed.

When the school called me to give me the results, they told me I'd missed getting a passing grade by one question. One question! They also told me that I could retake the exam the next week if I wanted to, and I said I would.

But now came the worst part: I had to call Doug, my new boss, and tell him that I had failed.

I could hear the shock in his voice; he was stunned. I could tell he was thinking, "She didn't pass? What have I gotten myself into?" I let him know that I was going back next week to retake the exam and knew that I would do better.

Well, wouldn't you know it? The following week, I was so run down from all the activity the month before that I came down heavily with the flu. As a result, I did very little studying, something I knew I needed to do if I wanted to pass. I tried very, very hard, but nothing was sinking in.

I drove to Perth that Friday and the new group of people to take the class were at the end of their first week. Everyone who was retaking the final exam had to sit in with them. I couldn't believe how many from my group were retaking it! This made me feel a little bit better. But, once again, when that paper was put down in front of me, I went completely blank.

I did the best I could, went home and waited until the following week to get the phone call to see if I'd passed.

I did. I passed!

I cried with relief, thinking, *I'm not a failure, after all!*

I rang Doug and he was overjoyed. The very next day, I was in the office ordering business cards and setting up my desk, getting ready to start a new adventure.

The Pursuit of Knowledge

Because I'd failed the final exam the first time, I now worked extra hard. I really had to prove to everyone that they hadn't made a mistake by hiring me. I believe my exam disaster happened for a reason: so that when I did start, I had to put my heart and soul into it. And looking back, I see that I did this not only for my bosses, but also for myself. I had to move forward and I felt this was the only way I could do it. I didn't wait for the business to come to me; I went out and found my own business.

When I started in real estate–and remember, this was before the internet – this is what I did:

I sent letters out to all my family and friends, as well as to all my Nutrimetics customers, telling them I was now a real estate agent and that if they needed any help or knew of anyone who needed any help, I would be happy to assist them.

If any of the sales representatives in the office wanted me to do their 'home opens' for them, I would do them. We did home opens every Sunday and I would do five of them. None of them were my listings, but I got a ton of leads and those leads were all mine. I followed each and every one of them up with a phone call over the following days. Once I had a buyer, I never let them go until they bought something. Back then, it was a little easier for us as reps to hang onto the buyers, as there was no internet and they relied on us, a sign, or the paper to let them know what was out there.

Starting with the leads from the home opens, I began to work with buyers. I know many real estate agents dislike working with buyers, but this worked out well for me. I figured that when buyers are looking for a house and they find one they want to buy, more than likely, they are going to sell their old house. As a result, I obtained listings using this method. In the beginning, I didn't mind how hard I worked, as long as I was able to pay back the money Doug had lent me for the course. I wanted everyone to see I would do anything to make it work.

I also did telemarketing, going through the phone book and calling people up to see if they would like an appraisal on their home.

Finally, I sent out flyers and letters to property owners to see if they wanted to sell.

I went on appraisals with the other reps in the office. There was one girl in the office I particularly observed. Her name was Karen. I hung off every word Karen said, as she was really good at what she did. I tried to learn by watching what other successful people were doing. Success books will tell you not to reinvent the wheel. After all, if people are successful, they must be doing something right.

Go to every bit of training the company has for you; you are learning from the people who have done it, so again, don't try and reinvent the wheel.

I learned from the best, and this was what got me to where I wanted to be. I listened to different speakers in real estate. If they were successful, I studied their strategies and put them into practice. If they didn't work out for me, I still kept moving forward and just tried another way. To practice my sales skills, I did role-playing and studied scripts. Knowing what you're selling and who you are selling to is important, so I made sure I got to know my product–which was the properties.

I admit that getting started in real estate was really hard. You had to be self-motivated. You couldn't procrastinate. I pushed myself because I so badly wanted to succeed in this industry.

All of the hard work paid off. Soon I got really busy and eventually, I was getting my own listings and doing my own home opens. I was totally committed and working seven days a week.

One day, we had a meeting in our office and our licensee asked everyone why he or she was in the real estate business. Most people said money, but I said I was in it for the knowledge. He really didn't understand what I was saying. He responded, "In it for the knowledge? No one is in it for that."

But I understood what I was doing. My goal was to get into buying property and I needed knowledge to do that effectively, to make that work and move forward to the next level.

You Reap What You Sow

In my first year in real estate with Elders, I received the award 'Rookie of the Year' for the whole of Western Australia. And I was the number two in sales the following year. I was only number two because my boss was number one, and he had a personal assistant.

The evenings I received those honours were so special. There was a presentation where I received beautiful trophies, which I proudly displayed in my office.

As I said before, you don't have to be a genius; you just have to have the passion and a burning desire to move forward. And—most importantly—you absolutely cannot give up.

Elders was a great company to work for as they were very goal-oriented, but you did have to work hard. That suited me. I was used to working hard.

I had been in real estate for two years when I advised our eldest son to invest his money by buying property, and not to waste his money on frivolous things. So our first property was with him, and we had that property for 10 years.

Being in the real estate game, I saw a lot of bargains and gained a huge amount of knowledge, but I found I was so busy that I had trouble keeping up with educating myself. I knew there was more to life than just work. Don't get me wrong, I loved working, but I was looking for a way of earning passive income as well. I was hungry for more knowledge, and to become more knowledgeable, I had to read and learn.

My husband was in Ireland working for three months (more about that later…) and while he was gone, I put a deposit on two canal blocks. He was not happy about that, to say the least! If I hadn't been in real estate, I would never have bought a canal block, but the potential was huge and I felt I had to take a chance.

When Rob returned from Ireland, we ended up selling one of the properties before settlement as we couldn't afford it—and made a nice profit. We then built on the other property and lived in it. It was never our intention to live on the canals, and I didn't like it. There was no privacy, and as my heart ruled my head, we sold it. We then built our dream home, thinking that we would never move.

If I'd known then what I know now, I would never have sold the canal block or the house. On the other hand, if we had kept the property, I probably would have become a little more complacent and not have educated myself as much as I did by selling it and moving on. Yes, things happen for a reason.

Over the years we have made a lot of mistakes, such as not financing the right way, selling when we shouldn't have, and so on.

But you don't know what you don't know. You definitely learn along the way–sometimes when it is too late to do you any good.

When those things happen, learn from them, as I have.

As we didn't have a great deal of superannuation, this was another reason why we did what we were doing. As Rob said, at least we tried.

One thing I have learned over these years is that when you make a mistake, you never forget it.

Kane often asks me, "Mum, why does this keep happening to me?" to which I reply, "It's because you haven't learned the lesson yet." Once you have learned the lesson life wants to give you, it won't happen again and you can move on.

Mission: Create Wealth

After a while, I moved from Elders to a smaller company, and then to another company where my friend Karen was the boss.

When I'd started at Elders, Karen was a rep there and I will be always indebted to her. She began as a colleague, but over time, she became my boss and good friend. I owe so much to her! When I was starting out, she was the one who showed me the way, even though she was just as busy as I was. She had three kids and a husband of her own, but nothing was ever any trouble for her. She was always willing to take time out and show me what to do.

I soon learned that selling real estate is more than just a full-time job. You are on call seven days a week/24 hours a day. As a result, there isn't much time for anything else. I needed to cut back on my workload so I could find more to time to read books, go to the seminars and start using the knowledge I had accumulated. The big picture became very clear.

I kept reading and going to seminars, but things came together in 2006 when I read a particular book on buying property and how to structure and access money to be able to do it. I signed up for their newsletter and soon, a newsletter arrived announcing a seminar in Melbourne.

It wasn't cheap, plus you had to pay for the accommodations and airfare. I decided to go. My husband Rob told me that he wasn't going to accompany me; however, we had gotten to a stage where I needed him to start doing "the journey" with me. I had seen too many other couples split up when one partner grew away from the other and I didn't want that to happen to us. I needed him to understand what it was all about.

It was the wisest decision we've ever made. It opened up a whole new world to us. It changed our mindsets, and showed us a way of doing things differently.

At the seminar, I bought everything they had to offer in the way of books and DVDs. I devoured them and then, most importantly, started to apply the knowledge I gained from these resources.

At first it was difficult because it went against everything that we had been taught over the years, and we had over 50 years of reconditioning to get through.

But this seminar was what changed our mindset. This was really the point when we started to do things differently and our journey to create wealth began.

When we came back from the seminar, I held my own mini-seminar in our home and started to teach people how to create wealth. I wanted to teach others a different way of doing things.

People needed to realize that you are never too old. Some people also think that they don't have enough money to start creating wealth, which simply isn't true.

In 2007, I started to work for some investors in Melbourne, finishing off their houses. One investor we worked for educated us regarding how he had started and the road he was on. Basically, he was teaching us what we had just begun to learn at the seminars.

Around this time, I gave up real estate, as I was working full on for the investors.

We built some properties ourselves and I began thinking about writing my story. This started my journey of doing what I most love to do, which is helping people, but in the right way–as you will find out in the later chapters of this book.

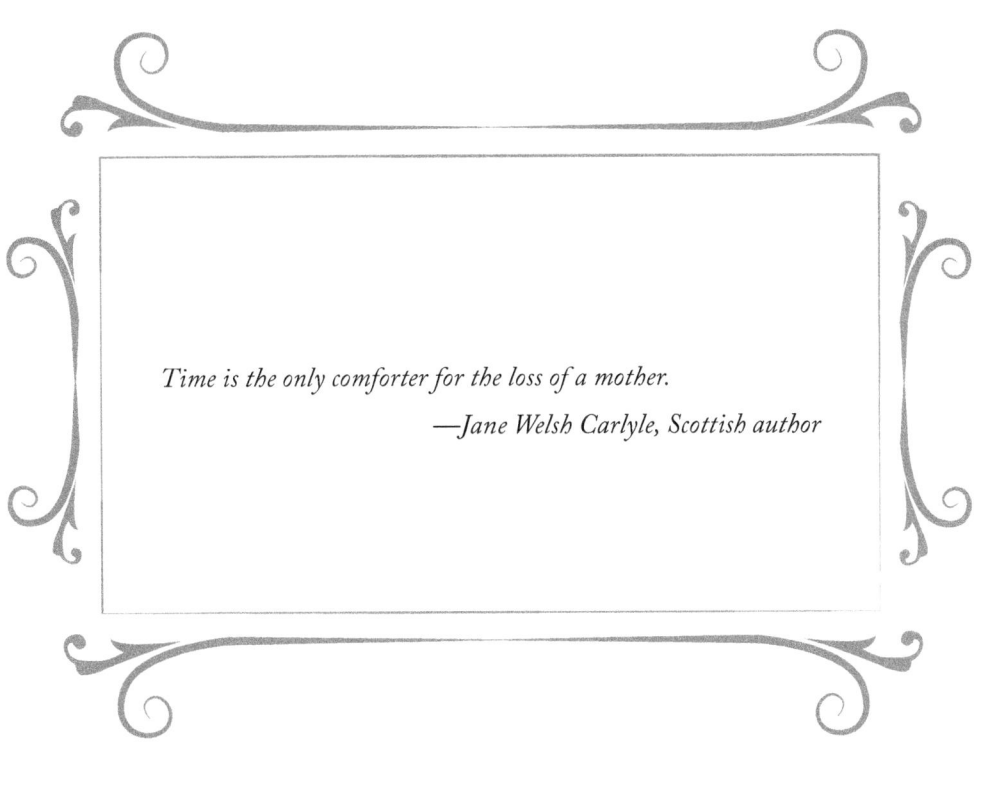

Time is the only comforter for the loss of a mother.
—Jane Welsh Carlyle, Scottish author

Losing Mum

I was still in the real estate business when Mum died. The night before she passed away, I travelled to the nursing home and went in to see her. She was unconscious and didn't know I was there, so I just talked to her about our life together. I told her that I really loved her, but I couldn't understand why she had been the way she was towards me.

I was there for ages, just talking. I told her that I forgave her for all the wrong between us, and I gave her a kiss and left. Early the next morning I received a phone call from the nursing home saying that Mum wouldn't last much longer, and advising me to come up.

We all were there, my brother and sister, with all the grandkids, at Mum's bedside. Mum didn't know we were there, as she had Alzheimer's. Sharon and I were on either side of her, and Mum simply closed her eyes.

We thought she had gone and we all started crying and hugging each other. Then, all of a sudden, Mum opened her eyes again!

It gave us a shock, so eventually when she closed her eyes again, we all just sat there and looked at each other and then at Mum, because we didn't know if she was really gone this time. Mum was playing one last trick on us, I suppose.

The nurse came in and confirmed that she had passed and once again, all our feelings came out. Even though I didn't feel a lot of love from Mum, she was still my mum. As I'd grown older, I'd come to accept the way she was. In the end, it really wasn't her fault, as she hadn't known any better.

This is what life is about, in a sense: if you don't know any different, you stay in the same place. That is why it is so important to stretch yourself and acquire knowledge to become stronger and grow; otherwise, you'll just stay where you are for the rest of your life.

When we were organising the funeral, they wanted some words for the eulogy and we really couldn't think of any. The people at the funeral home tried to be nice and prompted us with generic descriptions like "She was a good mother, wife, worker," and so on. Couldn't we think of anything worthwhile to say? It was awful. We all sat there looking at one another and we couldn't come up with one thing to say about Mum. This was our mother; surely we could have come up with something!

In the end, I didn't say much about Mum, but spoke about how I loved her. At her funeral, I decided to let go of all the bitterness in my heart. I wanted my children to learn that bitterness is not worth harbouring because of what it does to you and your family.

Be careful who you trust because as quickly as they say they are your friend how quick they can turn their backs on you.

— *Abhishek Tiwari*

Trashed!

In 2001, I was working in real estate when Rob decided to work as a bricklayer in Ireland. It was tough in the workplace here and bricklaying jobs were hard to find. Rob had some mates who had gone to Ireland for work and suggested that he come over. Apparently, there was plenty of work there.

I didn't want him to go, but Rob took pride in his work and his role of being a provider, so he took off to Ireland with a mate. It was a very teary farewell.

After a couple of months, I decided to go over and visit him. Travelling that distance on my own scared the hell out of me, but I wanted to be with him, even for just a while.

We hired a car and travelled all around the south of Ireland for eight days. The weather was glorious and the scenery in that beautiful countryside was breathtaking.

It was Rob's birthday and as he loved playing golf, I had booked us into a castle with an absolutely majestic golf course, for a couple of nights. I'd also hired a buggy. It was so enjoyable being with my man and watching him do what he loved to do!

Back home, my daughter Sharon was pregnant with Caitlyn. I had given her my car to look after and every day, she would drive down from Rockingham to Mandurah (she was doing some work for me), work and keep an eye on the house and Kane, who was already 18.

Kane had been keeping company with a guy we will call Fred. He seemed a nice kid. He'd had a bit of a sad childhood, so I felt sorry for him.

On the weekend we were away, Kane had a couple of mates around for a few drinks in the back yard. The garage door was up, so you could see straight through to the yard.

Fred turned up with some mates of his own, as well. By this stage, Kane had had way too much to drink and was quite out of it. Fred had sent word around that there was a party at our place, and it soon got completely out of hand.

Fred had planned the party because he knew I'd be out of town for a week. He took the spare key to my car, which was on top of the fridge. He also went to my jewellery box and took all my expensive jewellery. Someone told Kane much later that he was trying to sell it.

Fred then went into my office and stole all the money I had put away for Kane and Sharon, if they needed any. He took cheques out of my chequebooks, not just one after another, but in different spots within the book so you wouldn't know straight away, until you got to that particular cheque number.

He also took bankcards that I'd left in my purse at home. Luckily, the cards he was able to access didn't have much on them, so when he took the money out, there was not a great deal in there.

I always wondered how he knew the pin number. Then it came to me; just before I'd left for Ireland, I'd bought a video camera and Kane and Fred had accompanied me. When I paid for the camera, Fred had walked over with me and obviously seen what pin I put in. Even then, I had no idea what he was doing. The kids who partied at our place broke some of the tiles in our newly-built tiled water feature at home. With rubbish and food leftovers surrounding the area, I could just imagine how they used the tiled water feature as a target, throwing empty beer bottles at the waterfall, and then laughing as the tiles were smashing.

Someone also gouged our kitchen bench with a knife.

The place was trashed.

Sharon came over the next day and was in total shock. Kane couldn't remember what had happened. Neither of them could properly assess the damage and what was gone, so they just cleaned up the place the best they could.

A couple of days later, Kane was travelling up to stay at Sharon's and Fred asked Kane if he could get a lift. Fred said he wanted to see his mum, but all he really wanted to do was see where Sharon lived.

Early in the morning from her bed, Sharon heard my car start up and take off. She was beside herself, and so was Kane.

Back in Ireland, we were having fun, totally unaware of what had happened back home. When we rang Sharon and Kane to see how things were going, Sharon was too scared to tell me what had happened to our home and my car, but when I handed Rob the phone, she told him.

After a 24-hour flight back home, the first thing I saw was my car, which was now in an undriveable state. The police had only just found it at the beach, all smashed up–but it hadn't been broken into. At that stage, we couldn't understand at all what had happened.

I received a phone call from the mother of one of Kane's mates and told her what had happened. She asked me if my car was a Mitsubishi. She said she'd found a set of keys at their home with a Mitsubishi tag on it and she didn't know who they belonged to. We quickly went around there and sure enough, they were my keys.

It turned out Fred was staying with her. I asked the kids there if they knew anything, and they said they didn't, which I found hard to believe. I still had no idea that it had been Fred.

We found out later that Fred had also taken money from that family. As well, he took all their CDs, removing them from their cases then putting the cases back so they had no idea that the CDs were gone.

At the party, Fred had spotted the keys on top of the fridge and taken them. Sharon had a set of keys, so no one needed these others, and no one knew they were missing until I got back and noticed they were gone. At the time, Fred had made up the excuse about seeing his Mum, but he'd just wanted to know where Sharon lived so he could steal the car.

We found out later that Fred had asked Kane a few nights before the party if he could stay the night. He'd said that he would sleep in the shed. When he got up, he locked it up and returned the keys to

Kane, and as Kane had no reason to go in there, he had no idea that everything was gone until we came back from Ireland. What Fred actually did was steal everything valuable that we had inside that shed.

The police took fingerprints off my car. Fred had taken all my CDs and thrown away my real estate file from the car.

Then, just when I had my car fixed and we were starting to carry on with our lives, I received my bank statements and found out that two cards had been accessed and all the money was gone. Luckily, as I said, there wasn't a huge amount on them. Next, when I went to get the chequebook out to pay a bill, I noticed the missing cheques.

That was the last straw! I couldn't do this on my own any more, so I got on the phone to Rob and told him to come home, "Now!"

He did come home for me, just before Sharon gave birth to Caitlyn.

The police took my chequebook to look for fingerprints, but didn't find any.

Fred knew we were after him, and knew that if Kane got to him, he would be in big trouble. So he skipped town, and we have never heard from him again.

What was so upsetting about this is that I'd felt sorry for him. We'd treated him like family, feeding him and driving him places. He was our son's mate and we'd welcomed him into our home, yet he just treated us like dirt. Kane also had no idea that he was like this.

It feels awful when someone invades your privacy and goes through your personal belongings. The jewellery in my jewellery box meant nothing to Fred, but it meant the world to me.

We had just gotten out of bankruptcy and were so proud of what we had done to make our home a real home, and to have someone come in and trash it like that without the tiniest bit of respect for us and for the things we held dear, did not make sense to me.

My car was never the same, and not just because Fred had crashed it. It was because he had been in it and driving it. The thought of this repulsed me, so I decided to sell it.

The lesson here is to choose wisely who to trust. It is good to help others. It is good to be compassionate and to share what you have, but don't let anyone abuse your generosity.

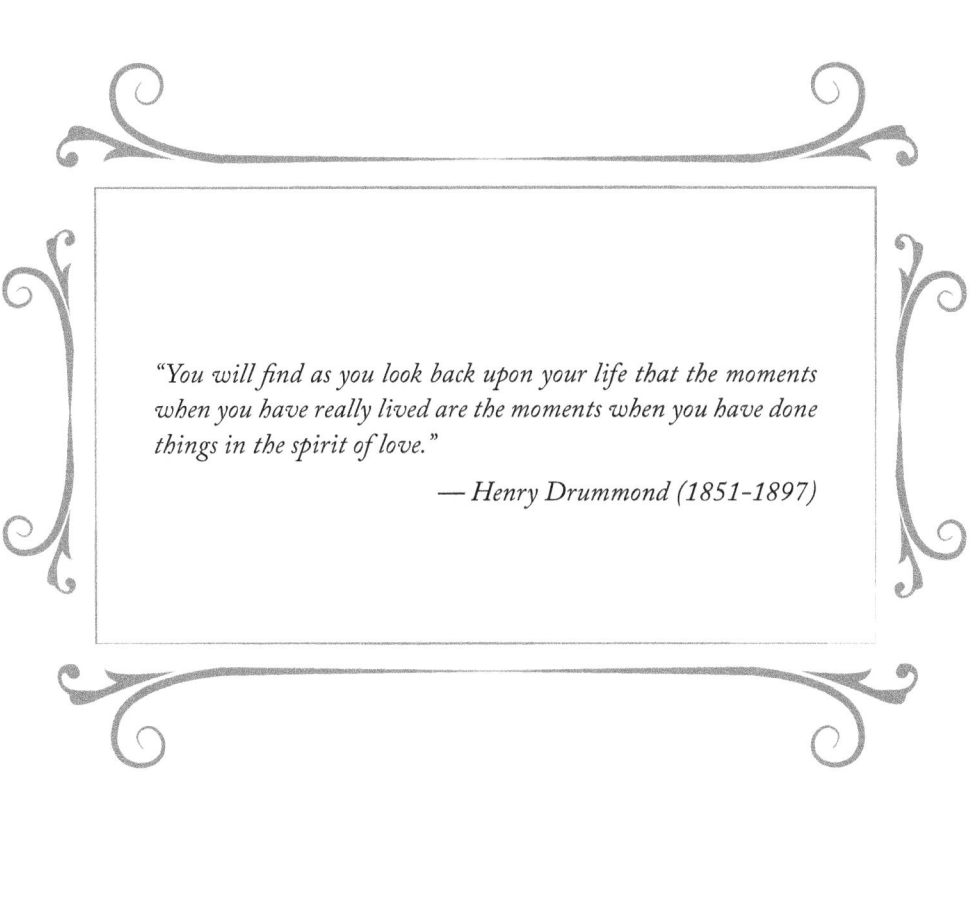

"You will find as you look back upon your life that the moments when you have really lived are the moments when you have done things in the spirit of love."

— *Henry Drummond (1851-1897)*

My Daughter Becomes a Mother

It had been wonderful going through pregnancy, but what I found even more pleasurable was going through my daughter Sharon's two pregnancies with her. Each time Sharon told me she was pregnant, I cried. "Yes!" I thought, "I'm going to be a nanna!"

Her first pregnancy went along without a hitch. And because my own mother had been of little help to me when I was a young mum, one thing I made sure of was to be there to help and support Sharon throughout the whole pregnancy journey.

As soon as I knew what day Rob was going to fly home (this was after the robbery), I rang Sharon and told her I had a surprise for her. She lived half an hour away from us and she had no idea that Rob was coming home.

On Sunday night, I picked Rob up from the airport and around 2 a.m., just as we were about to go to sleep, the phone rang. It was Sharon. Her water had broken and she was off to the hospital.

I asked her, "Do you want to speak to your surprise?" and handed the phone to Rob. Sharon cried; she was so happy to know he was home! How was that for timing?

I quickly dressed and got to the hospital. When I walked into that room and saw Sharon's face, I could tell how relieved she was to know her mum was there. She grabbed me and hugged me. I felt how comforted she was by my presence; it was a long labour for her.

Andrew—her then boyfriend and now husband—and I were a good team. He was the one with the flannel, cooling her down, and I was the one with the baby powder, rubbing her back.

Rob and Kane came up to the hospital and sat in the waiting room watching TV. Every now and then, they would check in to see how things were going.

Dinnertime came and I was starving, so Rob went to get some food. It was an odd time: I would eat some food and then Sharon would get a contraction and yell out "Mummy!" and I would run to her and rub her back. When her contraction passed, I would run out again and have something more to eat, then she'd call me again and I would rush back to her. It went on like this until I was able to finish my meal. It reminded me so much of when I'd given birth to Sharon, all those years ago.

The doctor arrived and it was time for the baby to come. Sharon pushed. Andrew was on the bed near her head and I was at her feet. When Sharon finally had Caitlyn, she gave birth on her knees.

When I had my own babies, I didn't see the birth, but here I was able to witness everything. There was my daughter, giving birth to my granddaughter! I cried, overwhelmed.

Caitlyn was born at 1.27 a.m. I hugged and kissed Sharon and told her how proud I was of her, and gave Andrew a kiss of congratulations. Then Rob and Kane came in and it was an emotional time. We all held Caitlyn, and Kane, who was 18 by then, was blown away. Caitlyn was covered with white fluid and blood, which shocked Kane. He hadn't realized how messy giving birth is; he thought babies came out clean!

We finally said our goodbyes and left Sharon, Andrew and Caitlyn to enjoy the moment.

It was Tuesday morning and the last time I'd slept was when I'd woken up early Sunday morning. I was running on pure adrenaline, so even when I got home, I couldn't sleep. I had my husband home, and my beautiful daughter had given birth to my first granddaughter. Life couldn't get much better.

Later that same day, we went back to the hospital to visit everyone. The nurse had asked Sharon to do something and she was having trouble with it, so Sharon asked me to do it instead. It reminded me of the time I'd had to ask my sister to put cream on me after that reckless skiing trip pulled open my then one-week old birthing stitches. They wanted Sharon to insert a condom full of frozen water to relieve her pain after such a long birth, but she couldn't do it. So, yes, I did it. Isn't that what mothers are for?

Sharon fell pregnant again, but lost her baby. She became pregnant a third time and this time, it was recommended that she be induced early, due to high blood pressure. The day arrived and Kane said he wanted to be there, so I picked him up at some ungodly hour.

When we all arrived at the hospital, Sharon was supposed to have been induced, but they didn't have her booked into a room, so they told us to go for a walk, which we did, down to the beach, returning later.

This time, Sharon was in a room with a lounge, her own bathroom and bath, and a separate room for giving birth.

Once again it was a long day. Andrew, Kane and I helped her, and every now and again, the nurse would come and check.

Eventually, it was time for the baby to come. The doctor wasn't there, just the nurse. She told Sharon to get on the bed and ordered me to quickly grab a leg. Sharon started to push and I helped deliver my grandson, whom they named Devon.

It was one of the most moving experiences of my life! But once Devon was born, blood poured out of my daughter like a tap, filling bowl after bowl. I looked at the nurse and said, "Should this be happening?" I could see the worry on her face. She quickly called for a doctor to stop the bleeding.

Relief, and then Andrew cut the cord. The placenta was pulled out and Sharon was able to relax. It was like a roller coaster ride, up and down, not knowing if everything was going to be all right. I hugged (a lot more than usually, as she had scared the hell out of me) and kissed Sharon and told her how proud of her I was. I kissed Andrew. Then I went up to Kane, who was 23 at the time, and had been there the whole time watching. Later on, he told me, "I will never look at my sister the same way again."

Words are not enough to express how much happiness and love I felt the first time I held my grandson, just as I'd felt when I first held Caitlyn. It is such a breathtaking experience to share these special moments with the people you love.

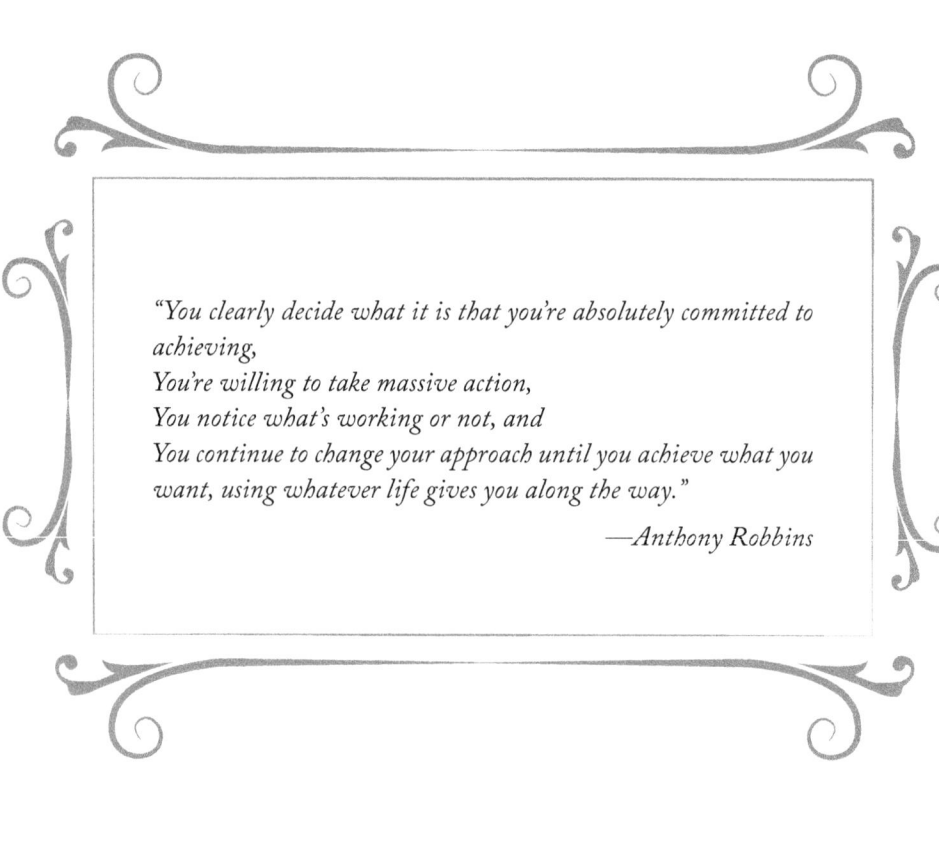

"You clearly decide what it is that you're absolutely committed to achieving,
You're willing to take massive action,
You notice what's working or not, and
You continue to change your approach until you achieve what you want, using whatever life gives you along the way."

—*Anthony Robbins*

The Fall: 2008

Rob and I didn't have much superannuation. To my way of thinking, it wasn't long since we'd lost the hotel and I was trying to make money so that I had something to give to my kids, as I felt they had lost their heritage. I was working hard, once again not seeing much of the kids, letting the almighty dollar rule me again without being completely aware of it.

Because I worked so hard, the kids would say to me: "Mum, what we want now is you, not what you'll leave us when you're gone." But I had progressed too far; I couldn't pull back.

We had six houses under construction and the market was falling. Throughout the year, it got steadily worse. It was difficult to sell the houses only half constructed as people wanted to see the finished product; plus, they were nervous.

You could feel the panic, tension, and uncertainty in the air. It was like a virus, and by the time the message got to the last person, it was out of control. The media was having a field day and that didn't help; it just helped spread the panic.

I believe everything I learnt over those years of building wealth was a great way to go – in a good market. In a good market, the concept is great, but the people who were teaching us had started earlier, before the boom hit, so had the luxury of time to reap the benefits. Not like us.

The following is our story. It makes me feel like a huge failure whenever I recall these things, but I am not holding back because I want you to learn from it. Learn from our mistakes so you don't have to tread a similar path. I hope my experiences will offer you a better way of looking at life.

The boom had started two years earlier and was now well underway. The property market was hot. We were buying land that wasn't going to settle for 12 months and as it turned out, when it did settle, most of the land had doubled in value, so we were able to take the equity out straight away. What this means is, say we bought the land for $100,000, 12 months later it was worth $200,000. We'd get it valued by the banks and the banks would give us the money. That is what the banks were doing: just giving money to anyone. Everyone seemed to be doing this and consequently, it was very hard to acquire land.

I knew the agent who worked for the developer, and he kept me in the loop as to what was coming up. This was the plan:

Use that increase in equity for the 20% the bank wanted and that same 20% the bank wanted for the building of the house. We had all of that, plus we had a buffer there to service the loan and finish off the other houses. What that meant was that once the land was valued an extra $100,000, the bank would keep 20% ($20,000) and give you $80,000 towards the building of the house.

Before starting to build, we would go to the bank, get the loan for the land, revalue it and then use that equity to start building the houses (as above).

The plan was that when the building was finished, we'd have the bank revalue the properties and access the equity so we would have more of a buffer to look after them, or even maybe to sell them. This part sounded great, but if you haven't a buffer for at least 7-10 years in equity, and when the rent doesn't cover the mortgage, you are in trouble. And because the market had died and was going backwards, this is what happened to us.

The market started falling in 2008 – now known as the Global Financial Crisis. It seemed to happen so quickly! One minute a house was worth $600,000 and the next minute, it would drop to $450,000. So, of course, when the houses were finished, there was very little equity left in them, if any, and we were having trouble finding money to finish off the other houses and meet the interest payments.

Because of the turn in the market, it was harder to sell. Of course, as the building of the houses wasn't finished, there was no tenant in place to pay for the mortgages—a catch 22 situation.

Even though there were three of us involved, Rob, Ryan and myself, I felt that the buying of this land and the building was my doing. I was listening to too many people and although the concept was great, as I mentioned, the market was falling. If it hadn't been for the market falling, everything would have been ideal. It would really have been wonderful if we had started two years earlier at the beginning of the boom, giving us time to build our wealth and obtain the benefits.

It was very hard to talk to anyone about this, including my family. The thought of failing again was killing me, so I felt I had to fix the problem and find a way to get out of it. But I was wrong.

I had already booked a Tony Robbins 'Life Mastery' seminar in Fiji. I was trying to pull out of the seminar as we couldn't afford it, but this was not possible, so Rob and I went. This was when I told Rob about the mess we were in. He'd thought that something was wrong, yet he didn't yell at me or tell me I was useless or that we were going to go bankrupt again. I felt relieved that I had my husband by my side to support me, whatever happened.

Now that I had someone to share with, I could work on trying to fix the problems. Going to the Life Mastery seminar was an eye opener for me. It really helped me get clarity on life, on a different type of life that I wanted.

As months passed, we tried to finish off our properties and the houses for the investor I was working for. He, too, was starting to get caught up in the tail end of the boom and going through the same thing as us. This particular investor was trying to keep above things, but he wasn't paying the tradies and this was coming back to haunt us.

You see, we were the ones who'd organized the tradies; the accounts came to us and we forwarded them on to the investor. The phone calls came to us whenever a bill wasn't paid. I would then pass the bill onto the investor and if it still wasn't paid, we'd get more phone calls, some of them nasty. We lost a lot of tradies this way, as now they wouldn't work for us, so we had to find new ones. The pressure was intense.

As more calls kept coming in, I started feeling depressed again. I remembered again how it felt after going through bankruptcy with the hotel. The phone would ring and I would cringe. I felt like throwing up each time as anxiety overwhelmed me. I no longer wanted to take these calls, so I started to screen them. Shielding myself from others didn't end with the phone calls. It extended into my social life. I soon didn't want to step out of our home or see or speak to anyone.

At that stage, our personal issues weren't huge and I was handling them, but the investors' problems that I was taking on board were becoming unmanageable. It was all starting to happen again and these weren't even our problems. And I was allowing it to happen, which I shouldn't have done.

I would wake up in a reasonably good mood and that would change as soon as I got that phone call from a tradie. I would become depressed and I wouldn't be able to do anything. And my poor husband copped it. Then, to top it off, the market was still falling, so of course it really started to affect us. It was as if everything had happened overnight.

I felt powerless, as if I had no control of anything any more. I felt I was a useless failure and I could no longer take the pressure. Rob knew things weren't good, but not to what extent. With the tradies and everything we were going through with our business, I didn't want to be here any more. It was all getting to be too much for me, and the feeling was torture. I just wanted to crawl up in a foetal position in a corner somewhere so no one could see me and hide from the world. Yes, I wanted to kill myself.

The only thing preventing me from committing suicide was the thought of leaving my husband and kids behind.

Rob and I decided to travel down south for three nights for a break from all this. We stayed in a secluded hut in the middle of the bush, and it gave me much relief, as there was no phone and I was able to spend quality time to think and be with Rob, and share with him how I was feeling and how it was all affecting me. I shared the big picture with him, and just how bad it was.

When I came back, it took a while before I let go of the problem with the tradies. That took a lot of coaching from Rob, with him reminding me, "It's not our problem". As soon as I started to let go of it, I began to feel a little better.

The time away gave me a space to clear my head. I realized that this problem was taking over my life to the point that it was paralysing me. I wasn't fixing our own problems because I was endlessly worrying about the tradie problem and that was making me sick.

I realized I had to get clarity about our business and where we were going in life.

We finished working for the investors. Rob went back to bricklaying and he advised me to go back to real estate. This meant putting on makeup and getting dressed up, cold calling, talking to people. It scared the hell out of me.

I was still suffering from depression and because of how bad I was feeling, didn't think it was possible for me to talk to people, let alone motivate myself. I felt sick just thinking about it. But I had to do it. Again, I had to push myself out of my comfort zone.

I started off doing home opens for one of the consultants in the office. I hadn't realized that I was missing that interaction with people–I actually enjoyed it–but I stuck to just home opens as there was no pressure of selling. I just handed the leads back to the rep.

Then came a phone call. The person on the other line asked, "Moya, are you still selling real estate? We'd like you to list our house." I knew if I did this that that would be it. I could pass the lead on and get a referral, or if I did it myself, I would once again be a full time consultant. Did I want this? Well, I had no choice; we needed the money.

I went into the lounge room and sat quietly. "Yes," I heard the universe saying to me, "just do it!" That phone call was a clear sign from the universe. So I rang my boss and said, "Craig, can I come back as a full time consultant again, please?" and he said yes. That was that; I was into it again.

I took stock and looked at the big picture, and I started to focus on what was important. Our son, Ryan, was involved in some of the houses with us, so I had to make sure his credit rating stayed intact. Our main aim was to sell all the properties we had with him, first.

Then Ryan lost his job in the mines. Luckily, he received a payout, so that carried him until he found another job, which didn't take long.

We started to put some of the properties on the market. I was still trying to hold off selling them, as it was so hard to let go. Once we put on more, they started to sell.

Now, when you sell a property, you have to pay agent fees, settlement fees, and capital gains. The upside in our case was we could get back the 20% the bank was holding as a deposit and we didn't have the interest payments every month; we had to access the money the bank was holding and not pay any interest payments, and all the other costs associated with owning a home.

Unfortunately, the small amount of equity was not as much as it had been a year before and it was falling every day, but at least it gave us something.

So every time a property sold, it gave us something, and that was one interest payment a month we didn't have to come up with.

If you plan to go into real estate as an investor, remember not to get personal with a property that you are going to sell or buy. It is business and the figures have to stack up.

Here's another story I would like to share with you that you may learn from.

When we were in the boom, it felt great, as everything was rising. It felt like it was going to stay that way forever. But it wasn't permanent. You should never get caught up in the hype. It's like an auction: someone bids and you just get carried away.

We were under the illusion that the boom was here to stay. But like many others, we made a huge mistake, not knowing that the boom was coming to an end soon. We bought four blocks of land through a major developer. The only way they would allow you to get this land was with a cash offer and a $5,000 deposit. They wouldn't let you put down "subject to finance". It had to be cash.

If developers make you do cash, please walk away! Anything can happen to you. You may think everything is fine, but you can lose your job or something else can change, but you are still obliged to buy that property. It is a legal contract when you put down cash, so you have to go through with the purchase. This is another area where we got caught badly.

The 12 months came around and the boom had finished. It was 2008 and we didn't have the money for the 20% deposit the bank wanted. The valuation was coming in $50,000 under what we paid for it and with the subprime market (making loans to people who might have difficulty paying it back) in the USA and the offshoots it caused, it was a lot harder to get money, not just to buy land, but also to get a house built.

Because of the boom, the developers got greedy, too. They were putting the land up an extra $50,000 to $100,000, so when it all went pear-shaped, they got burnt, as well.

We put a cash offer on a beautiful block of land for $515,000. If you built a two-storey home on this land, you would have stunning ocean views.

In that same street on the beachfront, this is what happened in the boom. The blocks were on the market for $750,000 and they were selling. An agent in Mandurah bought one and on-sold it before it settled–for $900,000! Since then, a lot of the blocks have gone on the market again–and sold for just $450,000. That gives you an idea how the market was going, and how the people were hurting.

Another issue we faced was the developer's refusal to talk to us. We tried to see them, but they wouldn't see us. We gave them our financials to show that we couldn't afford them, to no avail. They said we had to settle or they were going to take us to court.

We put all of this on the back burner, as there was nothing we could do until they pursued us further.

We just focused on what we had to do. As it turned out, we weren't the only ones in this situation. Eventually, the developers saw that they couldn't get money out of stone, so we ended up receiving a letter from them, terminating the contracts. We lost our $20,000 deposit, but at least they weren't going to pursue us. One problem solved, now onto the next.

There was one block we had bought where the interest payments were absolutely ridiculous. We just couldn't pay them any more, so we asked Rob's brother if he could help us out and make those payments for us and as soon as we sold our home, we would pay him back, which we did.

We sold our beautiful home, our boat, and Rob's car. I accessed my superannuation and we even had garage sales to try and get as much money as we could. With all of this, we paid the interest payments. All of our income was going on them, but it just wasn't getting any closer to finalization.

I rang the banks and tried to negotiate with them, but they were feeling the pressure as well and they weren't very helpful.

Before I move on, it's my pleasure to share a story here that saved us.

Rob had always wanted a dog, but I didn't. However, in real estate, you go on property tours, and one house we went to had puppies that were ready to be sold–for a price we couldn't afford. Well, I fell head over heels in love with one of those puppies!

When I got back to the office, I rang Rob and told him about this beautiful little Shiatsu/Maltese/Poodle cross. When I told him the price, he said we couldn't afford him.

When you want something badly enough, you will find the money, and I wanted this little dog badly! So yes, I found the money. I bought him and brought him home. He now sleeps with us and lives inside our home; he is gorgeous and his name is Teddy.

Seriously, this puppy saved our marriage. If Rob and I ever raised our voices to each other, Teddy would get upset and, of course, that would upset us, so we would stop.

If we were having our usual finance issues, there was just something about Teddy being so happy and showing us his unconditional love. He seemed to sense if we were in a bad mood. He would run up, jumping and licking you all over, melting away any stress or other negative emotions the day had brought you. Rob says he is spoilt. I say he is loved.

Thanks to Teddy, we had another wake up call.

Rob was driving on one of the main roads (with Teddy) in my car when a woman appeared out of nowhere and crashed straight into him. This wrote off my car, and when Rob got out of the car, Teddy took off, as he got really frightened. Rob called out to him, but in vain. Teddy was gone.

Rob rang me in a panic. He wasn't hurt, but Teddy had run away. I rang my daughter and asked her to come and get me and then we went and picked Rob up. Once we got to the scene of the accident, everyone except Rob had already left, and my car was gone. Rob was standing on the side of the road. As I approached him, my heart was pounding. I got out of the car and just hugged him and wouldn't let go.

He was terribly upset, as Teddy had disappeared. Worse still, Teddy didn't wear a collar and wasn't registered.

For hours Rob, Sharon, my grandkids and I walked the streets calling out for him.

We rang the ranger to let them know what had happened, and to let us know if anyone rang.

After a couple of hours, we received a phone call: someone had found Teddy!

We went to the caller's place and there was Teddy's little nose under the fence, as he looked up at us, wagging his tail. Apparently, to reach this place, Teddy had needed to cross major roads. We were approximately 2 kilometres away from where the accident had happened.

The lady let us in and we all cried. Teddy was going berserk, as he was so happy to see us. I picked him up and hugged him and then handed him to Rob.

The lady said she was out the front when she saw Teddy. She said to him, "I don't think you belong here," then brought him in and rang the ranger.

When we went to the car, I noticed Teddy had pooed himself, as it was all over his tail. He must have been dreadfully scared.

Once in the car, the reality of what had happened hit Rob. He fell silent and just hugged Teddy.

The car was a write off and we received a payout. Once again, this went on interest payments, but by then we had made a decision. We couldn't live with such stress any more.

The accident was a wakeup call. We could have lost both Rob and Teddy. Life was just too short. The universe was again trying to tell us something and this time, we listened.

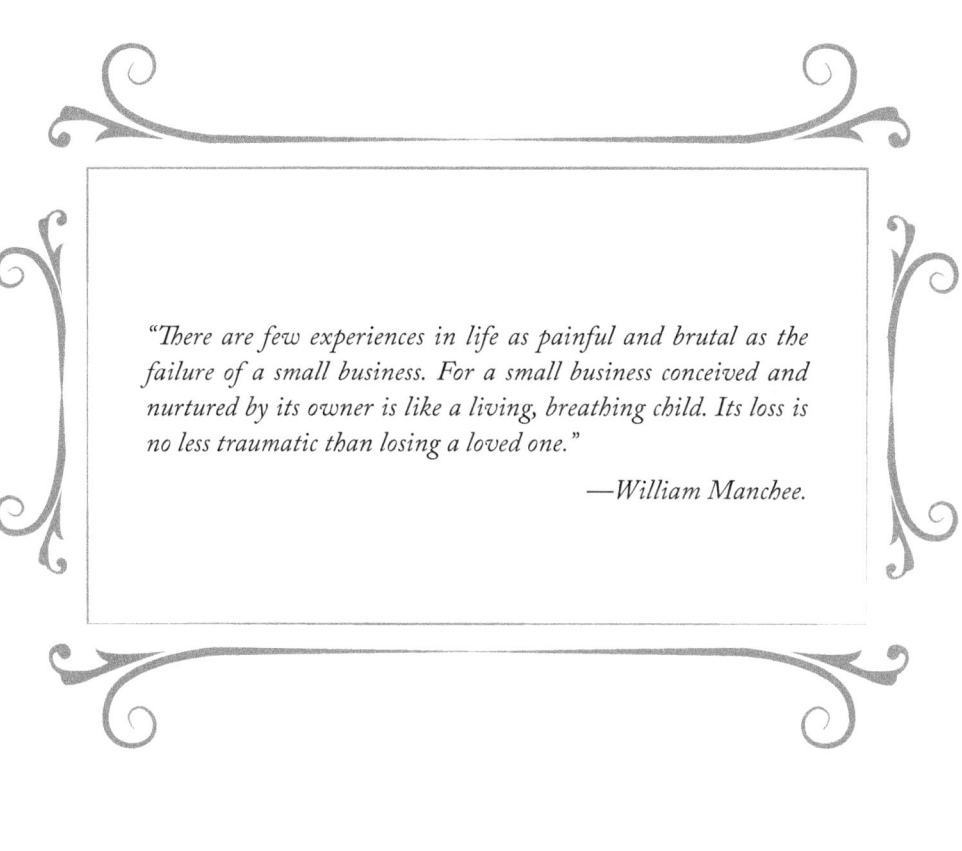

"There are few experiences in life as painful and brutal as the failure of a small business. For a small business conceived and nurtured by its owner is like a living, breathing child. Its loss is no less traumatic than losing a loved one."

—William Manchee.

Bankruptcy No. 2

We talked about our situation deeply and unlike last time, I did a huge amount of research on the internet, trying to hold off the inevitable. By the end, I knew so much of what we could and couldn't do, that in my heart, I knew we were going down the right road. Yes, we decided to go bankrupt again.

We looked at what was left. We still had one of our rental properties, which we'd moved into, another investment property, a block of land with Ryan and another block of land.

The plan was to walk away from everything that wasn't in Ryan's name and keep paying the mortgages and lines of credit that were associated with Ryan so that he would keep his credit rating and we would go bankrupt.

We had made one million dollars by the end of 2008! But eighteen months later, we had lost one million dollars and more. I remember saying to my husband that we needed this to happen so we could learn from it. Then I could share what had happened with other people, so they didn't have to go down the same path as us.

Before we declared bankruptcy, we obtained finance for a new car for me, because I needed it for work and we knew we wouldn't be able to get it after we went bankrupt.

One thing I'd learnt when we went through bankruptcy with the hotel was to not bury your head in the sand. You can't ignore the problem and hope it will go away. The problem will remain and it can get worse.

Instead, look at the problem and keep reviewing it until you have it solved. Then look back at what you have done and the steps you took to solve it and give yourself a pat on the back.

Why I am saying this?

This is because a bit of praise goes a long way. You feel good because you have knocked down another brick wall of learning and have grown and moved forward. If another problem comes your way, you can overcome it more easily. Better still, it won't happen again, as you will have learnt the lesson.

Life is about breaking down those brick walls. You always have to learn the lessons first; there is no shortcut. And quick solutions rarely work. Sure, you'll make mistakes. However, being willing to lose is part of the game of winning. As long as you learn from those mistakes and keep correcting, you'll do well in the long run.

I have to give credit to my husband, Rob. It took me a long time to turn to him to explain what was going on, but the advice I received, his love and understanding, pulled me through.

Don't feel like you have to take on all of the burden. Share it, like I did, with someone you trust and love. Don't bottle it all up inside, because this is what destroys and eats at your very soul.

Yes, we had been building wealth and doing really well, but the timing just wasn't right. And in my heart, I believe this was not the path I was meant to take.

My way of thinking was to not sell your properties, but there are times when you just have to let go, and this was one of them. Because of my feeling of failure, I was finding it very hard to let go.

So what did we do? We decided to bite the bullet. We had the knowledge and the tenacity to start again; we just needed to change a few things if we wanted to. But…guess what? I really didn't want to start again. I knew that this was not my life path.

When you go bankrupt, you are not allowed to go out of the country unless you have permission from the Trustee, and just before we went bankrupt, there was something special that Rob and I wanted to do, something that was important to us. On our 25th wedding anniversary, we wanted to renew our vows, and we wanted to do it in Bali with our children and grandchildren.

So we went ahead and organized the trip and booked out four double hotel rooms. We only invited a few friends, Rob's mum and stepdad and, of course, our kids; we didn't invite more, as we couldn't afford to.

We were all dressed similarly, and the hotel did an amazing job of setting the ceremony up on the beach, with the meal around the pool.

My sons walked me down the aisle, one on either side of me, with two of the grandchildren ahead, while at the front were our friends. Our daughter was there as a pretend celebrant, and she married us. What a glorious day! For a while, we forgot our worries.

We had two wonderful weeks in Bali with our family, with not a care in the world. And then, it was back to reality.

On our return, Rob and I declared bankruptcy, and we moved out of our rental into someone else's rental. Again, we were getting nasty phone calls from the banks, the only ones to whom we owed money. This time, our answer was, "We are bankrupt; do what you have to do." Relief started to seep in. I felt a sense of calm, and a huge weight lifted off my shoulders. I could step back and move on to the next stage.

Ryan was paying the line of credit, and the rent on the house was just covering the mortgage. We were paying two mortgages, our rent, two cars, plus all the other bills, including bills associated with the properties.

We were still hurting.

I had a buyer for the block of land, but the Trustee wouldn't sign off on it. One minute they told me that they would, and the next, they said that they wouldn't. The buyers were not happy, to say the least, as they had started getting plans organized for their home. They got really nasty and threatened to blacken my name. I couldn't have that, so I paid them $2,000 and they walked away.

The block sat there for another year, and we were paying the mortgage. Not knowing what to do with it, we moved onto the rental.

I wasn't allowed to sell it, nor could the agency that I worked for. It had to be someone independent.

As it was also in Ryan's name, he started to take more control. He was on the title, and was not bankrupt. The Trustee had to listen to him and did. The pressure was off me a little, which was wonderful.

Eventually, the rental went to another agency and it was sold, though there was a huge capital gain. (We'd owned the house for 10 years, so it had doubled in price). The Trustee received the money to pay some back to the banks, but we had to pay the huge capital gains bill, something else we didn't need.

Another one down, and another mortgage not to have to pay, even though we had the capital gains bill. We made arrangements with the tax office and paid it off. We were getting there.

There was another block of land we needed to get rid of. I rang the Trustee's office to see if I could sell it and they said yes. (We had a different case manager and she was lovely). I found a buyer, sold it, and that was that.

By paying the loans and liaising with the banks that Ryan was connected to, we were able to save his credit rating. Of course, ours was shot, but we didn't care. Our son was our concern.

You would think that when you go bankrupt, life would get easier, but it didn't.

All this time, Rob was working as a bricklayer and I was a real estate consultant. However, because you have to be really focused and motivated in real estate, I found it difficult to do my job with all the issues we were going through. The work that I should have been doing to bring in money wasn't happening, because my mind was somewhere else. So I began to work harder, not smarter.

I thought the harder I worked and the more money I made, we could pay off all the debts we had. But the more I was making, the more the Trustee was taking. When you are bankrupt, if you earn over a certain amount, you have to give 50% back to the Trustee, so for three years, it felt like the more I earned, the more I was giving away. Even though I was making money, the Trustee was taking a huge chunk of it.

We soon felt like we were going backwards again.

It's All Connected

In 2009, my son Ryan got caught up in the financial crisis. He lost his job in the mines, which he had had for over ten years.

When this happened, I believed that something good would come out of it, as it always does. Ryan sent me the following version of what he went through.

> Mum,
>
> *I'm a firm believer that things happen for a reason. The reason I say this is that somehow, everything we do is interconnected. Some may call this six degrees of separation, and this can be due to anything from a decision made, to a random meeting in the street. Looking back at all the events, meetings and decisions made throughout my life, they all led directly to where I am now.*
>
> *Recently, or more precisely, in January of this year, I was made redundant at my job in the mining industry. I was finishing my last night shift and at 5:00 a.m., we were given a message that there was a meeting in camp at 8:00 a.m.*
>
> *As we were due to fly out that morning, I rang dispatch to confirm this. What happened at the meeting was we were given a "state of the nation" speech by the General Manager of the mine. Then they asked to interview me separately. That was when I was told that my services would no longer be required, and I had to pack up my room before flying out from site.*

Overcoming Life's Challenges by Moya Mulvay

The next couple of hours were spent in a state of numbness. All told, 500 full-time and 300 subcontractors were let go. Thankfully, I was working full time, so I was eligible for a redundancy payout. The subcontractors, however, were not as fortunate, as they were employed as casual employees. It truly was horrible to watch grown men and women breaking down at the thought of what was going to happen to them next.

When I eventually got home, I contacted my family and told them what had happened. They were just as shocked as I was. The next couple of days were spent just trying to process what had happened. Word eventually reached a few of my closest friends, who called to offer their condolences, even from as far as Melbourne and Adelaide. Many offers of support and offers of visits were given. I thanked everyone, but at the time, I could not handle being around anyone. It took me quite some time to even consider what to do next.

Whatever reason I had for getting up in the morning was abruptly taken from me. This lack of "purpose" manifested itself as different sleep patterns, bad eating habits, weight gain and increasing levels of apathy. Life was looking increasingly grim.

The next month or so was spent just being with my family. It was important to have this support and unconditional love near me. They understood how difficult it was for me to accept help and, thankfully, they helped me any way they could. It was during this time that I started a long-distance relationship with a girl in Adelaide. We decided to fly over to McKay in Queensland on Valentine's Day to see if the relationship would work.

Unfortunately, things did not end up as planned. Don't get me wrong; she is a wonderful, caring and compassionate woman. The only problem was that there wasn't really a spark between us. I couldn't lead someone on, so I came back home after telling this wonderful woman that we could only be friends. Not pleasant, but it was better that, than living a lie.

Thankfully, when I came back, I had a job workshop to attend and that helped redirect my focus from thinking about what might have been. At the workshop, I caught up with one of the women I had worked with at the mines.

Overcoming Life's Challenges by Moya Mulvay

We learned various job-searching techniques, but the best thing was that I learned about the "stages of change" a person experiences after losing a job. The stages include shock, denial, anger, fear, grief and frustration. Another good thing that happened was that the lady I used to work with gave me the number of an HR representative who might be able to help me find another job.

Referring back to the stages of change, I realized I needed to work through all of the stages before I could move on to something new.

I contacted the HR representative and was told I would need to get my Heavy Vehicle licence, which led me to my next period of change. I had to start taking driving lessons, which meant that I had to leave my home or, as I referred to it at the time, my cave. This was quite difficult, believe it or not, as by this time, I was at my lowest ebb. The lessons went well, however, and soon I gained enough confidence to go for my test.

This ended up a bit of a mess, as I made the mistake of missing a gear and stopping on a turn during my assessment and unfortunately, it resulted in me failing the test. I started to nose dive again, but found I was just too stubborn to hit bottom. I immediately rebooked another test and took some more lessons. While at this training centre, I decided on a whim to renew my MARCSTA mining card and senior first aid course.

This was the time when I decided to take charge of my life.

This brings me to the next period of change. A friend of mine, who also got made redundant, called me, asking if he could stay at my place while he started his new job. As I had a granny flat that wasn't currently being used, and he was a friend, I said yes.

When he arrived, we ended up talking about things and I told him about the difficulties of finding work in today's environment. He then gave me the number of an HR representative to call. I called her and described my various skills and experience, and she asked me to immediately send my resume.

I went for my Heavy Vehicle license test again and believe it or not, I aced it! The following week, I received a call from the HR representative, offering me not one job, but two.

Overcoming Life's Challenges by Moya Mulvay

I accepted the job with the better roster; it has eight days on, six days off, which means more days home. The first HR representative called during this time offering me yet another job, which I had to decline. When it rains it pours, I guess.

I needed some further training before going back to work, and once that was done, I got back into the swing of work. During my break from work, I was fortunate enough to be in town for my mate's buck's night. The night proceeded along with much drinking and merriment, and fun was had by all.

While walking by the toilet, I saw a lady sitting at a table with a group of friends. I wasn't sure what it was that stopped me in my tracks, but it was enough for me to walk right up to her and introduce myself. I was then invited to sit at the table and I talked with her friends, until eventually, it was just the two of us left talking.

We exchanged numbers and both talked of catching up. I then caught up with my friends, who by this time were a little worse for wear. We grabbed a taxi and after making sure my friends got home safe and sound, I headed home and crashed on my couch.

The next day went reasonably well, with my head feeling slightly worse off due to the previous night's festivities. But it got a lot better when I received a message from the woman I was talking to the night before, asking to catch up. We ended having a relaxing light meal and coffee, and just speaking with this lady, I knew I wanted to see her again and told her so.

The next day, I had to fly back to work and during this stint, I kept in touch with this woman. Things have been progressing quite nicely and I definitely have hope for the future, for both this relationship and whatever else life may throw at me.

At the beginning of this story, I stated that things happen for a reason, and all these events led me to where I am now. I have so much to be thankful for. The time I had off from work gave me time to reflect on what's important to me, and this brought about many changes in how I view things. It also gave me greater knowledge about who I am now.

This knowledge of myself helps me deal with whatever comes my way. The time was also spent with my family and as such, we are all closer than we have been in years. Work is both challenging and rewarding, with more time spent at home. And the more time I have at home, the more time I can spend with my daughter and, as a result, we are having many adventures together.

I met and am currently dating a fascinating woman who intrigues me no end. But the greatest thing that I have learned from this experience is that life is full of challenges, and not to take anything for granted.

It's all connected and things always happen for a reason. It's the underlying message that's important.

— Love always, your son,

Ryan xo

All my children's lives, I have said to them, "Things happen for a reason," and yes, Ryan took it on board.

This chapter is about life: it will take you on many journeys and many paths, but it is up to us which path we take. If you look back and think that you didn't take the right path, or that you missed that window of opportunity, you have taken it for a reason you may not understand at the moment, but one day, you will look back and know why.

Me, for example, I look back on all the roads I have taken that have brought me to the place I am meant to be, and that is here. As I mentioned earlier, when my son Kane asked me, "Mum, why does this keep happening to me?" I replied, "You haven't learned the lesson yet and it will keep happening until you do."

So, if you are having a continuation of hard knocks and you don't know why, step back and look at what you are doing and ask yourself if you have learned the lesson yet. Because if you haven't, you won't move forward. If you don't know now, one day it will come to you and you will realize why you took the road you did.

"If money is your hope for independence you will never have it. The only real security that a man will have in this world is a reserve of knowledge, experience and ability."

—*Henry Ford*

Bankruptcy: the Full Story

Bankruptcy is a legal representation of a person's inability to pay and settle their debts.

In today's debt ridden society, many people are in severe financial difficulties, often for reasons outside their control. In fact, many people have gone bankrupt over unforeseen circumstances such as an accident, medical bills, unemployment and so much more. The daughter of a friend of mine had an accident and had to pay $3,000. She didn't have the money so she went bankrupt. So yes, it can happen to anyone.

If your debts are piling up, sometimes there is no way out but to file for bankruptcy. Your creditors can also make you bankrupt. They can also use scare tactics to make you pay by threatening to send you into bankruptcy. Once you are bankrupt, your assets can then be sold to raise money to settle your debts.

In our first bankruptcy case, with the hotel, we owed millions. The receivers had already taken the hotel and all the contents, and were about to take our home and car. On top of that, the bailiff began taking an inventory of what we had left in our home, including our furniture. It wasn't worth very much, so they didn't pursue it any further.

When we declared bankruptcy, we discovered we couldn't have a car worth more than $2,500 (the amount is higher now) and we couldn't write a cheque over $500–not that we even had $500!

If you earn over a certain amount of money, a percentage has to go to the Trustee of Bankruptcy. We couldn't get credit. We couldn't get a loan. We couldn't be a director of a company. These are just a few of the restrictions. Every country is different, I am talking about Australia, and when we went bankrupt the second time, it had changed. We were able to keep our furniture, our jewellery and a car worth about $7,600. (Remember, we just got a loan for a new car, and because there was no equity in it, they allowed us to keep it). There was also a way that we could have kept our home, but as the mortgage was so high, we decided just to walk away. This is why it is important to do your homework. If you are considering bankruptcy, visit http://www.itsa.gov.au/ and for a quick guide to Bankruptcy and regarding assets, go to https://www.afsa.gov.au/debtors/bankruptcy/bankruptcy-overview/asset-table to learn more about the insolvency and trustee services of Australia.

We were bankrupt for three years, and it was five years before we could even think about moving forward. (Credit agencies keep a report of your bankruptcy for up to five years or longer). And this happened to us twice. For our second bankruptcy, our five years is up in September 2016.

It wasn't so long ago that bankruptcy meant that bankrupts would carry a stigma for life. Many committed suicide rather than face such a disgrace. Throughout the Great Depression, a lot of people who went bankrupt spent years paying off their discharged debts as a matter of honour.

Nowadays, it's very different. It's not nearly as bad, because later on, you will be able to get credit and your debts will have been wiped away. We managed to get credit after our first bankruptcy.

What to consider before declaring bankruptcy

Don't think of going bankrupt as a last resort. If you are considering bankruptcy, think long and hard about it before you do. We did it the first time because we owed millions of dollars to many different creditors; the second time, we only owed the banks.

Most importantly, get "good" legal advice from someone who specializes in this area. Many people may not know that some debtors are willing to work with you to sort things out, to restructure payments, and so on.

When we first went bankrupt, we *thought* we'd had good advice before we declared bankruptcy. We were told we would lose our home, but found out later on that this wasn't true. We had only just bought the house and had no equity in it. In fact, it was worth less than what we paid for it. As I mentioned previously, we got a raw deal. This is where education comes into play: you need to know your options. This is why the second time around, I did a lot of research on what we could and couldn't do. Now, the internet has made it so much easier.

If you choose to file for bankruptcy, your life becomes an open book for the court appointed bankruptcy officials to see. They will pry into all aspects of your personal life and you have to give them everything they ask for, all your details. This includes all the information about your home, savings, bank accounts, investments and any assets you have including cars, boats, furniture and anything else they can sell for cash.

For this reason, if you feel that your debt isn't very much and that you could probably repay it over time, call your creditors and negotiate with them. Refinance your mortgage, but be very careful that you can repay the extra payments.

If You Can, Avoid Bankruptcy

If you have a mortgage and a home, think about selling it and moving somewhere less expensive. Make sure you buy a much cheaper house (don't forget all the fees you have to pay when buying and selling a home), or just rent.

Do you have a car loan? Try turning the vehicle in to the dealer and getting something used and without a car payment. If you own a car free and clear and it's worth something, sell it and buy something cheaper. If you are a two-car family, sell one car, if possible.

If you've got extra bedrooms in your house, take in a boarder, or even two. They can pay rent only, or you can also charge them for meals and washing and ironing. I used to cook meals and take them to Dad. I figured I was cooking anyway, so what's an extra meal? When I was working at the drycleaner's, I would take in washing and ironing. Don't let your pride get in the way; do whatever it takes.

Start selling your "stuff," known as your assets, either on eBay, Facebook or at garage sales. I have always done this. It is amazing what you accumulate and even more amazing what people buy. I had an old knitting machine, and someone bought it for the needles; the purchaser had a knitting machine but couldn't get the needles any more. One man's trash is another man's treasure. And all those little bits and pieces add up.

It's time to take control, take a critical look at your spending habits, and evaluate them. Try to understand where you have wasted and invested your money. In other words, think about what you did and what went wrong.

When your bills come in, pay them on time. If you are having trouble, don't bury your head in the sand hoping your problems will go away, because they won't. Call your creditor and work out a payment plan. With us, for example, one was the electricity account. I would ring the electric company and offer to pay $20 per week. You are showing them you are making an effort to pay. So, when you have finished, the next one comes in, and that's ok, at least the first one is paid. Do the same with the next one if you have to. This way your credit stays intact.

Prepare a monthly plan for your savings and expenditure.

Learn to go without. What I do is go away and think about it before I buy it. And more than likely, I don't buy it, because I don't really want or need it. Sometimes you can just get caught up with buying for the sake of buying.

Set aside money for emergencies and rainy days. By doing this, when a bill or emergency comes in, you will have the money to pay for it and you will be in control again.

Check all your statements for the fees you are paying and see where you can cut down. For instance, eftpos fees are huge, especially when you draw money out from a different bank. Over a year, that can cost a lot of money. That is money that has gone, literally, down the drain. Once again I did some research and found that ING direct don't charge eftpos fees over a certain amount, so if I draw out $200 from a bank, I receive that $2 back.

Go back to basics. When I was first married, I never had a credit card, but there were "lay-bys". This was great, especially at Christmas time. Wait until your favourite store has a sale, then go and lay-by what you want for Christmas, I would lay-by purchases in three different lots. So when one lot was finished (things I needed sooner), I would pick it up.

Start paying your lay-bys off. By doing it in three lots, when one lot comes out of lay-by, you feel great because you have something, and when Christmas comes around, you will have all your presents already wrapped without going into debt over Christmas, because it's all paid for.

Something I do even now is check on Facebook and Gumtree. Even garage sales are great for presents. I am collecting great bits and pieces that look like new for my grandkids for Christmas and birthday presents, so when the time comes, I don't have to fork out a lot of money paying full price for everything. Not just presents, but anything you need: furniture, sports equipment, the list can go on.

Actually, thinking about it, I rarely go to shops any more. I buy bargains online or at garage sales, and I get a real buzz from getting a good deal.

Buy Christmas cards, paper, decorations just after Christmas, when they go on sale.

When my children were growing up, I would wait until the sales started and go and lay-by their clothes for the following year. I didn't need them for a year, so I took as long as the shop allowed me to pay them off.

Some people are just not good with money. They see it in the bank and think it's all there to spend on fun things, instead of putting bits away for certain bills. There are two ways to tackle this:

Have a note pad, and with respect to the money in the bank that you need for bills, have each bill written down and accounted for in the notepad. This way, when you look at what is in the bank and what is written on the pad, you will know the amount of money that you really have. For example, you have $1,500 in the bank and on your pad your bills add up to $1,000; this means that $500 is yours to use. But please, don't use it if you don't have to. Save it.

When we went bankrupt, it was tight. Because of the work Rob and I were doing, there was never a regular pay cheque coming in, so it was hard to budget. When Friday arrived, we combined our money for that week and then put the money needed for bills in envelopes, and that is where it stayed until the bills came in. Or you could have a separate account linked to your main account and put it in there, and not touch it.

If you're not working now, if possible, start. There is huge satisfaction in working just because you have the ability to do so. When you are working on establishing or re-establishing your credit rating, a positive record of employment is essential. Steady employment is something that is looked upon favourably by the credit reporting companies.

Do some volunteer work; you receive fantastic gratification out of this, and it may just turn into work for you.

Find ways to earn extra money. Yes, working more cuts into family time, but realize it's temporary and use the additional money to repay your debt if you haven't gone bankrupt. This can help you avoid bankruptcy. You can get through this temporary period. If you have to get a second job, do it! I did everything from delivering papers to sewing zips into urine-soaked pants.

There are so many ways to help you get back on your feet and save money. Get on the internet and look around for tips. You will find information on my website, workbooks and links.

It will take a while to feel better again, to feel "normal." Think of this as a test: it is testing you and training you to acquire good habits.

It can be hard to get back on your feet, but combine smart choices with some hard work and heaps of determination. Read a lot of books. The book that got me moving forward was Robert Kiyosaki's, *Rich Dad Poor Dad*. Another fantastic book is Napoleon Hill's *Think and Grow Rich*, which I have for free on my website. Get back to basics.

It is totally possible to get your financial life back on track. Learn from your mistakes and make better choices next time around.

Don't try to keep up with everyone else. This is a big one: be yourself.

And there's no reason you have to fall back into your old habits. You have become so much wiser, haven't you?

Even if you do not have a lot of money, you still have huge potential for success.

Protect Yourself

I will be the first to say that I haven't always handled my money wisely. I have made some bad investment decisions. I should have kept more money aside in a savings account, but I chose to spend it.

A person can make money by being ethical and honest, working hard, making smart investments and looking for good deals. There will always be opportunities. We just have to decide when and how to go about them, decide which opportunities to take and which ones to leave. There is still no such thing as a free lunch, and any deal that sounds too good to be true probably is.

Over the years, I have seen it so many times: predators feeding off the fears of people who lack money, predators who see these people as targets and use get-rich-quick schemes and seminars to bring them in. When people are desperate for money, they really don't think. They want a quick fix, some quick money, and don't really think things through.

Do not get caught up in get-rich schemes! I have been to a lot of seminars and I do get bits of wisdom and inspiration from them. Some of them I have found to be outstanding and even life-changing. But not all seminars are as honest as they seem to be.

Learn from someone who has done it and has been through it. Don't just "book learn;" learn from someone who has really done the hard yards, someone who has been there.

Never put yourself in a position where you are uninsured, especially your home and its contents. Imagine if half of the furniture in your house is being paid for using a payment plan or credit card. If your house burns down, you are still liable to pay for it or, even worse, your house.

Insure your home and contents. Go without other things if you need to, but find the money. It is so important. This is where you live. Recently, we had major bushfires in Australia, and some of those houses weren't insured. They burned to the ground with everything in them. What are those people going to do? All their belongings are gone. Where are they going to go and with what?

This is especially important if you have children. If you won't do it for yourself, do it for them.

You're Not the Only One Who Has Faced This Situation

MC Hammer was a successful rapper in the late 1980s. You may remember his hit *Can't Touch This*. He earned a huge fortune of $33 million in a short amount of time. He should have been set for life. But he wasn't. He made bad choices, similar to a lot of people when they get a large chunk of money. He spent $12 million on a house and continued to live a lavish lifestyle. In 1996, his extravagant lifestyle forced him into bankruptcy.

Other well-known people have been bankrupt, including Walt Disney, Francis Ford Coppola, and Oscar Wilde, to name a few.

The above examples show bankruptcy can hit anyone, but it does not mean the end of the world for those who go through it.

In this world, there are so many more opportunities, just around the corner.

You just need that desire and fire in your belly. Educate yourself and take action.

After Bankruptcy: Take Responsibility and Prepare For the Future.

If you are now out of bankruptcy, that means you have spent the last few years watching every penny–every penny that you earn and, better still, that you have spent.

You have learned so much from this that you never want to go through it again.

You have sacrificed so much that you have learned restraint and patience in a world of instant gratification, and this is worth its weight in gold.

Don't get caught up with well meaning friends (this happened to me), thinking that to cheer me up, going shopping or retail therapy would help ease my worries away. No, don't do this because you will be going back to bad habits. It may feel good for a while, but then when you realize you can't afford it, it can put you in a depressed state.

Surround yourself with those who will reaffirm your sense of wellbeing and self esteem. Such people may offer to help you with a budget or other important information.

Always check your credit report after bankruptcy to ensure that you have been discharged completely. You might also wish to add a note on your credit file outlining and explaining your reasons for having to declare bankruptcy.

Take one step at a time and the process might not be nearly as complex as you think. It is not the end of the world. You may go through some tough times during or after your bankruptcy, but you will be free of the pain and pressure caused by your financial problems. You can rise above it and make something more worthwhile of your life.

This is what happened to me and no way is bankruptcy ever going to happen again. I have pushed myself, educated myself to overcome it. I don't mean just in a monetary sense; I mean in a spiritual way. I never want to go through that pain again.

If you are offered credit, rip it up. We haven't got a credit card, we don't want one and we will never get another one. We don't need it. If we haven't got the money to pay for something, we don't get it. You don't want to fall into the same trap again. We now know we can control our spending and budgeting, and we have learned a lot about money. You live within your means. If you haven't got it, you don't get it, simple. If you do have a credit card, pay it off in total when it is due. Never spend more than you earn. Spending beyond your means is the trap people fall into with credit cards.

It's going to be tough, but look on the bright side. It will be a good opportunity for you to start all over again with a clean slate. Yes, it might be tough to retain your good credit standing, but with a change in lifestyle, a good job and paying your bills on time, once out of bankruptcy, you will soon regain the trust of most financial institutions.

Be responsible. Don't get caught up in debt again.

When you do come out of bankruptcy, be very careful who you deal with. There are so many people out there who are looking to rip people off, so be sure you read the fine print before committing yourself to anything.

After our first bankruptcy, we went with just any home loan, happy that we could get a loan at all. Because you have been bankrupt, you may be charged a higher interest rate than people who have a good credit rating.

Do your homework. There are other options, if one bank says no, that doesn't mean it's written in stone. Go to another bank and don't give up. If only I'd known then what I know now, I would have done things differently. That is why education is so important. Don't rush into anything.

Please be careful of the loan sharks out there. They prey on desperate people who are trying to borrow money and have been refused everywhere else. They are not licensed and some operate illegally.

You all know how I feel about property; it is a love-hate relationship, but we have now made the big decision of not buying another home of our own. Yes, I know what you are thinking, that we are mad! (But read on a little bit more and you will see what a wonderful win win situation we are going to do). All that wasted money on rent; why are they doing this? It was a huge decision to make, but now we have made it, we are quite happy about it.

Because my children have always said to me, "Mum, we want you, not what you give us," they are now getting me, not what I will be leaving them in my will.

We live in a 3 bedroom plus study, 2-storey home, which is probably too big for us, but when the kids and grandkids are here, it's not.

The top floor has a lounge and main bedroom and I use the lounge for my office. You can walk out onto a little balcony and we have estuary glimpses, which is beautiful.

It is in a lovely street, with even lovelier people, and every morning it is just a quick walk to the estuary.

There is a park bench on the foreshore where Teddy and I sit. I close my eyes, meditate, take in the smell of fresh air, the sound of the water lapping on the shore, the birds singing.

This is what life is all about: being in the moment, helping people, loving life.

And there is now another chapter of my life regarding of where we will be living. My daughter, Sharon, and her husband live on 5 acres. They were going to downsize and build, once again looking at the cost of selling a property (agents' and settlement fees). Either building or buying, you also have stamp duty and settlement fees. And if you decide to build, you have the hassle of renting until you move in, so...we have been talking about putting a granny flat on the property. Rob and I could rent it off Andrew and Sharon, and Andrew would get the increase in the value of his property. As for us, we would have a smaller house to look after, we will build the granny flat and as it is on Sharon and Andrews land, and I can still claim all my expenses with work as I am working from home. Not only that; even though we will have our own space, we will be close to one another, which is a blessing. So all round, it is a win win situation.

We want to enjoy what life we have left, not be a slave to work.

"Education is the most powerful weapon which you can use to change the world."

—Nelson Mandela

Educate Yourself and Your Children

There is massive debt around us at the moment. As many children learn from adults, unfortunately, these adults are setting a bad example because they are having trouble managing their own finances.

Be certain that you have the right mindset. Don't talk about "getting out of debt" when what you really mean is "financial freedom." We must choose our terms carefully.

We learn our money skills mostly from our parents or other adults as we are growing up. For me, my parents were from the old school and they never spoke to me about money. Money management was never shown to me, so, not knowing how, I never passed these skills onto my children. I had to go out and learn those skills myself from whatever source necessary, and yes I made mistakes, but I learnt from them.

One subject that should be taught in school is Money Management—how to deal with money, how to budget, and how to plan. There is no education out there for the young or even the more mature.

Mary Hunt, the author of *Debt Proof Your Kids* says, "Values are more often caught than taught." Be very careful what you say around your children. They pick up things so easily. Of course, there are a lot of outside influences out there, such as TV, radio and friends, but it is our parents who influence us the most.

Over the years, here are some of the phrases I have heard. Think before you say them to your children.

"Someone has to pay the bills."

As adults, that is our responsibility, not our children's. Don't blame them.

When we say this to our children, it can cause guilt, a feeling a child may then relate to money. As they grow into adulthood, many struggle as they try to justify everyday purchases to themselves.

"I don't need it, but I really want it."

This phrase can cause impulse buying, which gives the illusion of instant gratification. It is a good idea to teach children how to evaluate purchases, rather than encouraging them to make buying decisions based solely on the fact that they want something. Remember, you can like something, admire it and appreciate it; that doesn't mean you have to own it. Think for a moment: you go out and buy something, you really *want* it, not *need* it, but you can't afford it. You have your quick fix, you then get home, a day may pass and you feel sick, as now you can't pay that bill that needed to be paid because you had to have your fix.

And the list goes on:
"We can't afford it."
"Money doesn't grow on trees."
"Money is evil."
"Money will attract problems."
"Money will make me a selfish person."
"Wanting money is greedy."
"Rich people are snobs."

These statements and beliefs reinforce a poverty mentality in children and teach them to shut their minds to other possibilities.

Explain to them why they can't always have what they want.

When you take the time to explain things, children learn that buying decisions are not always based purely on money. You work so hard for your money, so you feel you deserve to reap the rewards of all your efforts.

You want this money to work hard for you, not to line someone else's pockets.

It is so sad; most people will work like slaves all their lives to have little by the time they retire, that is, if they have anything at all. You don't have to be one of them.

It can be very challenging for most people to understand the financial world, as they find it confusing. Their environment didn't give them the encouragement and approval they desperately needed in order to learn. As a result, they either leave their money in the bank, thinking it will be safe there, or they hand it over to someone else to manage for them.

Change Those Voices in Your Head

Do you listen to the voices in your head? Do they sound like the voices you used to hear when you were young? Voices of negative beliefs and negative self talk, voices from your family, friends, from your past environment, and so on. These voices might be holding you back and these are some of the things they might be saying:

> *Who are you to succeed?*
> *You're not worthy.*
> *Success isn't natural for you.*
> *You're stupid.*
> *You are an idiot.*
> *You are a loser.*
> *You will amount to nothing.*
> *You're a failure.*

These voices are embedded into our subconscious. Without any real thought, someone could have said these things to us as a child, and this may have distorted our self-image.

They caused us to limit ourselves, fail when we did not need to, and perhaps fall into poverty.

This is unnatural.

We didn't know these voices were embedded in us, so we didn't know what they were doing to us.

Many people find it difficult to praise themselves and congratulate themselves. I know, because I used to be like this. We have to start reprogramming our thought patterns.

Many people never got the pat on the back or the "Great job!" for an accomplishment.

They got "corrections" along the way, seldom approval.

For many, this lack of encouragement, love and approval leaves a void in their self esteem. It beats them down and destroys their self worth.

Nobody told them they were great, special and talented.

How can you change this?

Be aware of your "self talk." Recapture the most powerful words in the English language, "you" and "I". NOW, say the following:

"I am born for greatness.

I am born to be a gift to someone else.

I am powerful.

Whatever I touch succeeds.

I have what it takes.

I was born to be financially successful."

Don't cover up the pain, like a lot of people do. Go to the root of the problem, and fix it.

How much are you willing to invest in yourself?

If you have put on weight and feel sluggish, are you willing to purchase healthier foods, pay for a gym membership or purchase exercise equipment? Exercise always makes you feel so much better and it puts you in a better state of mind.

Investing is not just about money; it is about time. Use that time wisely.

Are you willing to invest in educating yourself by attending seminars and buying books and CDs?

Are you willing to invest your time in learning a new hobby?

Are you willing to give time to help someone less fortunate?

Are you willing to invest in "you?"

Have you got a passion, so that you can move forward?

Have you thought about using that passion and your strengths to help people, and along the way, make money?

Another phrase that might pop into our head sometimes is, "I can't."

That phrase can stop people from living the life of their dreams.

"I can't do that."

"I can't afford that."

If this niggly little word gets into my brain, I say:

"How can I…?"

If you are faced with a challenge, stop and ask yourself, "How can I?"

If you don't, you won't move forward. Start reprogramming your mind right now.

You must constantly ask yourself these questions:

Who are the people around me?

What are they doing to me?

What have they got me reading?

What have they got me saying?

Where do they have me going?

What do they have me thinking?

And most important, what are they turning me into?

Then ask yourself the big question: Is that okay?

Believe In Yourself

Wouldn't you rather have control over your financial situation so you can make decisions and take positive actions that lead to long-term, sustainable wealth creation?

You know you can and I know you can. You just need to believe that you can.

Learn about money and investing wisely. Take control of your financial future and make your money work for you, so you don't have to be a slave to it. I have said so many times, bankruptcy was the best thing that happened to me. I have learned so much from it—and yes, twice, as I hadn't leant the lesson the first time.

I can't stress enough the power of ***applied*** knowledge. Yes, I have made some mistakes, but I am willing to lose because it is part of the game of winning. Just make sure, as I did, that you learn from those mistakes and keep correcting them. This way, you will do very well in the long-term.

Believe in yourself, that you have the potential to become richer (this may not only mean in a "money" sense, but a richer life) and happier than you have ever believed possible.

As I've mentioned before, when you are going for a goal and you achieve it, it's a victory, an obstacle you have just overcome. You have done a fantastic job. Give yourself a pat on your back and celebrate! There is way too little positive encouragement these days and this has a terrible effect on people's lives.

Without encouragement, people's self respect plummets; their self image gets distorted and they forget that they're better than the greatest diamond ever mined. I have received encouragement from other people, but when I give it to myself, I know the true worth of it, as I know how hard I have worked for it.

Try saying these words to yourself:

> *Today I am going to have the best day ever.*
> *My income is growing each day in a great way.*
> *My family is going to have its best year ever.*
> *People like me the minute they meet me.*

Respect yourself; this is the foundation of success. When you don't place value on yourself, your work, your time, your money, and your appearance, success becomes very difficult to achieve. Not just financially, but in all other areas of your life.

One thing to remember is that the work you do each day is important. You need to hear "Great job!" sometimes, then pay it forward and start looking for the best in others. Find someone today that you can sincerely compliment.

Work harder on yourself than you do your work. Change the inner person and everything else changes. I have done so much work looking for the "me" and at last, I have found her.

Have that attitude of *I can, I will, I must, and I will not be denied!*

Focus on building your character, as that is of real value.

You know what it takes; don't be afraid of your own power.

Don't be selfish, as that is the greatest threat to your wealth.

Do you have a passion, but you are so self-absorbed in your own fears, doubts and worries that your talent is buried? Remember, there are thousands of people starving for your given gifts.

I have books on my website by Wallace Wattles, Napoleon Hill and many more, all saying the same thing: What precedes Real Wealth is Real Service. This is one of the secrets of the ages.

There can be no HARVEST where there's no SERVICE first.

Everything you want in life you get from other people. The money you need to be financially set sits in someone else's pocket right now. How do you get them to be excited enough to share some with you?

Unselfishness = Gifts Shared = Problems Solved = Transfer Of Cash to You

Do you see more clearly how SELFISHNESS hurts everyone? You can't get what you first won't give.

Read this; it was written 100+ years ago by the GREAT Orison Swett Marden:

> "One reason why we get such stingy results from our life work is because we are not more generous givers of ourselves, our sympathy, and encouragement. We must give more in order to get more. He who is stingy of his sympathy, of his helpfulness, of his praise, and appreciation, pinches, starves, and strangles his own nature.
>
> It is the generous giving of ourselves that produces the generous harvest. Many people are so stingy of their sympathies, their praise, and appreciation, are so afraid of giving away something, they are so shut in—the shutters of their lives so tightly closed—that their natures are stunted and starved for the lack of sunshine and air.

> *It is astonishing how rapidly a person will develop when he opens up his nature and flings out his life with all his might in the service of others. There is nothing which will do so much for the life as the early forming of the good-will habit, the kindly habit, the habit of saying pleasant things about others."*

Living life is about development.

I am one of the blessed ones. Work to me isn't work, and my direction has once again changed. I thoroughly love what I do and I truly hope I can keep going till the day I die because it is so rewarding.

Challenges: Embrace Them

Successful (not necessarily seeing success as "money") people have the ability to bounce back. They don't necessarily have more knowledge or more experience, but truly understand that every challenge they face has the purpose of helping them grow and develop.

How many people out there today have stopped just inches from their goal because of some brick wall, some hurdle? How many people give up on fantastic business ideas because the first bank they approached turned down their loan application? How different would the lives of those people be if, rather than accept defeat first-off, they thanked the bank manager and then went into the next bank? And if they didn't get a loan there, they went to the next one?

Before success appears in any person's life, that person is sure to be faced with more than his or her share of temporary defeat and quite possibly, some failure. When defeat overtakes a person, the easiest and most logical thing to do is to quit. And that is exactly what the majority of people do.

Edison failed 10,000 times before he successfully made the electric light. Do not be discouraged if you fail a few times.

The blessed among us learn early and limit the effect failure has on us. Those are the ones who build wealth early in life. But, regardless of age, it is never too late to turn your financial life around. Any man or woman can be rich in their lifetime. We didn't start until we were in our 40's. Yes, we lost a fortune, but we found wealth in life.

It's about overcoming obstacles, beating setbacks (and I have had my fair share of them!) and moving forward. I see those brick walls now; I see each one as a challenge and say, "Bring it on!" because I know I will be moving forward when I break through it.

The most successful people face challenges and they all need to overcome those obstacles.

If you want to be successful, you have to get accustomed to challenges. If you find this too hard, well, you just have to learn, because problems and setbacks are as sure as taxes and death in business and life.

One way I handle challenges and obstacles is to self-analyse. I ask myself these questions:

> *What am I going to learn from this?*
> *What is so great about this challenge?*
> *What am I willing to do to make it the way I want?*
> *How can I appreciate this process and enjoy the ride?*

Sometimes I can get so overwhelmed with the problem and be in such a muddle that I forget to ask myself these questions. Eventually, I remember and then I do ask myself. I have to do this in order to change the way I perceive challenges. When I can view these challenges positively, I will be able to identify the opportunities and benefits that come from them.

Learn to embrace challenges.

You only have one life, so make the most of it. Self-improvement is about taking your life forward, making a major difference and impacting the lives of as many people as possible.

Winners have a clear direction and know exactly what they want, and nothing will stop them.

Walking tall and looking the world right in the eye demonstrates an air of confidence. The more you believe in yourself, the more you will have confidence in what you do. And the more positive your thoughts, the more likely you will be successful. Belief with conviction fuels the fire within.

Have a positive mental attitude, stay focused and be determined and have absolute faith in your own ability. What we used to say in Nutrimetics was, "Fake it until you make it."

The first time I did this was when I was going for the Nutrimetrics car. As I mentioned earlier, I went to the car yard to get the smell of the leather fixed in my brain. Afterwards, I visualized smelling the leather inside the car, and even though I was driving an old bomb, to me, I was in that Nutrimetics car. When I eventually achieved my goal, I knew this technique worked and now I do it all the time.

If you visualize something often enough, it will become your vivid reality.

Finally, once you have complete clarity, set a goal and a target date. Now you will have a definite and clear vision and together with the effort required, you will achieve your objective.

Many have overcome overwhelming adversity and extreme obstacles in their lives and gone on to become very successful. They have achieved greatness. These people have the Will, the Desire, the Power and the Passion to succeed. Along the way, they have acquired the knowledge necessary to succeed.

Believe in yourself and when you look in the mirror, believe in that person. You have got to get along with this person looking back at you. You have got to love this person.

It takes 30 days to change a bad habit. Do you want to change? You need to be determined, disciplined, focused and be sure to stay on course. I challenge you to do it and that old habit will die forever and be replaced by that new, winning formula you have now adopted.

Check out 8 of my 30 day journals with affirmations to help you move forward http://www.inspirational-quotes-and-thoughts.com/

(Disclaimer–The information presented here should not be interpreted as financial advice. If you think you may need to go bankrupt, please consult someone as quickly as possible.)

"The best way to not feel hopeless is to get up and do something. Don't wait for good things to happen to you. If you go out and make some good things happen, you will fill the world with hope, you will fill yourself with hope."

—Barack Obama

Just Do It

When we were building up our property portfolio, I knew what I wanted to do. Well, I thought I did. We had lost the hotel and I was trying to rebuild that million-dollar empire so that I could give my children back their inheritance.

The Global Financial Crisis took away that dream. I still think back and ask myself, if the world of finance hadn't turned like it did, would I have made it? The answer to that question I will never know.

One day during that time, my son, Kane, rang me from Queensland. His wife, Angela, was in hospital, as she had just had a breakdown. They were both full-time uni students with a beautiful three year old daughter, and both of them worked.

Kane was beside himself, a total mess, and there I was on the other side of the country. All I wanted to do was to hold my son and tell him everything would be all right. But how was I going to do it this time when work and money was such a huge issue? I needed to be there, but how?

Not knowing how I was going to manage it, I rang Kane and said, "I'm coming over." This is how he got me there.

He had $150 in the bank, and I had $160. I went to the bank to transfer my money into his account, then sat in the car while he was on the computer making the booking. I didn't want to leave until it was all done.

The phone rang. Kane was still looking for a cheap airfare to get me to Queensland.

"Mum, it was $312.00. Now it's gone up to $367.00!"

I dug into my purse to see what I could find: another $30.00. I started counting coins. We were both frantic. Where were we going to get the money from? Then the price went down to $312.00 again, so Kane quickly booked it. I just sat there with relief. *I can get there! I don't know how I'll get back, but we'll worry about that later.*

The next day, I was off. I didn't know for how long, and had no money for an airfare back, but my son needed me and I was going to be there for him.

Arriving at the airport resulted in the biggest kisses and hugs between a mother and son ever. It took me back in time to when Kane was a little boy, with me his loving mummy. I just hugged him, thinking, *Mummy is here. She'll fix it.* Being together again was pure relief for both of us.

That is the wonderful thing about being a mother, being there for your children, no matter what. It's one of the main reasons why I'm here on this planet.

The next day Kane picked up Angela, who didn't know I was coming. As she walked through the door and saw Ava (their daughter), she cried and hugged her. When I came up behind her, she looked up, burst into tears, cried, "Mum!" and just hugged me. I knew I was where I was supposed to be.

It was a wonderful week, and the start of "finding me" and what my purpose in life is all about. My husband, children and grandchildren are my life, and we would do anything for each other.

Once I was home (my daughter lent me the money for the return trip) and back at work, something had changed. I found it hard to get motivated. Nothing was working for me. I wasn't selling and I was listing very little. Then I came down with gastro.

I couldn't go to work, but I could still think, and I started to think about what I really wanted.

My website by this time was up and running and my book was on my site as an ebook. What I wanted was my website to inspire and help people to move forward, and to have books that they could download for free or for a minimal price. So I started to do more research, read and work out how I was going to move forward on this.

But first, let's just go back to the beginning, years ago when I started.

"You don't have to be a genius.

You just have to have passion and a burning desire to move forward".

— Moya Mulvay

Getting Real: My Website and Books

As I've mentioned so many times, I have a huge passion for helping people, and I've mostly been in sales or in some part of service. Real estate is great the moment you let the seller and the buyer know that their dreams have come true, the seller in selling their home and the buyer in buying their dream home. It's such a rewarding feeling to be involved in this process. But I needed something else.

I had always wanted to write my memoir–not just an ordinary memoir, but something that could help people overcome the challenges in their life. I wanted to share my experiences because yes, I have been through many obstacles, big obstacles, but I was able to overcome them. I wanted to share this experience with others, so that they knew that those obstacles could be conquered. And I wanted to explain exactly how I did it.

I don't know how it came about, but I received a phone call from Julie Matthews. By this time, I had already started my book. Julie's husband, Andrew, has written many bestsellers, such as *Happiness Now* and *Follow your Heart*, and the two of them asked me if they could put my story in a new book they were about to publish. This book was entitled *Happiness in Hard Times* and Julie said she would also put the name of my website in the book.

And so the pressure was on! I had to get my website up and running, and then I had to finish writing my book so that when people came to the website, they could find it.

Now I had obstacles of a new kind to overcome. First, I am not a computer whiz. I had to learn how to use a computer to write my memoir and set up a website where I could share my experiences. I didn't know anything about websites or where to start, so I began by buying bits and pieces of training, even though I had no idea what I was buying. Everything was so foreign and technical to me: keywords, AdSense, SEO... I had no idea what they were talking about! But I didn't give up. I did my best to learn, because I knew I wouldn't be able to do what I wanted unless I learned the language of the online world.

One tip that I will share with you is that when I was buying all those bits of training, hoping they would teach me, it actually confused me more. Now I have learnt to find one thing that works and work with it. There's a well known quote, "If it ain't broke, don't fix it." (If something is working adequately, leave it alone.) Chasing every option takes you away from what you are trying to achieve. And once you subscribe to one thing, all the emails start pouring in, trying to sell you something else, and it confuses and overwhelms you. Believe me, I've been there!

As I mentioned, the standout book that I'd read was Napoleon Hill's *Think and Grow Rich*. I learned it was in the public domain, and using this book, I started to play around on the internet. I had no idea what I was doing, but I knew what Google was and I had a lot of fun with it.

My passion and purpose, one I knew would be never-ending, was to have a website with my memoirs, combined with public domain books such as *Think and Grow Rich* and inspiring quotes. The purpose of setting up the website was and is to inspire and guide people to overcome life's challenges.

To tell you the truth, I don't know how I found a way to build a website. I had been searching for a few months, buying stupid things in the search for answers, when the answer seemed to just pop up on the screen. It was called SBI (Site Build It). I read about it, checked the reviews and thought, *this may be it: a step-by-step program*. For a yearly fee, you could buy the steps needed to build your own website. So I bought it.

So it was time to start building the website, a 10-day process with SBI. However, a "day" could take a week or more. Once, a supposed "day" took me a whole two weeks! I am not a patient person; I just want to get in and get it done. But SBI say to take it slowly (which sometimes goes against my grain) and not to rush, because if you do, you'll have to go back and fix your mistakes, which will take even more time. That's what happened to me.

Then I had to write this book!

As you will recall, in order to learn something, I find I have to do it myself. But this looked so complicated that I put it aside and kept researching and learning. Soon, all this was doing a number on my head, and my husband said to me so many times, "I can't believe you're still hanging in there!"

But I was determined; I had a purpose and that was what was driving me.

SBI has a 10-day step-by-step tutorial to take you through finding your niche (a subject that interests you), then seeing if it will work, and then the whole process of setting up your website. I printed out the instruction manual and started.

What I wanted to do was to have my public domain books, quotes, and an inspirational website. I skipped a day of the 10-day process, which was about researching whether it was going to be a good niche. An inspirational website was really what I wanted to do and I didn't want to change that.

I went to the SBI forum, letting people know my aims, and a lady came up with a domain name, "inspirational-quotes-and-thoughts" with a dash between each word. Maybe it was a bit long, but it perfectly suited what I was trying to achieve.

The website is inspirational–to inspire and help you grow and move forward in your journey of life.

It is filled with quotes—to guide you with words of wisdom in good and bad times.

It is filled with thoughts—to share with you the thoughts of our great world leaders, and for you to share your thoughts, whatever they may be.

Soon, however, I began to get overwhelmed with everything, so I decided I would ask one of the coaches at SBI to guide me through. She was great! I learned HTML and what tiers and keywords were. Not only that; I was also learning what the keys on my computer keyboard meant.

I was soon putting up my resources on the website like a pro, and beginning to have fun.

And it was all starting to make sense. I still had a bit of trouble with my website and the keyboard, but the more I applied myself, the more I learned.

If you keep doing something over and over, you become good at it.

Pretty soon, my website looked great. But I didn't yet know how to fully use it.

So all at once, I was trying to write my memoirs, find out what programs I needed for my computer for the e-books, and set up a website. Some days, it was totally overwhelming, but I had my values in place, a purpose, a huge passion, and a goal. With all of that moving me forward, I wouldn't – and I mean wouldn't–give up on what I was doing, no matter what anyone said or how hard it was. I knew what I wanted and what I wanted to achieve.

As I wrote each chapter of my first book, I would send it to an editor in America so she could edit it for me. When I was finished, she put the book together for me. Once the book was complete, I put it up on my website and built a lot of my content around that.

It was now up and running, I sent the section Julie wanted for their book, and my book was online as an ebook.

But the website just sat there, because I ended up going back to real estate and got so busy, I didn't have the time to do any more work on it.

I spent time trying to figure out how I could accomplish my goal. At the same time, I knew that I had to continue working in real estate to get my venture up and running. But I was willing to take that chance; I had to, because it was my passion.

The Universe works in mysterious ways. On Facebook I found a company that was offering their services for a fee (of course) to publish books. Needing some constructive criticism, I showed my book manuscript to a couple of people at work to see what they thought about this.

I decided to get my book published – but almost immediately, I got sick again. Pounding headaches and feeling bad; what was the universe trying to tell me this time? So I did some research on the publishing company. Well, the reviews on it were terrible, so I decided to can that wonderful idea of mine.

Work has always driven me. The only time I relent is when a drama or an illness stops me in my tracks. So when both these things happened to me, I listened to what the universe was telling me. And by opening my mind, things started to happen.

Next, I met a lady in Mandurah who helps publish books. She told me my book needed a lot of work, but that with a bit more information and cleaning up, it could be publishable. I felt I had so much more to share, such as our second bankruptcy, that I hadn't included in the first book. This is where my book, *Overcoming Life's Challenges* comes in. It is my life story.

Now I was in that dilemma again: how was I going to afford this? How was I going to have time to do all that I wanted to do? This was my passion, my dream, my purpose and I really wanted it to happen. My mind was going round and around: How am I going to do this? How can I get that energy back, that zest for life again, and work in a job that I've lost the passion for, when all I can think about is my book and website and helping the people who need me? And yes, I do have to make money at the same time. That will come, I know, but how?!

Check out this link: https://youtu.be/u4ZoJKF_VuA. It is what one of my trusted outsources sent me, and it changed the way I think.

I sat there thinking, trying to work out, in this headache of a head of mine, the how.

> *All right!* I thought; the universe guided me in the direction I had to go, and now it is up to me to "just do it." I have done it before, and I have to stop using the excuses, *I'm 63, I'm tired, I'm too old*, and just move forward.

Soon there was another brick wall, and another, and another, until I was crying with frustration, but I eventually got over each of those brick walls, step-by-step, and each time, I learned a little more.

Then I became so busy with work and life that the weeks and months flew by, and I did nothing to the website. During that time my computer crashed, and I lost a lot of the work I'd done, as I hadn't known to back up my data.

I forgot to mention something good: before our second bankruptcy, when everything was cruising along nicely, part of my life story was published in a book by Tony Melvin and Ed Chan called *Wealth for Life*!

I now knew I couldn't work on my dream alone, so I had to find people who would help me reach my goal. I started by looking for talents on Elance and ODesk (now Upwork). I studied the system, beginning with how others had put up ads to find the right person for the job.

When it comes to searching for the right person to work with, I don't pick someone just because they are the cheapest or because they are the most expensive (which would suggest they're the best), as this is often not the case. What I do is check out what other clients have said about that particular freelancer. I look at the work the person has done, ask him or her questions and give them a small job to see if they are the right fit. I will then negotiate a price, how many hours a week they will work for me and hire them. I also make sure their English is excellent, because it's important that they understand you.

Outsourcing is one of best things you can do if you need to do something and you have no idea how to do it. You may consider trying to learn a particular task, but of course, it could take you days or weeks to do so. Hiring someone else to do it gets the job done and because they already specialize in this area, chances are they will be able to do the job for you in less time, and with better results, than if you try to learn it and do it yourself.

One way that outsourcing benefitted me is that in 2015, I decided to create some Adult colouring books. Unfortunately, I can't draw, but there are many talented people out there who can. I had three people working for me. They all drew beautiful images, but one of them didn't speak very good English and we were having such difficulty communicating that I had to let him go. The other designers, a lady in the Philippines and a man in India, did the final images for me. I was so impressed with their work that when I do my next lot of colouring books, I will rehire them again. I had my granddaughter, Caitlyn, design and illustrate the back of the books. I then found a designer on Fiverr to do the cover of this book.

My colouring books offer something a little different to the colouring books you normally see in bookstores. They have quotes under the images. One focuses on stress and the other one on success.

Luckily, I joined some Facebook pages on colouring, because I was about to self-publish through CreateSpace when I found out they don't post to Australia, where I live. Someone on Facebook suggested IngramSpark, so I went through them. I am dealing with their office here in Australia, but if someone orders overseas, they have offices in England and the USA. The USA is the main place I sell my books, and they ship from either the USA or England to all over the world.

I couldn't get the pages in the correct format to send to the publisher, and they were going to charge a fortune to do it themselves, but through Upwork I found someone in Mexico, and they knew all about IngramSpark and exactly what was needed, so the formatting was done in a flash, at a fraction of the cost.

Now, with social media, the sky is the limit, and I want to be part of it. There is so much to learn and so little time to learn it!

I had to start promoting the books and my website, so I hired a social media manager from Kenya. He is now doing all my social media work as well. He is doing things with social media that I never even knew existed! You don't know what you don't know.

I wanted someone to help me with my website, so I hired a guy who said he would be ready in three weeks, and we exchanged Skype contact details. I contacted him by voice through Skype and he had no idea how SBI worked, so I had wasted three weeks. He might just not have been the right person for the job. Those three weeks may also not have been the right time for me to work on my website. There's always a reason.

I started looking on Elance again and one guy's qualifications jumped out at me. (It is funny how when I am looking for something, it often just pops up on my screen.) This particular person knew about SBI, so I checked him out. He was fantastic, spoke great English, and changed my website around to make it more mobile-friendly and easier to navigate. When I have new content going up, he helps me to put it in the right place. He has also put up AdSense for me, and so much more.

I found someone on Fiverr from the Philippines who told me where to go to get free images. I pick these out, then select quotes, and he puts these on the image and sizes them to the downloadable size they need to be.

Another freelancer from the Philippines has put my videos together and put them on YouTube for me.

Last, but not least, was a lovely lady in the Philippines, who has helped put this book together for me, making it sound right and editing it. She has written many articles for me, as well.

So here we are today. Yes, I am 63, and it is like starting my website and book all over again, but this time I feel I know a little more.

Of course, my wonderful editor in Australia, who encourages me every day with her inspiring words and has been so honest with me, is putting my book in a workable order.

There have been others over time. If I need them again, I know that I can go to the company where I first found them and hire them again.

The way I look at it, because I am very time poor, I need someone in the background to do the work for me, so that I can take care of my real estate, put content on my website and think of other wonderful ideas to move forward with what I want to do: working with my passion.

The lesson here is: don't try to do it all on your own! There are people out there who want to help and share their gifts with you. Remember, a lot of those people are in third world countries and would benefit from the work that you give them. I love helping and empowering them, so it is a win-win situation for all of us.

Yes, I have published these colouring books. Just type my name "Moya Mulvay" into your favourite bookstore and they will come up. I intend to do many more.

As I write this, it's winter and freezing. My husband is a bricklayer and gets up at half past 4 in the morning to go to work. Our warm and cuddly bed pulls me in and our dog, Teddy, jumps up with me and snuggles up. I don't want to get up, but I have to, because I am on a mission.

I have to have a routine and need to stick to it to make it work. Otherwise, I get overwhelmed and nothing gets done. The following is my routine:

Rob brings me my cup of green tea, which I drink. I get on my Ipad, check Facebook and my emails I get up have a shower, then take Teddy for a walk. When I am down at the park I sit on the park bench and just have some quiet time, listening to the birds and the water splashing. When I get back home I have my breakfast, do chores at home and then go to my real estate job, or my internet business.

Sometimes my routine may not happen according to plan, as someone might ring up to view a house, and that comes first. I never know what time work is going to finish, so I have to take this day by day, but I do stick to my morning routine and it has now become a habit.

And I do have a balance between my real estate job and my passion. If I keep this balance, I know it will work.

"By choosing healthy over skinny you are choosing self-love over self-judgment. You are beautiful!"

—*Steve Maraboki*

Weight Issues and Bulimia

An Overweight Child

I was overweight for most of my childhood. I remember going on my first diet when I was 14, even though I didn't even know what the word "diet" meant.

I was at boarding school and it was breakfast time, and the diet said "one cup of cornflakes." There I was, packing the cornflakes into the measuring cup as tightly as I could so I could get more. I didn't realize I was only cheating myself.

I wasn't bullied at school for my weight, but my son Kane was. I only found out about this recently. If we don't teach our children healthy eating habits, they run the risk of being called fat by schoolmates. As a result of this bullying, Kane felt isolated. I do have to add here, once again, that things happen for a reason. Because of everything that Kane has been through, he has educated himself with his food and exercise and has now got his own gym, which he loves.

I was the youngest in the family and I had never felt "worthy," I suppose that is what the word would be. I could never live up to everyone's expectations of me, so I went into my own world of comfort. That comfort came from food.

Bulimia Begins

My bulimia started when I was 15, and it wasn't severe at first. I didn't even realize what I was doing. I would just eat a bit too much, feel sick, and then make myself throw it up. This slowly progressed over the years, and got quite out of control when I was 23. That was when my first marriage broke down and I became a pill-popping alcoholic.

I never knew I had a problem, and I never realized what I was doing to my body. Consequently, I suffered from bulimia, serious bulimia, for almost all of 25 years.

I wouldn't say it was a daily ritual, but it was pretty close.

The cycle was this: I'd eat a wonderful meal, but I would eat too much, and feel sick. The food would be sitting there in my throat and I just knew I would put on weight. So very quietly, I would go to the bathroom, hang my head over the toilet bowl and push my finger down my throat. My gag reflex would kick in, sending my body into the violent convulsions I'd grown accustomed to.

Everything I'd just eaten would pour into the toilet bowl. It usually felt like there was still some more to come, so I'd stick my finger down my throat and throw up again. Now the convulsions would come, but nothing else would come up, so I'd stop. I'd walk out of the cubicle, wash out my mouth, and rinse with a mouthwash. I'd look in the mirror and see that my eyes were bloodshot, but I figured no one would notice. I'd walk out of the bathroom as though nothing had happened and just go back to what I was doing.

I now know I had emotional problems and a distorted awareness of a proper relationship to food. And even back then, I would sometimes think to myself, "Why am I doing this?"

What is Bulimia?

Bulimia is also called bulimia nervosa and is a psychological eating disorder.

It is binge eating (eating more than you can handle) and then vomiting.

It is usually a response to depression, stress, or self esteem issues. And yes, I had all of these. It started when I was young and became more pronounced as I grew older.

Someone with bulimia can look quite normal. Most are of normal weight and some may even be a little overweight.

The funny thing is, women with bulimia tend to be high achievers.

There isn't a definite cause of bulimia, but researchers believe it begins with dissatisfaction with the body and extreme concern with body size and shape. Bulimics also tend to have low self-esteem, feelings of helplessness and a fear of becoming fat.

Here is a list of things that bulimia can cause in you and your body, and how it affected me.

- Abdominal pain and severe weakness. *(I used to get this all the time, but thought it was just lack of food.)*
- Vomiting blood, which could mean a tear in the oesophagus or stomach.
- Contribute to clinical depression. *(Yes, I was depressed.)*
- The vomiting causes erosion of tooth enamel because of repeated exposure to acidic gastric contents.
- Suicidal behaviour. *(This was a common thought pattern for me.)*
- Decrease in sex drive. *(I didn't have this.)*
- Dehydration. *(My mouth and my skin always felt dry.)*
- Stomach ulcers.
- Inconsistent bowel movements. *(One day I had diarrhea and the next I would be constipated.)*
- Irregular heartbeat and in severe cases, heart attack.

- Tooth decay and sensitivity to hot and cold food and liquids. *(Yes, I have this.)*
- The salivary glands swell and become sore.
- Ruptures of the stomach and oesophagus. *(My oesophagus became very raw and it still is.)*
- Bloodshot eyes. *(This was the giveaway for me; this is when Rob found out what I was doing.)*
- Exhaustion. *(All the time.)*
- Irregular periods from the nutritionally sparse diet.

Are you bulimic? Is someone you love bulimic? Here are some signs:

Binge eating signs and symptoms:

- **Lack of control over eating.** Inability to stop eating. Eating until the point of physical discomfort and pain.
- **Secrecy surrounding eating.** Going to the kitchen after everyone else has gone to bed. Going out alone on unexpected food runs. Wanting to eat in privacy.
- **Eating unusually large amounts of food** with no obvious change in weight.
- **Disappearance of food**, numerous empty wrappers or food containers in the garbage, or hidden stashes of junk food.
- **Alternating between overeating and fasting**. Rarely eats normal meals. It's all-or-nothing when it comes to eating.
- Purging signs and symptoms:
- **Going to the bathroom after meals** – Frequently disappears after meals or takes a trip to the bathroom to throw up. May run the water to disguise sounds of vomiting.

- **Using laxatives, diuretics, or enemas** after eating. May also take diet pills to curb appetite or use the sauna to "sweat out" water weight.
- **Smell of vomit.** The bathroom or the person may smell like vomit. They may try to cover up the smell with mouthwash, perfume, air freshener, gum, or mints.
- **Excessive exercising** – Works out strenuously, especially after eating. Typical activities include high-intensity calorie burners such as running or aerobics.
- Physical signs and symptoms of bulimia:
- **Calluses or scars on the knuckles or hands** from sticking fingers down the throat to induce vomiting.
- **Puffy "chipmunk" cheeks** caused by repeated vomiting.
- **Discolored teeth** from exposure to stomach acid when throwing up. May look yellow, ragged, or clear.
- **Frequent fluctuations in weight**–Weight may fluctuate by 10 pounds or more due to alternating episodes of bingeing and purging.

If these signs sound familiar, it is time to get professional help.

How Socialising Contributed To My Bulimia

As an adult, I got caught up in the social scene, partying and going out to clubs. I wanted to look good, so before I went out, occasionally—only occasionally—I would have some dinner. But if I did, I would bring it up before I left the house. I had to feel slim to go out and have fun.

Then to make sure I had the energy to party the night away, I would pop a slimming pill so I could go until dawn.

But that wasn't the only time I threw up.

I had a real sweet tooth. I remember one particular day I was craving for a lolly, so I bought a big packet and absolutely gorged myself on them and then threw them up. Because of my sweet tooth, I would eat a load of "junk" and then bring it up.

Even when I married Rob, I was still throwing up. After I induced vomiting, he could tell, as he could see it in my watery and bloodshot eyes. He used to get so angry with me and tell me how bad it was, but I just couldn't beat it.

Stopping my bulimia was by no means an instant fix, and even today, I sometimes feel the urge. Once again, I had to find the root of the problem.

Eventually, with a new attitude to life and in particular, my role in it, I was able to free myself of this destructive daily habit.

It has taken years of self inquiry and a new approach to eating and exercise, with many stumbles along the way, including an addiction to slimming pills.

I am not naturally that thin, so I had to go through everything from using drugs to diet pills to laxatives to fasting. Those were my main ways of controlling my weight.

—*Carre Otis*

Slimming Pills: An Addiction

When I started on the slimming pills, I wasn't really overweight, in fact, not even close to obese, even though back then I thought I was huge. It was the "in" thing to be skinny.

I wasn't eating properly; I was working long hours, drinking too much alcohol and not exercising.

Somehow I got it into my head to use diet pills, so I went to the doctor to get a prescription. He was a bit hesitant, but gave them to me anyway. This turned into a real roller coaster ride. I actually became dependant on them. They became a habit with me.

When I started to take the pills, they were great; I hardly ate and I was losing heaps of weight. My energy level was huge, although I found it hard to relax or sleep at night. What I couldn't see was how they were destroying me.

Effects of Slimming Pills

Does not eating, losing weight and having tons of energy sound good? Well, think about these side effects:

I constantly had a dry mouth. Back then, I never drank water, only cool drinks, to quench my thirst.

Insomnia and sleeplessness were an issue; I hardly slept at night. So I would take a sleeping pill; yet another pill.

I was irritable and cranky all the time, very jumpy and nervous. I felt like my heart was going to jump out of my chest. I am so lucky I didn't have a heart attack or stroke.

I used to have bouts of dizziness, which I thought were from not eating, so I would eat a little something. Sometimes, I would eat too much, so then I would bring it back up.

One day, while I was working at the hotel and I hadn't eaten for a couple of days, I began getting shocking pains in my back. I went to the doctor. Boy, did he tell me off! My kidneys were shutting down and I was totally dehydrated.

I would get severe headaches, so of course, to get rid of the headaches, I would take a headache tablet; yet another pill.

I was depressed, so I would take Zoloft for the depression, another pill.

I would shake and I found it hard to breathe.

What slimming tablets really do is "speed up" your body artificially to suppress your appetite. Prescription-based diet pills are often nothing more than speed, but I thought they were okay because they were given to me by a doctor.

Diet pills should never be taken by anyone with glaucoma, an anxiety disorder, thyroid problems, diabetes, epilepsy, a history of substance abuse, or high blood pressure, just to name a few. I had a thyroid problem and a history of substance abuse, but I didn't know that at the time.

Of course, by taking the pills, I was consuming fewer calories than I usually did. On the surface, this is good for losing weight, but ultimately, it will lead to your natural metabolism slowing down. And when your metabolism slows down, so does your weight loss. What was happening was I would lose the weight, but when I eventually weaned myself off the pills, the weight would come back—plus some more! No matter what I ate, I would put the weight back on.

Looking at all the symptoms I was experiencing, you are probably asking yourself why I took the diet pills. Well, to be honest, I took them both to lose weight and because they gave me a high.

"I've come to believe that all my past failure and frustration were actually laying the foundation for the understandings that have created the new level of living I now enjoy."

— *Tony Robbins*

The Anthony Robbins Seminar That Changed my Life

I had been to a lot of Tony's seminars before this particular one.

One of the earlier seminars was called *Date with Destiny*. If you have ever been to one of Tony's seminars, you will know what I am talking about. He gets you to think about an issue you are currently dealing with, and mine at the time was my weight. Back then, I was 54, and I needed to beat my weight issues; I had to find the trigger that made me eat junk food.

When you attend a seminar, Tony takes you to a place in your mind where you really don't want to be and gets you to feel what you were feeling during certain situations. He then slowly brings you back to the present, making you feel better about yourself each step of the way, and on that journey, you find out what is causing the problem.

When I attended that seminar, after we finished the exercise, he told us to write. I wrote and wrote, and when I finished, I just cried and cried, and jumped up and down. At last I knew the cause of the problem and it all made sense to me. Here is what I wrote:

> *I saw young Moya always sitting alone. Never with my family, eating in the dining room, either at school or the hotel – lonely, unloved. Food was my love and comfort, I had nothing else. I remember never having a meal with my parents, not even at*

Christmas. Never had a birthday party, I was a very lonely little girl, food was all I had. It was my comfort. I had a terrible sweet tooth and this was because I was trying to sweeten myself up to be loved.

Now I understood it, but I was still having an issue with how to fix it.

When I was 55, I attended Tony's *Life Mastery* seminar in Fiji with Rob, and this changed me in unbelievable ways. I finally dealt with issues I had regarding my weight, exercise, and eating healthy food.

At this seminar, I stepped out of my comfort zone, big time.

When we first arrived, we were told we were going to climb a 50 ft. telephone pole. I told Rob, "No way am I going to do this."

I looked at those poles and thought, *nope; this isn't for me.*

Everyone lined up and started to climb and I was the only one not doing it. I had to get out of my comfort zone. I had to just do it.

The people running the seminar put the harness on me. (You are in a harness with a rope attached and someone on the ground is holding the rope in case you fall.)

I started, inch by inch, step-by-step, climbing the pole.

Fifty feet may not sound like much, but I was overweight and incredibly unfit.

I stopped halfway, because I thought I was going to have a heart attack. I was 25 ft. off the ground, the pole was swaying and I was so, so scared. I thought I was going to die right there. I asked if I could jump to the ground from where I was, as I just couldn't go any further. Then everyone started to cheer me on. "You can do it, Moya! Come on!"

Overcoming Life's Challenges by Moya Mulvay

I had been watching everyone else and they just climbed their pole like it was nothing. It looked so easy for them. But that was them. This was *me*.

Take it easy, I thought to myself. *There's no rush. Go step-by-step.*

Finally, I reached the top. The pole was swaying and I was hanging on for dear life. Most of the other people who got to the top were getting up and standing on the top of the poles, but I just couldn't get my leg up.

I was hanging onto the pole, but to get back down, you had to jump into thin air–just let go of the pole and jump.

It's just not natural to let go, 50 ft. in the air, and then jump out into nothing, and it took me a while to build up the courage to do this. Finally, I let go and jumped!

The next thing I knew, I was on the ground, flat on my back. Rob and everyone else were standing over me saying, "Moya, are you okay?"

I'd fainted on the way down; the whole journey must have just overwhelmed me. I gurgled a little and then woke up. But I'd done it!

Rob was the last person to climb. He has a bad knee and is petrified of heights. Step-by-step, he climbed and when he reached the top, I could see absolute panic on his face.

Then he stepped off the pole and jumped. I was so proud of him! He'd done it, too.

We both learned so much at that seminar. It was fantastic and life-changing. The best part was we did it together, so we could work towards the common goal of getting our life and health back on track.

When we returned home, we changed our way of eating. Rob now has breakfast in the morning–which he never did before–and we take a small mixture of vitamins and nutritional supplements.

Our bodies and health have changed in so many ways. Consider this: Rob had a wart on his foot for years. He would go to the doctor, have it burned off or cut out, but it would keep coming back. It was so bad that it even affected the way that he walked.

Since we changed our diet, that wart has completely disappeared.

Hypnosis and Visualisation

Because I am an emotional eater, I was still having a huge problem with my sweet tooth. At the seminar, I'd discovered the root of the problem, but I still didn't know how to fix it.

Your brain is a complex organ that works on several levels, including your subconscious, which directly affects your conscious level. Your brain is complex, but you can control it. You can change your needs and wants.

To tackle my sweet tooth, I went through hypnosis, and it was going great until "it" hit me again. I suppose you could say I fell off the wagon.

At Tony Robbins' *Life Mastery* seminar in Fiji, he had a man come up to the stage who loved chocolate cake. So Tony brought out a chocolate cake, then put big slabs of beef fat on it and asked the man to eat the chocolate cake with the fat on it, which he did. Tony kept instructing him to eat more fat than cake and little by little, eventually, the man just didn't have that craving for the cake any more.

I decided to do a mixture of visualization and hypnosis, as I really wanted to get rid of my problem and I needed all the help I could get.

I went to see a hypnotist, a lady, who did hypnosis on me, and taped the session so I could take it home. Now, when I fall off the rails, I put that CD on at night, visualizing what the hypnotist is saying to me, and the scene I described from the seminar. Each time

I think about eating junk food, I also visualize maggots crawling through the food.

The day after the hypnosis session, when I got up, I had no desire to eat sweets whatsoever. However, it wasn't long before I was having a horrible day and started to crave them. In my mind, I knew that I didn't really want the sweets; I was just remembering what it was like, back when I needed sweets to make me feel better. But that particular day, I felt like someone had just put me through the ringer, and old feelings started to resurface. I desperately wanted something sweet, so I ate some apple pie with ice cream. But this made me feel really sick.

What I realized at that moment was, when I got into this emotional eating pattern, it was just a habit – the habit of having something sweet to make me feel better. And I hadn't broken the habit yet.

I had been changing over the months, but I needed to find out *why* I would still have these cravings, and why, year after year, I kept destroying myself.

Lying in bed with my husband the next morning, I was trying to analyse why I did this. And then it came to me.

I remembered what I had written at Tony's seminar, and I decided to read it again.

Again, the old feelings came rushing back. I needed love, protection and comfort, and food was all of this to me. What I needed was to remember that food doesn't really make me feel any better.

I now get it; I know the cause of the problem and with a little help from hypnosis and visualization, I have beaten it.

Now, I don't need junk food or sweets any more. I am a sweet person and I love my family and am loved by my family. I no longer need junk food to compensate.

"There is nothing more rare, nor more beautiful, than a woman being unapologetically herself; comfortable in her perfect imperfection. To me, that is the true essence of beauty."

—Steve Maraboli

Life as An Overweight Adult

Why do we put on weight?

As children, we are not taught properly about food, which of course leads to bad eating habits.

We are not active enough and we spend too much time looking at TV, on the tablet, internet and all the other electronic devices of today.

Comfort food is more readily available.

So many people these days have low self esteem. Whenever we get a compliment, we tend to shrug it off, when we should be proud of ourselves.

We let the scales rule our lives.

You make one little mistake and you think you have blown it, so you give up.

We get so busy that we choose to pick up quick, unhealthy snacks.

The media doesn't help with the "skinny" models and all the "diet" stuff on the market.

I got caught up with this. I even had food delivered once and yes, I lost 10 kilos and yes, I put it back on when I finished the program. Do you really look at what you are eating when you are on a program, and educate yourself? No, you just eat the food.

I really needed some new clothes and I knew that shopping was going to be totally depressing. I have so much trouble just picking clothes off the shelf and I fall into the same old rut. I take a couple of sizes, always the same colour, black, and the same loose baggy clothes. I go into the changing room and what's with the mirror? It's like the mirror at the carnival that makes you look "big." *Am I really that big?* I try on what I've brought in and the clothes don't fit. *Surely I am not the next size up?* But I am, aren't I?

I didn't feel comfortable. Shopping was meant to be enjoyable, but it made me miserable. I would go home and sit down to a nice piece of chocolate. Ah yes, that made me feel better.

Scenario: You are feeling overweight and uncomfortable, and as you and your partner are getting ready to go to bed, you turn the light off to get changed. Once in bed, your partner wants a bit of loving, and as his/her hands are caressing your body, you become self-conscious and wonder what your partner thinks of all those rolls of fat. You've probably told your partner, "Don't touch my stomach! It's too big." Or "Don't touch here" and "Don't touch there!" You aren't "in the moment" with your mate, because you feel uncomfortable.

Now it's over and you are huffing and puffing. Your partner is excited, thinking it's because of them and that is why you are exhausted. You haven't got the heart to say that you just ran out of energy.

Do these two scenarios sound familiar? How many more can you think of?

I was feeling like this. I became more comfortable when Rob said he loved the way I was, no matter what. Now that I have been eating right and going to the gym, even though I still have a few rolls, I feel firm. I am more nimble, and have a lot more energy. Because of that, when we are together, I am now totally there, enjoying every moment.

If you are overeating, your children see you self-destruct. And what habits are you are teaching them? I have got a lovely friend at the gym, Kelly, and she has done so well losing weight–doing it the right way, by eating healthy food and exercising. It is now starting to rub off on her children. They can see the change in her and they are getting into "good" habits. She goes on bike rides with them and as a family they are enjoying a fit and healthy lifestyle. I am so proud of her.

What are the emotions you are running from? Face them head on. Believe in yourself.

"To insure good health: Eat lightly, breathe deeply, live moderately, cultivate cheerfulness, and maintain an interest in life."

—*William Londen*

The Journey to Better Health

At 56, I had got myself to a place where I understood what exercise could do for me and, along with the right mindset, how food and exercise had put me on the road to success.

You can exercise and diet as much as you like, but if you haven't got the right mindset, it's just not going to work for you. That is what I had to work on. I had to really want to do this, not just for me, but for the lifestyle I wanted with my family. I wanted to be around long enough to be at my great grandchildren's weddings.

To get the right mindset, I had to get rid of everything from the past that was holding me back. I had to get to the root of my issues.

Writing this chapter has been quite interesting for me; I had to do some research and didn't realize just how naïve I'd been about certain things. I also realized that there was a lot of information I just didn't want to know about. By not knowing, I had an excuse not to live a healthy lifestyle. I thought that being healthy was going to be just too difficult.

So I started to educate myself because not only did I want to share this journey with you, but I also needed to understand more about it for myself. I am sharing what I did and what I do, but as this may not suit everyone, please take steps to educate yourself. Get on the internet (if you haven't got a computer, go to the library) and do some research. If you join a gym, take classes and ask questions. Whatever you do, don't just sit there and do nothing!

This is the story of my weight loss journey. While I don't profess to be an expert on the subject, it is my story–what I have been through, what I have done in the past, and the steps I have taken to overcome being overweight. Through learning and education, I have done what I feel suits my body and age–and have come to enjoy it. Making healthy choices is no longer a chore.

My mentor is my son, Kane.

When Kane came home for Christmas 2008, not only were his father and I proud of his achievement; when the rest of the family saw him, they were surprised and full of admiration. He'd lost 30 kilos and looked fantastic! Everyone was quite impressed with how he did it

Now, I like recognition for my achievements, so when I was listening to all of this, I thought I would like to get in on the act. I figured, *if he can do it, so can I.*

I had been going to the gym for a couple of months, and I confess I wasn't in the right mindset. I wasn't focused. I didn't have a plan or a goal. But after that day, I made the decision to do this the *right way.*

My goal was to have the body that I wanted and to be fit and healthy. And having the right relationship with food was very important to me, as I didn't want to just "go on a diet."

I wanted it to be a lifestyle for me. And it was about how *I* wanted to look and feel, not what everyone else wanted for me, so the pressure was off, as I was doing it for myself. It's not about how much you weigh, but being happy with yourself.

I'd had eating disorders for years. The heaviest I weighed was 95 kilos, and that was when I wasn't pregnant! I stopped weighing myself after that, as I didn't want to know any more.

I tried going to a naturopath. She told me that if I didn't lose weight, I would get diabetes, as I was already a borderline case. This scared me for a while and I lost some weight, but I soon fell back into my bad habits. Even something as life threatening as diabetes didn't push me to change.

My husband Rob never once said to me that I was fat. He said he loved me for what and how I am. But when I decided to go on a diet here and there, he would always encourage me. He knew me so well and knew what I wanted.

I used to say, "I'm ok; I'm comfortable with myself just as I am. I just want to be healthy," and eventually, I started to believe it. I've since realized the source of the problem.

Getting to the Root of the Problem

I am an emotional eater. I eat when I am happy, sad, lonely, unloved and stressed.

I also tend to get so caught up with work and life in general that I would rather not worry about dieting or going to the gym. It was just way too hard! It was just something more that I had to think about, and I felt nothing else could fit into this brain of mine.

I hired a personal trainer for a bit, but just couldn't get into it. I would lose weight, put it back on, go to the gym, not go to the gym; it didn't matter, I just wasn't focused.

One gym I joined had a whole circuit of exercises that you were supposed to complete: leg curls, bench presses, squats and lunges and so on. You were to do three sets of each exercise and increase the weight each time. Well, I would start off by doing the first one, but then couldn't remember what came next. I would ask someone what the next exercise was, do it, and then couldn't remember the following one. It was getting too hard. I didn't enjoy it at all and I couldn't wait until it was over.

I am a morning person and my brain races like mad thinking about everything I have to do during the day. The last thing I wanted to do when I went to the gym was think about the exercises. So my solution was to stop going.

My daughter was going to a gym near her, so I decided to try that one. The circuit took 29 minutes. It was fantastic! I got in and got out. I loved it, so I stuck with it.

After Kane came home and showed us all what hard work can do to a body, I decided I was going to do this the right way. Kane and I talked about what I wanted to do, and he became my mentor. He encouraged, educated, and pushed me.

He knew the type of workout I was doing and said, "Mum, I want to see you do more cardio." So I put in another half hour doing cardio exercise and was at the gym for a total of one hour. I did 30 minutes of cardio, as well as weight training. (The gym I go to now is so friendly and happy, and I am having fun and getting fit at the same time. I love it.)

Kane even took me grocery shopping and showed me how to read the labels on the back of the food; now, that was a real eye-opener.

As Kane worked in the mines, he called me almost every other night and checked to see if I had been to the gym and if I was eating right. I was having a ball, and the part that I found most encouraging was that I was doing the journey with someone I loved—my son.

I'd always dreamed of pumping iron and lifting weights. I realize now it wasn't the pumping of the weights I wanted, it was that feeling you get from doing it when you do it right.

Diet is a Four-Letter Word

I used to think that if I didn't eat, I would lose weight, that if I skipped a meal, I would lose weight. Sometimes, even now, I get so busy that I forget to eat or just haven't got the time.

Over the years I tried many crazy diets. The soup diet, the grapefruit diet, the popcorn diet; I tried them all. These types of diets may help you lose weight in the short-term, but in the end, you will put the weight on again, and most of the time you will put on even more.

Even worse, you are not learning the basics of nutrition and healthy eating.

Say you have a goal to lose a certain amount of weight for a big event, like a wedding. The day arrives and maybe you achieved your goal. But time passes and the weight creeps back on, and the next thing you know, you are back to square one.

As I have said so many times before, have a goal, but make it a goal with a purpose, because a purpose is never ending. If you make it a purpose, you will make it a habit, which means it will be a lifestyle for you and never again will you have to go on a diet.

Excuses, Excuses

When it comes to excuses, I have used them all. Every time you make an excuse, counter it with a personal challenge to yourself.

"I can't find the time."–You're right, you're never going to "find the time." You have to *make* the time. Get up earlier, watch less TV; go to the gym instead of going shopping.

"Exercise is boring."–Find something you enjoy and change it, when you need to, in order to keep it interesting. Take different exercise classes at the gym; don't let your workouts become "routine." Challenge yourself by trying new things. This is going to be a lifestyle for you, so you have to enjoy it.

"I'm too tired."–Exercise gives you more energy. If you're a morning person, do it in the morning; if you're a night owl, do it then.

"It's too hot," or "It's too cold."–Most gyms have heat and air conditioning. If you exercise outside and it's cold, you will warm up quickly once you start moving. If it's too hot, do it in the morning when it's cool. Just get moving.

"It might be too hard on me,"–Check with your doctor and once you get permission, get going. A little sweat won't hurt you.

"It's too expensive."–Walking and running outside are free. Buy some inexpensive free weights and use those. As I mentioned, you can exercise without it costing you.

If you haven't got the money to join a gym, remember, you don't need a gym to exercise. Buy some dumbbells (check local garage sales; someone is always selling a weight set). Dumbbells and a good brisk walk are all you need to get started.

Combine this with a reasonable nutrition program and once you start exercising, not only will it improve your physical wellbeing, it will change your whole state of mind. And you'll be on your way to a fitter, healthier, and longer life.

What is Your Passion and Your Goal?

To keep motivated, I remember how great I feel when I exercise. Look at positive motivation, not negative motivation. Think, "I'll feel great!" instead of "I don't want to be fat."

Set a realistic goal, and it won't be long before you're there.

A goal, or better still a purpose, is what pushes you; it keeps you going when things get tough. You are doing these things for a reason. You have got to have energy and focus to achieve your goal and live your purpose.

Learn to love getting up. Get excited about it, and be passionate about going to the gym. When you have passion, it makes it so much easier to get out of bed. Find that passion.

I've found that it's important to start out with the right motivation, because a good start can build momentum that you can sustain for a long time. If you start out right, you have a much better chance of succeeding.

For example, I think of something that happened to me before I started exercising. We live just near the sea and one day, the grandkids came over. My son Kane was home for a visit and we all decided to go to the beach. I had on a t-shirt and short leggings, but I didn't get too involved with what the grandkids were doing; it was mostly Rob and Kane playing with the kids.

I felt sad and uneasy that day. Kane didn't say anything to me at the time, but later when I had made up my mind that enough was enough and it was time to get in shape, he said, "Mum, you know when we went to the beach with Caitlyn and Devon? You looked and felt like you were really uncomfortable."

I told him that he was right about that and that is why I felt so sad that day. I don't want to have to sit on the sidelines and watch my grandkids play. I want to join in and run around with them and not get exhausted. This became a huge motivation for me. I didn't want to be an old Nanna.

Here are some tips to help you get started on your own weight loss journey:

Start out small and set small goals. For instance, set a goal of getting up earlier, but don't try to go from getting up at 8 a.m. to getting up at 5:30 a.m. Try getting up at 7:30 and walk outside for 30 minutes. You don't have to do it every day, just do a few days a week. Start with small, tiny step exercises. You don't have to go for the big, grueling workout at the beginning. Once you have started, do this for a week, and let it grow from there.

Thinking about how hard something is can become a big problem for most people. Waking up early sounds so hard. Just thinking about it makes you tired! But instead of thinking about how hard something is, think about what you will get out of it.

For example, instead of thinking about how hard it is to wake early, focus on how good you'll feel when you're done, and how your day will be so much better. Thinking about the benefits of something will help energize you.

If you are getting bored, change your routine; get creative, keep new ideas and techniques a primary focus. Variation in any fitness routine will help you to not only develop different muscles, increase endurance and greater skill, but it will also develop variation in your *mental* routine. You won't be limited by the false barriers that kill your motivation to exercise.

One thing I used to do was go full hog, and then hate it, as it was too much, too fast. I would get busy at work and because I needed so much time to exercise and it wasn't yet part of my daily routine, exercising got to be too much and I would give up.

Set a date to start, and have a plan in place.

The next week, get up a little earlier, do a few more exercises and put another day in your routine.

Keep remembering and focusing on the goal, the reason you are doing it. Be passionate about it. Workout time is time you are devoting to YOU. And you're worth it. You're not doing this for anyone else but yourself.

Let friends and family know what you are doing. This is what I am now doing and what I now realize I never did before. I never used to tell anyone, because I thought I would fail.

I love to visualize myself exercising but more importantly, I love how I feel when I exercise: energized, strong, alive and alert. I am ready to take on the world. Visualize what you want to look like.

Have a poster or a picture of something that will drive you towards that goal and keep it somewhere where you will see it all the time.

Maybe your goal is starting to fade, and maybe you missed a couple of days at the gym. Maybe you're getting busy at work, and maybe you feel like all this effort isn't amounting to much. Maybe you're not seeing results quickly enough. You're getting discouraged. It's taking up too much time and exertion.

Well, take some time to sit and think. Why were you excited to do this in the first place? Why have you lost your motivation? Get rid of that negative self talk. Replace thoughts of "This stinks. I can't do this any more!" with thoughts of "I can do this," and "I *will* do this!" I used to look at Kane, thinking, *if he can do it, so can I!* Refocus yourself and get energized again.

To keep my motivation up, I would read my goal daily—mine is my purpose in life. I read why I exercise and what it does for me. I also remember why I eat healthily and do not eat junk food any more.

Find someone you can talk to, someone with similar goals. I have my son Kane. At one time I told him I was going to do the six-week challenge at the gym and he said, "That's great Mum, imagine how you will feel and look after you finish!" And, "If you don't finish, I will be so disappointed, but if you do finish, I will be so proud of you!" So now every time I have trouble getting out of bed to go to the gym or lose my focus, Kane's voice is in my ear and it pushes me on.

Read inspiring stories or success stories; they can move you so much and push you forward.

It is also very important to celebrate along the way. Commemorate every little step and celebrate your milestones.

Take that feeling of success and build on it with another little step. These steps are going to add up and before you know it, your little steps will add up to a lot of progress and a lot of success.

Keep track of your progress; you may feel as though nothing is happening, but I know I have looked back and thought, "Gee, I've come a long way, and it was painless."

If at all possible, never miss two days in a row. A little slip up can make you feel lazy—or you might suddenly feel like a complete failure. If you do backslide, recognize it as a bump in the road and just pick yourself up and get going again. Don't let a little lapse in effort make you think all is lost.

There has to be fun, pleasure, and joy in it, every day, or you won't want to do it. Find those pleasurable things; they are there.

The Benefits of Regular Exercise

Exercise is an investment for your health.

Remind yourself of the benefits of exercise. I'm sure they have a lot to do with why you decided to begin in the first place. They range from preventing chronic health conditions to boosting confidence and self-esteem. Here are a few more:

The higher your proportion of body fat, the greater your likelihood of contracting a number of medical conditions and diseases such as cancer, heart disease, diabetes and obesity. More muscle = less body fat.

Healthy human blood vessels widen (during exercise) in order to accommodate increased blood flow, which means you have less risk for a heart attack or stroke.

Exercise delivers nutrients and oxygen to your tissues and, of course, your heart and lungs work more efficiently and you'll have more energy to do the things you enjoy.

Exercise will help you lose weight and firm and tone your body.

Exercise helps you manage stress and depression, and it can help if you are having trouble sleeping at night. Depression will not directly affect a person's ability to exercise, but the willpower to commit and participate may be affected. Exercise can contribute to positive feelings of wellbeing and increased energy levels. In fact, studies have shown that exercise is just as effective in the treatment of depression as medication.

Menopause causes a decline in the hormone estrogen, which impacts bone strength. So it is important to take adequate calcium and vitamin D, combined with adequate exercise.

In addition, the more muscles you have, the more your body will naturally burn calories, because your muscles need calories to function and stay alive. Don't be worried about building *big* muscles; you can build muscles that are just enough to tone you up nicely and at the same time, enjoy the calorie burning effect.

The Difference Between Strength and Cardiovascular Training

Aerobic exercise, or "cardio," as it is known, strengthens your heart and lungs; it works large muscle groups and causes you to breathe more deeply. It consists of smooth, rhythmic, continuous movements. It forces your heart to work harder to pump blood and causes you to emit carbon dioxide and other waste products, so your body burns more calories.

Strength training or weight lifting helps to build strong bones and muscles. With more muscle, you burn more calories. You are burning calories 24 hours a day.

Cardio Exercise:

- Reduces stress
- Strengthens the heart
- Reduces depression
- Relieves anxiety and improves your mood
- Helps you sleep
- Relaxes tense muscles
- Improves lung capacity
- Lowers cholesterol
- Lowers blood pressure
- Helps you lose weight
- Boosts the immune system
- Enhances self esteem
- Builds energy levels
- Strength training:
- Improves muscle tone and strength
- Strengthens and builds bones
- Helps reduce body fat
- Makes you look fit and healthy
- Can lower your blood pressure and cholesterol
- Strengthens your muscle and bones
- Improves your circulation
- Keeps your joints flexible
- Both forms of training:

Reduce your risk for many diseases and conditions, including heart disease, stroke and certain kinds of cancer, such as colon and breast cancer

Improve your chances of living longer and living healthier.

My Diet and Exercise Routine

As I have mentioned I wrote the first draft of this book years ago, before our 2nd bankruptcy.

I was younger of course, which really means nothing, since then I have put in the next chapter of what happened to me, but then something else happened to me when I started on my book again and started reading my "Journey to better Health" that feeling I had back then start to excite me, and reminded me of how I felt.

So I am leaving in what was written years ago, as I will get there again.

When I have to get up at 5 a.m. and it's freezing cold, I need to keep my motivation up so I will still go to the gym and eat right. I have made it a habit.

I know it's not always easy, and it may seem harder because you didn't sleep well the night before or it is raining outside, and doing it day-in-day-out is no picnic. But remember, you want a long and quality life.

Here is an expanded example of my daily eating and exercise routine:

5 a.m.: Alarm goes off. I get up before Rob. I have a quick look at my e-mails, then make breakfast for us. I also make Rob's lunch. (This is something I never did before; he used to buy his lunch and a lot of times, it was rubbish.) I then sit down and have a cup of green tea with lemon and honey.

6 a.m.: Off to the gym, arriving at 6:20. I work out until 7.30, go home and have a shower.

8.15 a.m.: Have breakfast, and a cup of green tea with lemon and honey.

9 a.m.: Start work.

11 a.m.: Have a snack.

1.30 p.m.: Have lunch.

4 p.m.: Have a snack.

6.30 p.m.: Have dinner.

The food plan below (which is not a "diet") is how I started to get in the habit of eating the right foods. Now that I know what to eat almost instinctively, I can't handle eating greasy food any more. When looking at the TV, for instance, Kentucky Fried Chicken advertisements turn my stomach. How did I ever eat that stuff?

I try to follow a few simple rules:

Eat every 2 ½ -4 hours.

Drink at least 2 litres of water each day.

Try and eat carbohydrates in the morning – avoid eating them in the afternoon.

Try to avoid carbohydrates (pasta, rice, potatoes) at night.

Stick to low glycaemic index foods, as they release energy slowly, so you don't "crash" as the energy wears off

Have one day where you eat whatever you like. As you get healthier, your "cheat meal" will also become healthier. You'll find you no longer want that greasy burger or pizza the way you used to.

Moya's and Rob's Breakfast

Every morning we have Bircher cereal, which consists of oats soaked overnight in lemon juice and water. I then add some grated coconut, yoghurt, honey and grated apples. This lasts for a week. In the morning, I take one big scoop and then add flax seeds, oat bran, ½ banana, slivered almonds and crushed hazelnuts. On mine I add a large teaspoon of protein powder, while on Rob's, I add some Udo's oil.

The pills we take are greens, probiotics, wheat grass, Udo's oil, plus I take thyroid tablets, a troche for my menopause, and Rob takes a vitamin B.

Other Breakfast Options

½ cup of rolled oats, or
2 pieces of Burgen bread + 2 poached eggs (Sunday Breakfast), or
Bowl of (200g) low fat yoghurt + grapes+ ½ cup of rolled oats, or
Banana smoothie, or
Protein shake.

Snack Options

4 Cruskits, topped with cottage cheese, tomato

4 Cruskits and peanut butter
4 Cruskits and tuna slices
200g low fat yoghurt + 6 strawberries (or a handful of blue berries)
Handful of almonds+ piece of fruit (apple)
Protein shake
Half a carrot+capsicum+celery and hummus/Philadelphia cheese (25 g low fat)
Banana Smoothie (250g low fat milk, banana, ice, cinnamon, 100g of low fat vanilla yogurt)
Apple
You can mix and match (apple and yoghurt)

Lunch Options

95 g Tuna or 90 g Chicken breast Or 90 g lean ham, plus
100g lettuce, plus
40g capsicum, plus

40g tomato, plus
100g cucumber, plus
30g tomato.
If you are on the run, Protein shake.

Dinner Options

110g chicken or 110 red meat or110g fish, plus
100g steamed spinach, and/or
1 cup of zucchini, and/or
1 cup of broccoli, plus
30g steamed sweet potato.
Soup (minestrone for example)

Dessert Options

150 g Yogurt + blueberries or strawberries

Meal replacement protein shakes will give you the protein you need, along with vitamins and minerals. They are tasty and if you make them properly, you won't experience diet-killing hunger. However, watch the calorie content.

You will find after a couple of weeks you won't have to weigh your food. You will have become attuned to how much you can have.

My Routine at the Gym:

5 minutes on the bike

10 minutes on the cross trainer. In those 10 minutes I will have 3 big bursts forwards and 4 going backwards.

The circuit (to keep my heart rate up). The circuit consists of 10 machines and I do 15 reps on each one. I go around twice in between the machines. I do some cardio on the springboards and four lots of boxing with the trainer. (She uses focus gloves, which are padded flat gloves, so when I hit them with my boxing gloves,

I can hit as hard from one hand to the next and get a really good workout.) I do 120 punches each set and if my trainer isn't available, I will use the punching bag.

15 minutes on the rower

Stretches

You have to want it, you have to believe it and you have to come up with a plan. Believe me, it's not hard when you put your mind to it. Starting an exercise program is fun, enlightening and empowering. But, if you fail to plan, you plan to fail.

I was doing the six-week challenge as I wrote the above. When I got weighed and measured, there wasn't a great change, but when I came home, I tried to explain to my husband that I felt like I had lost weight "inside". My insides felt strong and taut, and I felt tall and strong. I felt energized and healthy.

Please don't get too caught up with what the scales say. Muscle weighs more than fat. I have lost many centimetres, which is amazing!

The best plans for weight control are those that re-educate your way of looking at food and how you make healthy choices.

Expect success, forgive yourself if you miss a day or two and **don't quit**.

My goal is to get to the weight where I am most comfortable. By having a healthy eating and exercise routine, I will never have to worry about my weight again, as it is now my lifestyle. I will never have to diet again.

I feel more confident and positive about life and better able to cope with stress.

That takes me just over an hour and I feel fantastic – exhausted, but fantastic.

I printed out, laminated and put in my office the reasons why I was exercising, because that's where I spent most of my time. This is something you can write out yourself and use to motivate yourself daily.

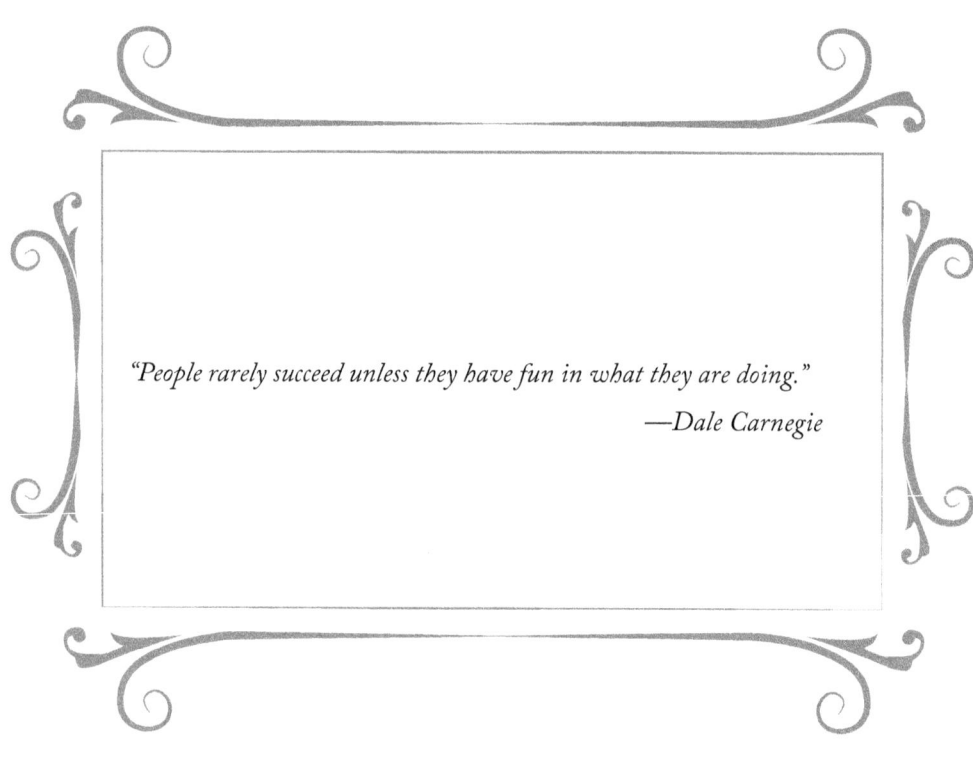

"People rarely succeed unless they have fun in what they are doing."

—Dale Carnegie

Falling off the Rails: Don't Belt Yourself Up

Around 2009, I totally fell off the rails. This was the time we were going through really hard times, emotionally and financially. All of this took over my life, so I wasn't focused any more on looking after myself. In my head I felt a failure–so why not become a failure at everything? In addition, I started to have trouble with my hip, which didn't help when I wanted to exercise. It hurt so much, and it seemed to be getting worse.

Please, if you do fall off the rails, don't beat yourself up. I did – big time.

I put the weight back on, and had to restart my journey to get back into a routine. It was a lot harder because of my hip, although I managed to walk, which I do now, every day. I just had to start again with my eating patterns.

My weight has always been an issue, but by this stage, I felt I was in the right place to understand what had gone wrong. Over the years, the amount I have learned about health and exercise continues to astound me. I realize that you don't need money to be fit and healthy. Lack of money should never be an excuse to not exercise or eat healthily.

During those horrible years of stress, the emotional roller coaster ride, being a comfort eater, everything I had been doing right, went straight out the window. I put back the weight, and I stopped going to the gym—not only because of my hip and because I couldn't afford it, but because the gym I loved closed down. I eventually joined another one, but it was as uninspiring as the very first gym, where I'd had to think about what I was doing. I didn't want to think; I just wanted to do it.

I remember one funny experience at the gym. I got on a machine. It was an arm exerciser, where I had to pull the bar down. As I started to do the exercise, it felt uncomfortable, so I got up to see what I had to adjust. But no, nothing worked there. Meanwhile, the guy opposite me was just staring (and he must have thought what an idiot I was!). I kept trying to exercise, even though it was so uncomfortable. Eventually, I realized I had been sitting on the apparatus back to front!

Another thing I didn't like about this particular gym was that no one was friendly; it was so hard to get a hello out of anyone. The atmosphere was depressing, and when you're working out, being part of a community that shares your goal can really help motivate you. I did not find that factor at all in the new gym, plus my hip was getting worse.

So I began to ease myself back into an active lifestyle. I walked Teddy every day, no matter what time I started work, and this has become a habit. I pass people and say hello and get a hello back, and I thoroughly enjoy it. That is what it is all about, enjoying the journey.

I also had to listen to my hypnosis CD again to get myself back on track.

I am now eating correctly, and even re-reading this chapter of my book helps keep me on track. I may be a little overweight, but I am becoming healthy and that is my main goal.

I notice now that my mind is clearer, and not so cluttered that it overwhelms me.

It's called the "KISS" method: "Keep It Simple, Sweetie!"

At 63, I want to keep learning and expanding my knowledge in this area and apply this knowledge to help make it easier for people to lose weight. I want to live a long and healthy life for my husband, children and grandchildren and, one day, great grand children.

"Becoming a mother has been the most amazing experience—in an instant you become strong. You have to be a little bit wiser; it's the most important job you have in the world."

— Katie Holmes

Stories of My Family

If it seems as though something that happened to you was bad or unfortunate, just think about the path it has put you on. All things happen for a reason and I first started to believe this when my youngest son Kane was born.

Kane's Story

We did not plan to have our son, but we've never felt that Kane was a "mistake." In fact, he was the exact opposite–he was a pleasant surprise. But Kane has had some death-defying moments, moments when he was lucky to walk away with his life.

As a baby, he wasn't home from the hospital long when I would lie him down on one particular spot on the rug, on the floor. Next to that spot was an air cooler.

One particular day it was raining and the spot where I would normally put him was wet because of a leaky roof, so I lay him down in a different place. I was sitting on the floor playing with him when I heard a big crash.

I looked behind me and there, right where Kane would normally have been lying, was the air cooler. It had fallen over–right onto the spot where Kane would have been had it not been for that leaky roof! He would have been crushed.

Even though Kane was safe, I picked him up and looked at him with tears in my eyes. Right then, I knew something special had happened.

Another time when he was about 18 months old, Rob and all the kids were home (or so I thought). I was working at the hotel next door and it was time for morning tea. I just happened to be looking out at the beautiful water surrounding the hotel when I saw a toddler walking towards the river. I did a double take: it was Kane! Somehow, he must have got out the front gate.

Sheer panic tore through me and I have never run so fast in all my life! As I took off, I told one of the staff to ring home and tell them what was going on.

I made it just in time; Kane was right at the edge of the water when I reached him. I picked him up, and there he was with just a nappy on and a dummy in his mouth, not a care in the world. I hugged him so tight, thinking of what might have happened if I hadn't been looking out over the water.

Our house (next to the hotel) was on the corner of two busy roads. One Saturday night, when the roads, as usual, were extremely busy, we had just returned home from getting takeaway. We all climbed out of the van and went inside, the kids into one room to watch TV, Rob and I into another. We were sitting there eating our tea when there was a knock at the door.

We opened it and to our shock, there stood a man holding Kane. Kane was about three years old at that stage. He had been out on the busy road and this gentleman had stopped and brought him in. The kids had thought Kane was with us and we'd thought he was with the kids.

When Kane was 21, I was in real estate. I never suspected he was using or abusing alcohol or drugs because he wasn't living at home and I just didn't see the signs. But even if he had been at home, I wouldn't have known what to look out for. One morning at 5.30am, during the silly season between Christmas and New Year, we had a phone call from Kane.

On the phone, he told me how much he loved me, and said to tell Dad he loved him too, and that he was sorry that he had caused us so much grief. A shiver went down my spine. I knew what he was about to do and tried to keep him on the phone, but he hung up.

I remember that terrible feeling of uselessness, of not knowing where he was, and knowing what he was going to do. Rob was already out of bed, looking at me anxiously. I told him I thought that Kane was going to kill himself and Rob said, "No, he won't."

I was already in a state, not knowing what to do. I was crying and my heart was pounding so hard I thought I was going to have a heart attack. The thought of losing a child is every mother's worst nightmare.

We rang all of Kane's mates to no avail, then began pacing the floor. What could we do? We didn't even know where he was! Then we got a phone call from the police to say Kane was in jail. He had been in his mate's car, put his foot on the accelerator, flat to the floor, thrown his arms in the air and closed his eyes. He'd crossed traffic lanes and ended up in a paddock. Luckily, it was early in the morning and nobody was around, as he could have hit someone and killed not only himself, but them as well.

That drive to the police station was the longest three hours of my life.

When we got there, all I wanted to do was hug my son, but I wasn't allowed in the jail. Kane was angry due to the drugs and alcohol. Eventually he was released and I hugged and hugged him, so hard. I didn't want to let him go.

Kane had to see a physiatrist before they would allow him to come home. In the meantime, we sat with him and talked. I had been telling him for years that he was here for a reason and this just proved that it was true. Kane told us he'd felt disappointed when he didn't die, so he'd tried to start the car to do it again, but the car wouldn't start. Subconsciously, he hadn't wanted to die after all; he never wore a seat belt but on that particular day, he had put the seat belt on. I rest my case. Deep down, he really didn't want to die; he was crying out for help.

We brought Kane home and I didn't let him out of my sight. He came everywhere with me and I wouldn't let him go anywhere without me.

That New Year's Eve, Rob and I were going to Perth and staying with friends. I really didn't want to go, but Kane said he would be fine. I wasn't much fun that night as I was so worried about him, even though I knew he was at home. The whole time at the restaurant, despite all the drinking and partying, I just wanted to leave. We had planned to stay the night, but I couldn't leave Kane for that long. I had to get back home.

On the ride home, I wanted to drive my car as fast as it could go; I needed to get home "now!" As soon as I walked through the door, I went straight to Kane's room to make sure he was all right. He was awake. I hugged him and felt a huge relief and calm come over me.

When eventually Kane broke away from me, I still worried. This feeling is difficult to explain. Always in the back of your mind is the question, "Is he ever going to try it again?"

Sometimes, I think about how I would feel if I had lost Kane, or any of my children. I also think: that's what I would have put them through if I had succeeded in killing myself. If you ever get into this mind space, think about that. It just may stop you.

I drank when I was pregnant with Kane. This can cause foetal alcohol syndrome, (FASD) which I believe my son may have inherited from me.

Kane was also born with a severe club foot, he had two operations on his foot: one when he was six weeks old, when they cut the tendon at the back of his heel (he had no heel and the doctor said it was the worst case he has ever seen). He was in plaster for months. The second was when he wore callipers to push his heel out, and he wore these for six months. It is amazing how children adapt. Kane never had a problem with the plaster or callipers, and he would still crawl and try to walk with them.

Kane's foot was corrected as best as it could be, so he could walk, but his left foot is two sizes smaller than his right foot, and his left calf muscle is smaller. He can build up the strength in this calf, but it will never match the other one in size. And his left leg is shorter than his right, which has caused him some problems with his back.

He had some further problems related to drugs and alcohol, but we have worked with him and sent him to see Anthony Robbins. I also gave him the books *Follow your Heart* and *Being Happy* by Andrew Matthews to read. These things have helped him, but it still took years to realize just what alcohol and drugs were doing to him.

We are so proud of Kane, as he has broken free of his addictions and is on the way to recovery with goals and, most important, a future.

Here is a recent story that can happen to anyone…

It was Christmas, and Kane, Angela, and their daughter Ava had gone to Bali for 3 weeks. For their last week, they stayed at the time-share we have over there.

Kane hadn't been drinking for quite some time, but in Bali, he came down with the flu and was feeling a bit low, so thought he would have a cocktail to cheer himself up. Well, that was it! That is all he remembered.

I received a distraught phone call from Ange. She was beside herself. From the time he'd had a cocktail to the moment when he'd come back to their room, Kane had smashed up over $700 worth of furniture in the lobby of the hotel, caught a cab into Kuta, lost $1,000 and hit a policeman. We are talking Bali here, if you know what I mean.

The police found a key to the hotel Kane was staying at and brought him back. Fortunately, the security guard on duty was a policeman and talked his mates out of laying charges. Also, the staff at the hotel knew this was totally out of character for Kane and helped him as much as they could.

After a few well-placed phone calls, the hotel moved Angela and Ava to a different room. At that point, Angela felt like she was over the marriage and didn't want to try any more. Kane eventually went to his room. Angela was on the phone to me; she could see Kane sitting on his veranda.

I felt so much for Angela. She has been through a lot. Even though Kane has never hit her or Ava, he can get very angry and naturally, she gets scared. It isn't nice for your daughter to see this behaviour, either.

I rang the hotel and talked to Kane. He was beside himself, as he couldn't remember anything and didn't know where Angela and Ava were. I told him they were all right, that they were in the hotel, but that they didn't want to see him. I talked to him for a while, then hung up, rang the hotel and talked to Angela again. I kept doing this until I could bring them together.

Angela had asked Kane on many occasions to stop drinking and he'd promised her, but he'd still messed up. This time, he had his daughter of three years standing in front of him, saying, "Promise me, Daddy; please don't ever do that again." At first, he couldn't make that promise. He'd tried so many times with Angela and hadn't been able to keep it.

But here was his little daughter getting angry at her father, saying over and over again, "Promise me, Daddy, *please* don't ever do that again." After the third time, Kane relented. "Yes darling, I will never do this again." Kane told me he would keep that promise, and I believed him.

They still had a few days in Bali, and it was probably a good thing to be away, like this, from people they knew, people they could run away to. Instead, they had to stay together and sort it out. And they have.

I've mentioned that Kane used to ask me, "Mum, why does this keep happening to me?" and I'd reply, "You haven't learnt the lesson yet". What happened in Bali was a wakeup call. He was so lucky he wasn't locked up–or worse. This had to happen for him to learn the lesson. And no, he hasn't had a drink since.

Kane's Story

Foetal Alcohol Syndrome or FASD

I drank when I was pregnant with Kane and I am sorry that this might have contributed to Kane's suffering.

Drinking alcohol during pregnancy can cause foetal alcohol syndrome, and as I mentioned earlier Kane may have received from me.

When I was growing up no one told me anything, everything was so hush hush, you just don't talk about sex or any of those things, it was a very naive world back then and 33 years ago, yeah I probably knew that I shouldn't drink alcohol, but never in my wildest dreams did I think that it could cause problems to my baby. Otherwise, I wouldn't have done it. Back then, we could eat processed products, and so many other things that you shouldn't eat, and not worry about it. We ate and drank whatever we wanted. We didn't have the internet then to educate ourselves about what not to eat or drink during pregnancy, and nobody told you not to, not even the doctors.

I have recently discussed this with a girlfriend of mine also told me how she drank during pregnancy. She didn't know any different as no one told her what she can or can't have while carrying her baby inside her womb.

Foetal alcohol spectrum disorders (FASDs) are a group of conditions that may come to a person because their mother had been drinking alcohol during pregnancy. Here are some of the problems people with FASD could suffer from:

- An abnormal appearance, short height, low body weight, small head size. *Kane is a good looking man, tall, good body weight and a normal head size.*
- Poor coordination *Kane doesn't have this problem*
- Low intelligence, *Kane is highly intelligent*
- Behavior problems, *Kane did have behavior problems*
- Problems with hearing or seeing. *Kane doesn't have a problem with hearing or seeing.*

Those with FASD have an increased risk for having trouble in school and run ins with the law. They also tend to participate in high-risk behaviors, and have trouble with alcohol or other drugs. I believe this is what happened to my son Kane. The worst part is that the symptoms may not be noticed until school age. And we did notice that Kane just wasn't fitting into the school system from the age of 13.

He always felt like a failure and now he feels that there was a reason why he felt that way. He has an answer to it, because he couldn't work out why he acted like he did. He has always been blamed for being that "problematic" kid, but the truth is that he simply wasn't given the best start. Now he understands why it has been harder for him. He got his answer and the mystery is finally solved. He is happy in his life now we are so proud of him as he has broken free from his addictions and is on the way to recovery with goals and, most important, a future.

Kane looks back now, he seems angry and upset about it, but not blaming anyone. He just wish he knew that FASD may have been the cause of the many problems he experienced since childhood, and so do we.

I have always said to Kane he is here for a reason: for great things! And I have said to him now, if it hadn't have been this way, he may not have turned out to be the incredible man that he is now. Sometimes we need to go through rough challenges in life to reveal our real strength and potential.

I knew I wrote this book for a reason, one of those reasons I now realize was for my son to have closure and for myself and Rob to understand why Kane was like he was.

It wasn't until I was writing this book, that I learnt about FASD and what it can do to the unborn child, I really had no idea.

Once I found out about it, I was able to research on the internet (back when Kane was born there wasn't any internet) but also back then I wouldn't have done any research as I didn't know there was a problem.

I gave my book to Kane, it was a real emotional time for him, finding out about what myself and his father went through. The main part of the book that resonated with Kane was my drinking and FASD and what it can do to the unborn child, him, and he started to understand his behaviors, why he was like he was. He couldn't comprehend "why it was always happening to him" and how he would say he was just a fuck up.

We have talked in length over this and now he is understanding that is wasn't all his fault.

Kane thought, which we have talked about, that I was feeling guilty so I would make up for it in everything I did for him, with money and love.

I can honestly say I felt no guilt because I never knew it was partially my fault, everything I ever did for Kane was out of unconditional love, as I love his so much I would do anything for him, to help him, to be there for him.

Now this is the way I think, and I have said it so many times throughout my book "things happen for a reason" Kane getting the short straw made him so strong, determined, man, most would just roll over and say this is my mum's fault I will blame her for everything, it wasn't me at all, so I will just be the dropkick that I am, because it is all her fault.

I am sorry it happened but I don't feel guilty because it has made him the man he is today and I will say again, he is here for great things, his passion is to help people with their addictions and that is what he is doing, he is going to save so many lives, helping so many people, and is a true inspiration to them all including his father and myself.

Our son, stood up, fought it and is winning, day by day he is getting stronger and stronger and we are sooooooooooooo proud of him.

Where Kane is Now

I don't know if it was because I drank when I was pregnant with him that he got FASD. Yes, he fell into the wrong crowd and got caught up in drugs and alcohol and he could have stayed there like a lot of people do. But he didn't, he packed up to go 1000s of miles away with no money to start a new life, and HE did this, he pushed himself and conquered his addictions.

I may have given him a bad start, but he has fought the battle and is winning.

Kane is an intelligent young man. In fact, he went to university to study bachelor of psychology, so that he could further understand addiction and learn how to help people, was an achiever, and still is, receiving many distinctions. He can converse with anyone on any level, is a fantastic sales person, and a wonderful husband and father (and of course son).

He is loving, with a heart of gold, and wants so much to help people with their addictions, and help them to move forward. I think to myself if he hadn't have gone through what he did, he may not be on the path that he is now. With everything he has been through, he also is going to write a book, and I am sure it will be a best seller, and help many people.

Kane lives on the sunny east coast of Australia and is happily married to his beautiful wife Angela and they have a gorgeous daughter Ava who is nearly 5 years old. Angela is a pillar of support for Kane and they are the best parents to Ava. Ava is a happy child and they are bringing her up the right way.

He doesn't drink alcohol or take drugs. Yes, the urges are still there and it is a constant battle for him, but now he understands how addiction works and what he can do to stop it. He fights it every day.

Kane is now running a gym with a business partner. He did the business plan, painted, met with the franchises, ordered the equipment, unwrapped each piece of equipment and set the whole gym up. To understand what he teaches, he is also taking courses on nutrition and exercise.

Kane is a natural businessman and people gravitate towards him because of his energy and infectious personality. At the gym, he is in his element and he absolutely loves what he does. He gets up at 3.30 a.m. every morning and drives 45 minutes to work. That's how dedicated he is to his business. He is living his dream, as he is helping people and that is his passion.

I have said throughout my book that things happen for a reason and that Kane is here for a reason and these are two of the reasons: to bring joy to his family and be an inspiration to others, yes I could give many more.

My heart swells with pride as I look at my little family, how far they have come, leaving the west just after their wedding and moving to live in a tent. Where they are now, what an achievement!

Kane's story proves that you can overcome any obstacle and achieve anything in life. If you really want something, put your mind to it and go for it. Kane is living proof of this.

I could go on writing about what a wonderful mentor he has been to me, and how proud his father and I are of him and how much we love and respect his fighting, tenacity and guts to break the mold and just do it.

Kane sent me this message that I believe everyone should hear:

As we grow older, and hence wiser, we slowly realize that wearing a $1,000 or a $10 watch–– they both tell the same time. Whether we carry a $500 or a $50 wallet/handbag–– the amount of money inside is the same. Whether we drink a bottle of $100 or $10 wine–– the hangover is the same. Whether the house we live in is 100 or 1,000 sq. ft.–– loneliness is the same.

You will realize, your true inner happiness does not come from the material things of this world.

Therefore, I hope you realize, when you have mates, buddies and old friends, brothers and sisters, who you chat with, laugh with, talk with, have sung songs with, talk about north-south-east-west or heaven and earth–– That is true happiness!

To end this chapter, I am sharing six undeniable facts of life and the six best doctors in the world that I have discovered through our family's journey with Kane:

1. Don't educate your children to be rich. Educate them to be *happy*. So when they grow up they will know the value of things, not the price.
2. Best awarded words: "Eat your food as your medicines. Otherwise you have to eat medicines as your food."
3. The one who loves you will never leave you because even if there are 100 reasons to give up, he or she will find one reason to hold on.
4. There is a big difference between a human being and being human. Only a few really understand it.
5. You are loved when you are born. You will be loved when you die. In between, you have to manage!
6. If you just want to walk fast, walk alone! But if you want to walk far, walk together!

SIX BEST DOCTORS IN THE WORLD:

1. Sunlight

    Taking a walk and getting sun exposure are sometimes all you need to brighten up your day. Natural light has been found to help improve mood and ease depression.

2. Rest

    The body and mind need rest to repair itself and renew energy. You need to sleep at least 7 to 8 hours per day to keep your brain healthy, to regulate your metabolism, to protect your heart and boost your immune system.

3. Exercise

Every adult needs at least 150 minutes of moderate physical exercise per week. Exercise isn't just for losing weight and maintaining health, it also helps you de-stress, improves your memory, boosts your confidence, and helps you live longer.

4. Diet

    A healthy and balanced diet are essential to help you maintain good health and protect yourself from diseases, so you feel good and function at your best every day.

5. Self Confidence and

    Self-confidence is an important ingredient for success. You need confidence to say yes or no to many things in life. You need confidence to overcome fears and have the courage to just start taking action. Confidence means you believe in your ability to win in life.

6. Friends

    Friends add meaning to our lives. They contribute to our happiness as they make us feel we're loved and never alone in our problems. We need a strong support system through our family and friends to help us conquer challenges and attain success.

Maintain these six and you will find it easier to enjoy life.

Ryan's Story

An incident occurred with my oldest son, Ryan. He was 18 at the time, and I was working at Nutrimetics.

We received a phone call from Ryan's mate saying that my son had passed out at a party and had been taken to a hospital. Immediately, we jumped in the car and ended up behind the ambulance. My heart was pounding, knowing my son was in front of us. I wanted to fly into the ambulance and be with him. We got to the hospital and as the ambulance door swung open, I could see Ryan's feet and lifeless body.

I didn't know if he was dead or alive, and felt sick to my stomach. As soon as he was carried out of the ambulance, I was beside him, hugging him, talking to him. He wasn't responding, but he was alive.

I then found out that he had alcohol poisoning. If he hadn't received help when he did, he would have died. In the hospital, they put him on a table and inserted a drip. As they pumped fluids into him, I had to keep pinching his ear, as this kept his breathing and heart going.

After a while, when everything had calmed down and he was okay, the doctor told us to go home. Ryan was going to be fine. So we left and went home to rest.

Later on that morning, I had a phone call from Ryan to come and pick him up. When I arrived, he was chirpy; they had pumped so much fluid into him that he had no alcohol left in him and had no hangover. I was happy he was feeling better, but I just wish he'd felt some after-effects so he wouldn't do it again. It would have been a lesson to him. But thank goodness he survived!

That night I looked at Ryan and felt useless. Here was my son lying in hospital for something that was his own fault. I felt a mixture of thank-God-you-are-okay, and wanting to shake him for being so stupid.

Please, educate your children about binge drinking and alcohol poisoning. These can kill them.

Sharon's story

I was still involved with Nutrimetics, but was right on the edge of pulling away. It was a weird feeling, as if something wouldn't let me go.

I went to one of our shows and met a wonderful young woman who became a consultant of mine. By working with her, I got to know a lot about her. She told me that she had just joined a dating agency and she described the nice guys she had met through the agency.

Sharon was single at that stage and having a ball with her friends, so she really wasn't thinking about a serious relationship. Even so, I told her about the dating service and suggested she give it a try, which she did. She joined and went out with a few guys, but then she met one guy she was really taken with.

To cut a long story short, Sharon and her guy ended up getting married and now have two beautiful children.

Think about it: if I hadn't stayed with Nutrimetics (even though I wanted to leave) and met that young woman, Sharon wouldn't have joined the dating agency and found the love of her life. And I wouldn't have my beautiful grandchildren, Caitlyn and Devon. Things always happen for a reason!

My Daughter's Stroke

One of the most beautiful experiences in the world is giving birth to your child. But to me, even more beautiful was when I had the pleasure and privilege of witnessing my daughter, Sharon, give birth to our granddaughter.

I don't want to focus on the details of the birth. Instead, I want to tell you what happened to my daughter a short time after her daughter was born.

Caitlyn was born 10th July 2001, and everything was fine until ten weeks after she arrived. The day was 18th September 2001. This is a day I will never forget.

I was on my way to work when I received a phone call from Sharon. She told me that something was wrong, but she wasn't sure what. At that stage of my life, I was a real workaholic and was torn between rushing to my daughter and my duties at work. I called a co-worker and she told me not to worry about work, just to go to my daughter's home.

Since that day, I have totally changed. Work no longer dominates my life.

When I arrived at Sharon's house, she was sitting in a chair and had a strange look on her face. She told me Caitlyn had woken up at 5.30 a.m. for a feed and that she had fed her and changed her nappy, and at that point, she was feeling fine. As Caitlyn was taken care of, she decided to go back to bed. She'd then woken up at 7.30 a.m. feeling "weird." She had trouble balancing, walking, talking; in fact, she couldn't function at all. She had just managed to get to the phone to ring me to say something was wrong.

By the time I arrived, Caitlyn was awake again, lying in her cot, making happy sounds.

As soon as I saw Sharon, I felt a wave of panic. Something wasn't right. I helped her get dressed and then packed up a few of Caitlyn's and her things. I called Andrew, Sharon's boyfriend, now husband, told him what was happening and let him know that Caitlyn and Sharon were with me.

I drove them straight to the hospital, where the doctor informed Sharon that she had a virus and should go home and get some rest.

I wasn't convinced, so both of them came to my place, and I told Sharon to sleep on a mattress in the living room so I could check on her frequently to see how she was doing. She was very weak and couldn't do much of anything; in fact, when it was time for Caitlyn to feed, I had to hold her against Sharon's breast. I burped and bathed Caitlyn, washed nappies and clothes and tended to Sharon.

Sharon slept a lot. She felt so weak that she needed help to do even the simplest things, like going to the toilet, taking a shower, and getting dressed. In addition, she couldn't eat much.

I timed my real estate work for when Sharon slept. I would strap Caitlyn to my front and do some work, show houses, fill out papers and so on. She was wonderful; you didn't hear a whimper from her and she slept most of the time.

One evening as I was looking at Sharon, I noticed that the left side of her face seemed to have drooped. And then she said she was having funny feelings down the right side of her body. Right then I knew, *this is no virus*.

I had no idea that it was a stroke; it didn't even enter my head. I just knew we had to find out what was really wrong with her.

Over the next few weeks as Sharon began to feel better, we rang up doctors and specialists and made appointments. We wanted to research the problem and what caused it. This went on for no less than two years!

We began by visiting a local doctor, who confirmed that Sharon had suffered a mini stroke. After numerous tests on her heart and circulatory system, Sharon also underwent a cervical biopsy and on 24th February, 2003, the doctors told her that there would be a high risk of another stroke if she were to have more children.

I will never forget the look on Sharon's face: total devastation. I felt for her so much, recalling my feelings at the time I'd had my hysterectomy. It all came flooding back to me, that terrible thought: "You can't have any more children." It wasn't a case of not wanting any more; it was a case of not being *able* to have any more. It devastates you.

Not only was Sharon shattered, so was I. After the initial shock wore off, we started to talk about finding a surrogate or starting the process of adoption. Sharon was desperate to have one more child, which I could totally understand as she was, and is, such a wonderful mother. It just wasn't fair.

She continued to have more testing, including an MRI Cardiovascular EXC Investigation, and in June 2003, a neurologist told Sharon that she could, indeed, have more children. But we still wondered: what had caused her stroke in the first place?

It turns out the left vertebral artery hypoplasia, or the blood vessels that run up the back of the neck and join at the base of the skull, had formed a thrombosis, which is a clot of coagulated blood. That was the cause of her stroke.

Because of this, Sharon has to take the blood thinner Cartia, a low dose aspirin that helps prevent blood clots and reduces the risk of a stroke, for the rest of her life. She has now been taking Cartia for eight years and hasn't had any problems since.

Christmas 2003 arrived and we went up to Sharon and Andrew's home to hand out presents. Sharon handed Rob and I each a card.

"Congratulations!" mine said. "You are going to be a nanna!" On Rob's, it said "poppa."

Sharon was six-weeks pregnant. I burst into tears with a mixture of joy and fear–although I really think the fear took over. I was so worried that the same thing might happen again.

On Boxing Day, Sharon had some spotting, and a blood clot came out. We now think that must have been the baby. Because it was a holiday weekend, she couldn't get in to see her doctor until first thing Monday morning and of course, I was there with her.

Tests were done and Sharon was told she had lost the baby. She was inconsolable. I told her it is nature's way of saying that things aren't quite right. This helped a little. As a mother, you just hate it when your children are in pain. Words can help, but sometimes just being there for them, consoling and hugging them, is all the help they need. These are the times you have to be strong for your loved ones.

Yes, there was a reason for the miscarriage, but that story belongs to Sharon and Andrew. However, I will say it was the best of reasons.

Sharon became pregnant again in 2005 and I was worried. I didn't tell Sharon this, as I didn't want to upset her. When she called to tell me, she was very excited but after we hung up the phone, I just had to sit down. I thought about what might happen and knew I had to be with her the whole way to support her if anything went wrong.

When Devon was born on the 24th February 2006, the doctors took into consideration Sharon's previous stroke. But, even though the medical team were fully aware of everything that had happened, the doctor wasn't there when Sharon delivered her baby; only the midwife was present. When it was time for the baby to come into this world, the midwife told me to "Grab a leg." I did as she told me.

When Devon arrived, blood was pouring out of Sharon like a tap. I couldn't believe my eyes. I looked at the midwife and asked if this was normal, hoping she would say yes. She didn't answer me, as she was quickly on the phone with the doctor, at the same time using kidney bowls to collect the blood. Sharon lost a litre of blood that day.

Sharon didn't realize what was happening. I kept looking at her with all my love, tears in my eyes, praying that everything would be all right. My heart was pounding out of my chest; I wanted to do something—anything—but didn't know what.

Eventually the bleeding stopped, but my emotions didn't. I was terrified I was going to lose my precious daughter and seeing all that blood—and the fact that it took so long to stop—scared the hell out of me.

For 12 weeks after Devon was born, Sharon had to give herself daily injections in the stomach with Clexane to stop blood clots from forming. If another clot formed, she ran the risk of having another stroke.

But our story has a happy ending. Sharon now has two healthy children and I am a proud nanna. Most importantly, Sharon's children have their beautiful mother and I have my wonderful daughter.

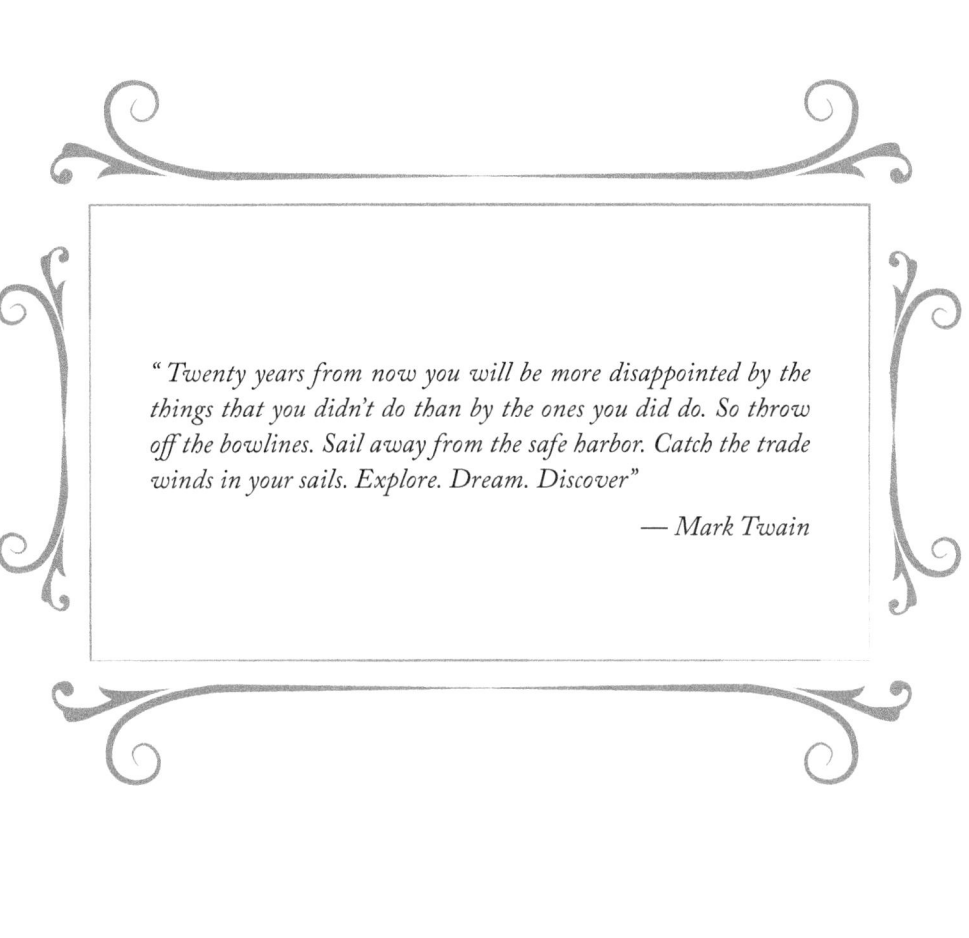

" Twenty years from now you will be more disappointed by the things that you didn't do than by the ones you did do. So throw off the bowlines. Sail away from the safe harbor. Catch the trade winds in your sails. Explore. Dream. Discover"

— *Mark Twain*

Living the Dream: Backpacking through Egypt

From the time he was little, my son Ryan and I shared a fascination with Egypt. It was our dream to travel and see the pyramids in person.

Ryan was 30 and I was 53 when he suggested that the two of us travel there. Ryan is a bit more adventurous than me and after doing some research, decided we should "backpack it." I went along with this because it was what he wanted. (The things we do for our children!) But because I like a bit of luxury, we compromised, so on the way back, we would spend time in in a nice hotel in Dubai, and relax.

I looked on this trip as the opportunity of a lifetime and was also honoured that my son wanted to go backpacking with me. What son wants to go backpacking with their mother?

Then I saw the age group for backpackers and got a bit nervous. If you were 60 years old, you needed a health certificate from your doctor stating you were fit enough for the trip. I suddenly wondered, *what am I getting myself into?*

I was already going to the gym, but now had to train to get fit enough to climb Mt. Sinai, which is 7,500 feet high! I told a couple of the girls I was going to Egypt and immediately they said they would never go there, telling me horror stories about snipers on the side of the Nile, shooting at people while they were going down the river. They went on and on about murder on the streets and so on.

Going on the internet to check it all out made me feel even worse, as there were warnings not to go to Egypt because of terrorism. We also planned on going to Jordan, where someone was shot and killed the week before we left. I voiced my concerns, but Ryan said it would be okay, that he would look after me. I was more concerned about him than me. He was my son and if I lost him, I would never forgive myself!

We registered with the Department of Foreign Affairs, and Ryan convinced me that we couldn't let the fear of terrorism rule our lives. We have a life to lead, and no one should be able to tell us what to do and what not to do. Especially not terrorists.

I went shopping for my backpack, thermals, torch, toilet paper and all the bits and pieces they recommended for the trip. We planned to go for 3 ½ weeks and when it was time to pack, I lay all my clothes out on the bed for Ryan to check. I asked him to "go gentle on me, because I am a woman". He didn't.

By the time he was finished, I was left with less than half of what I'd put on the bed. I began to wonder how I'd survive.

Departure day: Saturday, 21st October 2006.

The flight to Dubai was 11 ½ hours. Dubai's airport is enormous, with fake palm trees everywhere, and it took 15 minutes by shuttle to get from the terminal to our connecting plane to Jordan. Luckily, the flight to Jordan was much shorter.

In Amman, our tour guide was waiting for us. We stayed at the Dana Hotel, but I wasn't allowed to use the lifts: Ryan insisted that I climb up five flights of stairs to our hotel room with my backpack on, then took me to the gym to do a workout! Even though the trip had started, Ryan was still trying to get me fit, so any time he spotted stairs, he made me walk up them. I was never allowed to take a lift or escalator; he wanted me to reach the top of Mt. Sinai.

Jordan was quite a culture shock and I didn't feel comfortable there. It seemed that few people spoke English and they stared at you as you walked by. No one acknowledged me, or if they did, they would call Ryan "Sir." When we walked around, Ryan would joke, saying, "Get behind me, woman!"

We paid for a bit of washing to be done. Then Ryan informed me that this was the last time we were getting our clothes washed; it was time to go feral. Oh, poor me!

And we were off and running.

In Jordan, we visited the Umayyad desert castles (qasrs), built in the 7th and 8th century AD, used as fortresses and leisure resorts for the caliphs, where they could hunt and race their Arab horses. Our driver raced down the highway at 170 km an hour, and lining the side of the road were tyres that had blown from cars. The driver couldn't speak English. He just drove. Fast.

All along our route were road blocks with armed police, and we were stopped several times as they checked our credentials, guns pointing at us.

We visited Qasr Amra, the most famous desert castle in Jordan and deservedly, a UNESCO World Heritage site, with its mixed style of Roman, Byzantine and Eastern frescos and mosaics, roofed halls, siesta rooms and steam baths with painted frescos. Inside the dome on top of the hot room was a magnificent painting representing the heavens, with the twelve signs of the zodiac spread over a round surface. Amazingly, they had hot running water. They also had a well, which appeared bottomless, but would have to have been cut out by hand.

Our next stop, Azraq castle, was 100 km east of Amman in the heart of the Azraq Oasis. Amongst other things, it had served as temporary headquarters for T.E. Lawrence ("Lawrence of Arabia") during the Arab Revolt in the early 20th century. It had the only permanent source of fresh water for 12,000 square miles.

Kharaneh castle, 17 km west of Qasr Amra, and 60km east of Amman, was built by the Umayyad, with heavy stone walls for defence purposes. We climbed up to the roof, and the views were really outstanding. There was desert all around, and it just went on forever.

The next day, Ryan and I stood at the edge of the Dead Sea. On the shore, crystals of salt covered everything.

The Dead Sea is beautiful. It's called the Dead Sea because nothing can live in it. You won't find any seaweed, fish, or plants. You can swim there, although you won't really be swimming, more like floating, because of all the salt. The water is almost six times as salty as the ocean.

Jerash is approximately a fifty-minute drive to the north from Amman, Jordan's capital and is home to some of the best-preserved and most extensive remains of the Roman Empire, with a really well-preserved Greco-Roman city. We saw ancient city walls enclosing colonnaded, paved streets with chariot tracks worn into the original stone. Standing there, looking down, you could just imagine the chariots riding into town.

Back at Jordan airport, I was frisked twice by female security guards, but when we checked in to get our boarding pass, the steward said something beautiful. "What is better in life, a friend or brother? It is when your brother becomes your friend. What is better in life, a friend or a son? It's when your son becomes your friend." It was very touching because Ryan said he'd realized this a while ago; not only is he my son, he is my friend. I feel the same way.

As we flew into Cairo, we were speechless as we looked out the window. Out one side of the plane was a vast desert, which seemed to be never-ending; in complete contrast, on the other side was a busy city that looked like a modern day oasis.

Arriving in Egypt is like plunging yourself into the past, but there are also very modern aspects. Cairo is breathtaking; I couldn't believe how big it was–and clean, even with 20 million people in one city.

The tour guide, Ahmen, was at the airport to meet us. He spoke English – what a relief! He took us to the hotel, where, just as in the previous one, we had to walk through a metal detector. Then we were off to the museum.

At that moment, a well-dressed man came up to us and said he was waiting for his wife, but that he "wanted to do the right thing by us." He told us about a shop across the road having a sale. Forgetting the many warnings we'd had, we accompanied him. We hadn't yet been shopping, so didn't know the prices, and we got caught out big, big time. You learn by your mistakes, and we'll never make that one again.

Our tour of Egypt had started, and with us on the tour were 12 women and 3 men, with me about 20 years older than everyone else on the tour.

First, we headed to the edge of the desert to explore the pyramids and the nearby Sphinx. We also visited the beautiful Valley Temple of King Chephren.

The Pyramids of Egypt, built at Giza during the 4th Dynasty, are the oldest of the seven wonders of the world and the only ones remaining intact today. You really can't tell the immense size of them until you see them in person. Each building block alone was nearly at tall as me!

Next, we were off to ride the camels. I didn't like their grunting, and the prospect of riding them made me nervous, but I mounted one and rode around the outskirts of the three pyramids–and loved it!

Next was the Sphinx, one of the best known monuments on earth, 73.5 metres in length and originally sculptured from a limestone outcrop and dating back over 4,500 years. They say the head of the Sphinx depicts King Khafre, and it has the body of a lion.

On the way back, we visited a papyrus museum and saw how they used to make paper from the pith of the papyrus plant.

On the train to Luxor we were given a little breakfast box for the morning. It was an 11-hour train ride, the light was on all night, and I was freezing; one thing we should have bought was sleeping bags.

I woke up during the night and walked into the toilet. Water was sloshing back and forth on the floor and the smell was so horrific that I almost threw up. I really needed to go, but couldn't find any way to flush the toilet when I was done, so had to leave it. When I got back to my seat, I could smell the urine on my shoes. That was not water sloshing on the floor...

In Luxor, we checked into the Hotel Tutotel, and took a horse-drawn carriage to the temple at Karnak. What an incredible place! It had hieroglyphics honouring the many different gods, and has been called the world's greatest open air museum—and it is. The temple of Amun is amazing. It is the largest temple supported by columns in the world.

That night we went to an English-style pub called The King's Head. Our tour guide, Ahmen, drank 35 shots of tequila and you couldn't even see a difference in him! Afterwards, we caught a horse and buggy back to the hotel.

We rose early and walked to the Nile, then caught a boat to the other side where donkeys were waiting to take us to the Valley of the Kings. We headed off just as the sun was rising. My donkey, George, was a natural leader; we started at the back, but quickly caught up. Then George ploughed through the middle and took the lead, with me shouting "Yella!" ("Come on!") and throwing my arms around to make him go faster. Riding was both fun and nerve racking. There were times when I felt like I was going to bounce right off!

We rode for an hour and half, through small villages, on a mix of roads. Once we encountered a car coming in our direction and this turned into a major and very funny bottleneck of donkeys, as we couldn't really guide them. That ride was one of the highlights of our visit to Egypt.

The Valley of the Kings was nothing like I expected. There were tombs dug into the sides of mountains, and we went through four of them. The artwork and colours were out of this world.

As we were leaving, we had a group photo taken with the Colossi of Memnon.

We went to an alabaster factory, where we were shown how they make the figures and vases, and we all received a necklace from Ahmen. Later, Ryan and I caught a horse-drawn carriage to the Luxor museum, where we saw even more carvings.

That night we took a boat across the Nile and went to a pretty restaurant on the top floor of a building. It was very open and scenic, and we ate a variety of delicious local foods before catching the boat back.

We left early to travel to Aswan, Egypt's sunniest southern city and ancient frontier town, about 81 miles south of Luxor and a four-hour bus trip. Aswan has a very African atmosphere and was easy to walk around; the pace of life there was slow and relaxing.

The Nile is at its most beautiful at Aswan, flowing through "amber desert and granite rocks, around emerald islands covered in palm groves and tropical plants."This was one of our favourite places.

Next, we met up with some other buses and went in a convoy, armed escorts in both front and in back.

The number of police and police stops along the way was unnerving. Along the way, we saw people living in the same kind of mud huts they had in Biblical times. I watched people harvest their fields using a donkey, with no machinery at all. It was like stepping back in time.

We checked into the Cleopatra Hotel and in the afternoon, began a four-hour trip to the Philae temple and museum. They had moved the entire temple–40,000 pieces – to a different location, taking 10 years to put it back together again. The temple was stunning, set on its own island, with a magical view.

When we got back, we did a one-hour power walk to the Aswan museum, which I loved and thought was better than the Luxor museum.

I decided not to go to dinner that night in order to give my tummy a rest, and when Ryan came back, he fussed over me, making sure I took in enough nutrition and fluids. (He's great at looking after me.)

At 3.30 a.m. we met the armed convoy to take us to Abu Simbel, one of the most impressive temples ever built, and another of the highlights of our visit. We followed the shores of Lake Nasser and arrived at the temple just after sunrise. We loved our tour of the site! Then we left by bus, convoy in tow, with armed guards at each end, and went back to have our last shower for a while. In Aswan, we bought some munchies, then headed to the Nile to board a *felucca* and sail north toward Kom Ombo.

The best way to sail the Nile is by *felucca*. It's a simple sailing boat made of wood, with no engines, toilets or showers. One great sail is attached to a mast at the stem and one man can single-handedly sail the boat. Most of our crew were Nubian, dressed in the galabiya, the loose Egyptian shirt reaching to the feet.

An Egyptian proverb says: "The one who voyages the Nile must have sails made of patience. If Allah wills it, the wind will come and give speed for your journey. If the river is flat calm, you must wait in patience. You cannot force the Nile…"

Sailing down the Nile is a magical experience! There is a single deck and you lie on thick mattresses, which you can stretch out on during the day under the shade of an awning, watching as the dark waters glide past. It is a dreamlike way to travel.

Meals were simple, prepared by our crew. They included chicken, rice, and local bread and vegetables, and the cooking was done in a small area between the sleeping section and bow. A big tablecloth was spread out on the mattresses and we would sit around them, with the food in the middle.

If you needed to go to the toilet, you had to tell the crew and wait until they got to shore. If there was no wind, it could take them an hour to get there…

We had a roster and after each meal, would wash the dishes in a bucket. Ryan took a photo of me because he said he couldn't remember the last time I'd washed dishes! Our lights were candles in plastic bottles. There was an esky for drinks, which people brought themselves. We would sit, eat and sleep on the mattresses.

The captain's room, under the bow, was where you changed your clothes. However, our captain had the flu and slept there most of the time, so we didn't get changed at all.

During the day we relaxed and enjoyed timeless scenes of local life as we sailed slowly down the Nile. We played cards, told jokes, drank and read. We all shared toilet stories. (This was a big thing, because either you needed to go and there wasn't a toilet in sight, or there were bathrooms that you didn't dare go into.)

Each evening our crew would pull into shore and find a flat, sandy area for the night, and we would sleep under the awning on the mattresses. It was freezing; as mentioned, Ryan and I hadn't brought sleeping bags, only our thermals and a sheet. On our last night, I asked Ahmed for a blanket, and Ryan and I cuddled up.

If you wanted to go to the toilet, you had to take someone with you, so with torch and toilet paper in hand, you would head off into the bush. All of the woman were on a ledge, and after you did your bit, you had to burn your toilet paper so it didn't blow around and create litter. When you got back to the boat, you could see little bonfires of toilet paper along the shore.

We weren't allowed to wear shoes on the boat and when we got off the boat, we would put our shoes back on. Then, when we came back on board, it was shoes off and they sprayed everyone's feet with antiseptic.

The last of our three nights on board, we had a party. We pulled up on shore and collected firewood for the bonfire, and other boats and people arrived.

That night, Ahmed and I had a great conversation. He told me what a gentlemen of a son I had, and of course, I agreed. He also said that when he'd seen my age on the itinerary, he was a bit worried about me, but he quickly realized he didn't have a thing to be concerned about, as I could keep up with everyone. Yes, all that stair walking had paid off!

After dinner, we danced around the fire to the guys playing drums, and although I don't smoke, we all sat around and had our first *sheesha*. It was very sweet.

When we docked at Edfu, we farewelled our Nubian friends, which was a little sad after spending so much time with them on the boat.

Edfu is located about halfway between Luxor and Aswan. The Temple of Horus in Edfu is considered to be the best-preserved cult temple in Egypt and gives you a great idea of how all the temples once looked.

When we arrived at the temple, there was a "taxi" ramp of about 50 horse drawn carriages. I then got an urge, and when I have to go, I have to go, so I just took off to the toilet. It was getting time to leave, so from the toilet I headed straight back to the bus.

As I was standing at the bus, I saw Ryan storming towards me and when he got to me, he was furious. "Where were you?!" he asked, shaking his finger at me "Don't you ever do that to me again!" The guys from the bus told me that he was so worried about me that he'd walked through the temple, yelling out for me. When he saw someone from our group, he asked if they had seen me. I actually thought it funny, but under the circumstances, and given where we were, I should have had a bit more consideration. But I just wasn't thinking.

Returning to our hotel, it was heaven to have a shower after four days of not washing! We took a nap, and then it was off to the Mummification Museum by horse and cart. The Museum was remarkable; they even had mummified fish, cats, and crocodiles!

Afterwards, it was the dreaded train trip back to Cairo in the evening. I made sure I didn't drink anything, and I took an Imodium. There was no way I was going to go to that toilet again!

After 10 hours, we arrived in Cairo and headed for the hotel, then visited the Cairo Museum. It was sooooo big! I've never seen anything so huge. The museum collection exceeds 120,000 objects, from the prehistoric era to the Greco-Roman period.

We walked around the lower floor, then headed for the bazaar through the absolutely hair-raising traffic.

What a place the bazaar was! Massive stalls in all directions, as far as the eye could see.

That night we went to the sound and light show at the Sphinx and Giza pyramids. It told the history of Egypt and the Sphinx and like so much of what we'd seen, was spectacular.

Up early again, we travelled by bus to Mt. Sinai, armed escorts in tow. The trip took eight hours, and we drove through a tunnel that passed underneath the Suez Canal. We spent the night in a simple, multi-bed hostel near Mt. Sinai.

The alarm went off a 1.30 a.m. and at 2.15 am we left to catch a bus to the foot of Mt. Sinai. We would start the climb at 3.00 a.m.

Mt. Sinai is the mountain where God spoke to Moses, and pilgrims all over the world go there. On the way up the mountain, you see ancient chapels and structures honouring saints and the Virgin Mary. Close to the summit is an amphitheatre where the 70 wise men waited while God spoke with Moses, and right at the top of the mountain is a small chapel and mosque.

The climb was a 7,500 ft. stairway made up of nearly 4,000 steps. We were there to climb the mountain and watch the sun rise over the southern end of the Peninsula, a glorious, untamed wilderness of immense beauty, with jagged pink granite mountains punching into clear blue skies.

For a price, you could hitch a ride on a camel, and after about 30 minutes of power-walking up the mountain, I thought, *If I keep going like this, I'll never make it.* So I was the first one to catch a ride. It was scary, as it was pitch black and the camels tend to walk right on the edge of the cliff. At times, I was sure I was going to go over. At the end of the trail, we then had 750 steps, which weren't like steps at all; there were jagged rocks all over the place. It was so dark, you had to use your torch, and it was hard going.

When we reached base camp, I sat with Ryan and suddenly thought: *This is the end. We're done. We made it!* Then he told me there were another 150 steps, straight up! The air was getting thin and it was freezing, and it was also getting harder to breathe. Those last 150 steps took me an hour!

Ryan was at the top of the mountain waiting for me with a rug, and we huddled together while we waited for sunrise. We looked at each other and told each other how proud we were that we had made it; all in all, it had taken two and a half hours to reach the top. The beauty of it was breathtaking.

The descent was easier said than done. I got about halfway down when I felt my knee start to give, but stupid me kept pushing. About three-quarters of the way down, my knee completely seized up, and I couldn't walk. At our request, the man came with a rather dodgy camel, and off we went. Finally, I hobbled onto the bus, where Ryan and the crew had been waiting for us.

Back at the hostel, we ate some much needed breakfast, then caught the bus to Dahab, a relaxing town in the middle of the Gulf of Aqaba and a great place to chill out. There's a beautiful beach, good snorkelling and windsurfing and you can also arrange a day dive. Unlike the big, touristy-type places, it had a small, bohemian centre with a lovely promenade through the town.

The restaurant that evening was beautiful! It was open air and right on the water; in fact, you could get splashed by the waves. We sat on the floor in a cornered off section and had dinner and a send-off cake. Then, around 10.30 p.m., a few of us decided to do some shopping, arriving back at the hotel at one in the morning.

Dahab has some of the best diving you will find in the Red Sea, so Ryan went diving in a paradise of warm water, coral and exotic fish.

The next day I felt very sick, with a headache, chills, and a sore throat, so when the bus came, Ahmed set me up in the back seat with pillows, a sleeping bag and towels. It took us nine hours to get back to Cairo. There, we said our sad goodbyes to everyone, before catching a taxi to the Sheraton Hotel.

Located on the West Bank of the Nile, the Sheraton is one of Cairo's greatest landmarks. Ryan and I stared out at the truly magnificent views of the city and the river. And the hotel had just what I needed: a luxurious room! There was a lounge, a king-sized bed and a bed for Ryan, two TVs and a huge bathroom full of lovely smelling goodies.

After a rest, we headed off to the Cairo Museum and this time did the second floor, where we saw heaps of mummies. They had fingernails and hair, and you could even see the wrinkles in their skin. The highlight was the tomb of King Tutankhamen. There were over 3,500 artefacts from the King's life: a decorated chest, ivory and gold bracelets, necklaces and other jewellery, alabaster vases and flasks, and weapons and instruments. The most extraordinary piece was the Gold Mask, which rests over the bandages that wrap around the King's face. The mask weighs 24.5 pounds of solid gold, and is believed to represent what the King really looked like. It was stunning.

Afterwards, we returned to that beautiful place of luxury, our hotel, and totally vegged out. Then, at 6.30 a.m. we were off to the airport for the three-hour flight to Dubai.

To say Dubai is impressive is an understatement; its skyline aspires to be the world's biggest, brightest and tallest. We decided to catch the "Big Bus" to do a tour, a great way to see the sights.

We visited the Al Fahidi Fort, now the Dubai Museum, built in 1799, which gives you a glimpse of the incredibly rich culture and heritage of Dubai, and a real insight into desert life, the traditional Arabian homes, mosques, fishing, pearl diving and local trade.

Next stop, gold…

The gold souk is one of the largest retail gold markets in the world, selling everything from ingots to intricately worked jewellery, at bargain prices. There are street-front stores and side alleys of smaller shops, with glittering show windows–literally wall-to-wall gold! I did a lot of shopping here.

We did a bit of men's shopping for Rob and Ryan, then the beach tour, where we saw Burj Al Arab, a five star hotel unofficially known as the world's only seven star hotel. It is built on an artificial island, with a sail-shaped tower 321 metres high. We also saw The World, an exclusive development of private and commercial islands, just off the coast of Dubai. At Jumeirah public beach, we took some pictures, and finally, we bought golf shirts for Rob at the Dubai Golf Club. Perfect.

On the flight home, Ryan and I had the whole middle row to ourselves.

When we got off the plane in Perth, all I wanted to do was hug and kiss Rob – which was unfortunately made difficult due to the cold sores I now had on my face. During the trip, Ryan and I had lost four kilos.

The lesson of our adventure was, for me: think for yourself! If I had listened to all the negativity and stories of threats of terrorism before I left, I would never have had such a fantastic adventure. I achieved things I really didn't think I would have the energy and stamina to do, but I did it and I'm proud of myself for achieving it. I got to see one of the most beautiful places in the world, and to do this with my son was even more special. On this trip, he and I formed an extraordinary bond.

"No matter how much it gets abused, the body can restore balance. The first rule is to stop interfering with nature."

-Deepak Chopra

Back to Daily Life: More Health Issues...

The Nail Biter

A few years ago, my husband said to me, "If I give up smoking, will you stop biting your nails?" I had been nagging him for years to give up smoking so, of course, I said yes, but I still couldn't stop. For a year he nagged me and used to get very angry with me.

I used to bite my nails unconsciously, that is, without even thinking about it. And I didn't "bite" my nails; it was more of a nibble, combined with aggressive picking. The worst times would be when I was driving, especially long distances. I would actually take my hands off the wheel and steer with my knee so that I could pick at my nails.

I would bite and pick at them well past the nail bed until they became so sore that they bled. When it got to the point where there was no more nail left to chew, I would start on the skin around the nail and then travel down my finger. Ironically, my favourite target was my right pointer. I am right handed, so this was the finger everyone saw first, and it was a bloody mess.

I found that this habit got worse when I was anxious, stressed, frustrated, depressed or angry–which, to be honest, was most of the time.

Sometimes I would realize what I was doing, but still feel compelled to continue, using snags or tears in the nail as an excuse to bite them. I would think, *I just need to get rid of this little bit.*

Yes, it was a habit, and all behaviours and habits are maintained at an unconscious level.

I tried so many times to stop. I used nail-biting creams, which had a bad taste that would deter you from putting your fingers in your mouth, and I even got false nails, but still picked at them. False nails are quite hard at the top of the nail, so I would pick at the base and work my way up.

Rob was always nagging me, telling me how ugly my nails looked. What made it worse was that in my job, I dealt with the public, so I was self-conscious about it.

When I was a Nutrimetics consultant, you were naturally expected to have perfect make-up and nails. Not me; I just couldn't beat it. I remember I was on my way to a show and was picking at my nails the whole way there. At the show, when I was doing the facial, I realized my finger was bleeding, quickly wiped it with a tissue and hoped no one had noticed.

Even that embarrassing moment didn't stop me.

The situation became even worse when I became a real estate agent. I was always using my hands to write contracts. The job required me to be up close and personal with the clients and I didn't feel comfortable because of my hands. But, again, I wasn't uncomfortable enough to stop.

Then I attended one of Tony Robbins' seminars, where he told us how he used to bite his nails, without even realizing he was doing it. Once he was on a business appointment with a very attractive lady and wanted to ask her out on a date. Everything was going well professionally and personally, but then the woman grabbed his hands because she'd noticed he was biting his nails.

She told him that she was disgusted by this and said it demonstrated poor personal restraint. To top it off, she told him she couldn't work with him, and got up and walked out of the restaurant.

A while later, when he was at the cinema, he noticed he was putting his fingers to his mouth to bite his nails. He suddenly remembered the disastrous dinner date and the incident about his nails and has never bitten his nails since.

Famous nail biters are Lisa Marie Presley, Phil Collins, and former U.S. First Lady, Jacqueline Kennedy Onassis. So even the most talented and beautiful among us find it hard to stop.

What damage can biting your nails do?

Nail biting can cause your fingertips to be red and sore, and your cuticles to bleed. Nail-biting also increases the risk of infection around your nail beds and in your mouth. Many bacteria are found under nails, especially on unwashed hands. In some cases, a type of bacteria called Staphylococcus can be found. This causes illnesses such as impetigo, and even toxic shock!

Dust and harmful bacteria can travel from the nails into the stomach during biting, and this may lead to stomach ache. Nail biting can also cause damage to teeth; despite nails being made of keratin, the same substance that hair is made of, teeth can become damaged when they bang together quickly and from the force it takes to bite through a nail.

WebMD.com says dental problems and infections of the gums can be caused by nail biting. Long term nail biting can also interfere with normal nail growth and cause deformed nails.

I was pretty lucky with my nails; they are now strong, although the index finger nail is a little off centre. When I finally stopped biting them and let them grow, because I'd bitten the nail down so low, the tip of the finger would start to come over the nail. As a result, when the nail started to grow, it had a ridge. Fortunately, after about a year, this disappeared.

Nail biting can cause your nails and nail beds to weaken. Bacteria and fungi could enter these small cracks and lesions on your nails made by your persistent biting. Although some types of nail infections are easy to manage, others, like nail fungus, can be very hard to get rid of.

If you bite your nails, please stop! You might think it's a harmless habit, but it's not.

Tips to Stop Biting Your Nails

Eventually, I just had to stop, but it took time. It's the same with everything I do in life when I'm trying to change: I take little steps. Step-by-step, you will get there. Don't try to do it all at once, since you're just setting yourself up for failure.

When I stopped biting my nails, I didn't go "cold turkey." I started off by making one nail on my little finger (one I didn't especially like biting, anyway) off limits, so I was limited to just nine nails. Then I ruled out my ring fingers, then my thumbs. Slowly, I kept narrowing down which nails I could bite, until it was just my right pointer. Being able to stop chomping on that one took me another two years.

As my nails began to grow after years of neglect, I would see a little bit of nail and nurture it, file it, rub cream into it, and when that nail was starting to look good, I would move onto the next one. One thing I never did was use nail polish, because when it started to peel or needed a new coat, it was an invitation to start playing with it. I would pick at the polish to get it off without realizing that I was also picking the nail, and before I knew it, the nail would be gone again. Everywhere I went, I had a nail file. In the car, in my glasses case, next to the chair where I watch TV, in the drawer near the bed, in the drawer in the office, so if I felt a tear, I would file it off instead of biting it off.

Try to keep your hands busy, for example, when you're watching TV or talking on the phone. Squeeze a stress ball. And if you truly bite your nails (I was more of a "picker"), paint a bitter tasting polish on your nails. The awful taste will remind you to stop every time you start to bite.

I also recommend hypnosis. Although I did not use it for nail biting, I have used it to break other bad habits and found it extremely helpful. Hypnosis can be used to control and influence the subconscious mind, which begins to have a conscious effect in controlling the urge to bite nails.

As I mentioned, even after I stopped biting most of my nails, it took another two years to stop biting the right pointer. To stop once and for all, I made a New Year's Resolution and said, "As of 1st January, 2009 I will never bite that nail again!" And I never have. I still can't believe it. It was like when I stopped drinking. I said I would never do it again and, just like that, I haven't.

I now have beautiful nails and no inclination to bite or pick at them again. Instead, I am always filing and putting cream on them. I have some beautiful rings which before I would never wear, as they just drew attention to my messy hands. Now, after all these years, I can show them off with pride.

Health Risks Associated with Nail Biting

- Fingertips can be red and sore, and your cuticles can bleed.
- Increased risk for infections in and around your nail beds and in your mouth, including Staphylococcus.
- Bacteria found on your hands can cause stomach ache.
- Damage to teeth, dental problems and infections of the gums.
- Deformed nails, weak nails and nail beds.

Tips for Breaking the Nail Biting Habit

- If you are a true nail biter, try using a bitter tasting nail coating.
- Begin to narrow down which nails you bite or pick. Make some nails off limits. Slowly limit them until you're down to a couple.
- Take care of the nails as they start to grow back, but do not jump into wearing polish right away. Use nail creams, instead.
- Keep a nail file handy at all times to file down rough edges, as tears or rough spots are an invitation to start biting.
- Keep your hands busy; buy a stress ball, take up knitting, anything.
- Tell people around you what you're doing, so if they see you slipping, they can tell you.
- Consider hypnosis to help you break the habit.

Panic Attacks

Panic attacks are something I know all too well. I still get them at times, but I know what they are now, so when I feel one coming on, I go into a quiet space and just try to relax. I tell myself that I am not dying and eventually, I know it will go away.

As mentioned earlier, I was sitting for the real estate exam when I suffered a panic attack. And during the course, I was having a lot of trouble concentrating. I used to think it was just because I was getting older when, in fact, it was the result of the hormonal imbalance in my system.

When that exam paper was put in front of me, I found it even more difficult to focus. I felt disorientated and experienced a state of mental confusion. This was because I was going through a mid-life transition, and these symptoms can be further exacerbated for women (like me) who have undergone a hysterectomy.

Melanoma: A Health Scare

One night about 12 years ago, I happened to be watching TV and I saw something that literally stopped me in my tracks.

The program featured a young man walking around Australian beaches talking to people about melanoma, a deadly form of skin cancer. He showed viewers just what the spots looked like on his own body and, frankly, they didn't look that bad. He had told everyone that he had had just a small mole on his back, but by the time he went to see the doctor, it had spread. The doctor cut out as much as he could—the poor young man was cut from back to front—but it wasn't enough. He died a short time later.

This program saved a lot of lives, including mine.

I had a mole that I was all too happy to ignore. One day, I happened to be driving in my car with a girlfriend when she noticed that I kept scratching at it. She told me to have it checked by the doctor.

Yeah, yeah, I'll go when I get time, I thought to myself. Then I saw the TV program and thought I'd better go.

The doctor looked at the mole and took a biopsy. At the time, he said that it looked benign, but he would send the biopsy to the lab and let me know the results.

He called me just a few days later, and I will never forget that phone call.

I stood there dumbfounded as he told me, "You have a fast-growing melanoma on your arm and I have booked you in for surgery to have it cut out straight away." The doctor was serious; I was booked in the day after next! There wasn't time to waste.

I felt sick, as once again, it was the waiting game, which I hate. I always work myself into a panic and the worst part was it was the first time I'd ever seen Rob a mess. He was beside himself, thinking he was going to lose me.

I felt like I had bugs crawling through me. I couldn't sit still, couldn't sleep, and couldn't relax. I just couldn't wait to get the mole removed from my body. Knowing it was there and growing gave me the creeps.

The surgery itself was a breeze, just a simple outpatient procedure. After they'd numbed the area, I actually watched as they cut the mole out. And then they kept cutting and cutting to be certain they'd got all the cancer cells. After another period of waiting for lab results, to my relief, they told me they'd got all of it.

After the surgery, they told me to keep an eye on the spot and if I noticed anything different, or if I discovered lumps under my arms, I had to see the doctor immediately.

It has now been 12 years and I have had no other symptoms. If you get it taken care of quickly, melanoma is treatable.

Even with all the efforts to make the public aware of melanoma, tragedies still happen. Not too long ago, a young man in his early 30s from our hometown in Mandurah was diagnosed with a melanoma on his ankle. Six months later, he was dead.

Just recently, my son Kane was home from the mines when I saw him without his shirt on and noticed how many moles he had on his back. He also had a mole on his face that he said was itchy. I told him I wanted him to get checked out and got the usual, "Yeah, yeah, Mum, whatever." I made an appointment for him, which he missed, so the next time I booked him in, I made sure he went, and I also got checked myself. It was a really quick examination and everything was fine, but what if it hadn't been?

Gallstones: A Pain in the Back

I had been getting terrible pain across the lower part of my back for about six months. At the time, I had changed doctors, and the new doctor told me that I had slipped discs in my back.

The pain would get worse at night, right after dinner. One evening, I got up around 2.00 a.m. in excruciating pain and this time, it wasn't just my back, but also my right shoulder. I put a hot water bottle on it and took some painkillers, but the pain just wouldn't go away. By about 4.00 a.m., the pain had subsided enough for me to go back to bed.

The next day, I decided to see my old doctor, and as soon as he examined me, he knew what it was. Even so, he booked me to have an ultrasound.

Sure enough, it was gallstones. And I had acute cholecystitis, which is inflammation of the gallbladder caused by the duct being blocked by the gallstones. The bottom line was that I had to have my gallbladder removed.

I was in my 40s when this happened, but my daughter, Sharon, had to have her gallbladder out when she was only in her early 30s, so it can happen at any age.

What is the Gallbladder, and What Are the Symptoms of Gallstones?

The gallbladder is a small, pear-shaped organ on the underside of the liver in the right upper quadrant of the abdomen.

Its main function is to collect and store bile, which is used by the body to digest fats. The liver produces bile and the gallbladder stores it, then releases it when partially digested food is absorbed inside the small intestine. Bile is very important in the digestion of fat.

There are a variety of symptoms of gallstones, such as:

- Nausea
- Vomiting
- Indigestion
- Pain in the right upper abdomen, which can then go to the lower back
- Fever
- Abdominal bloating
- Severe heartburn and gas
- Diarrhea
- Jaundice
- Bad breath
- Clay-coloured stools (The lighter colour results from insufficient bile–that is, blocked gallbladder ducts).
- Itchy skin rashes
- A white-coated tongue
- Offensive body odour and yellowish skin
- Yellow, discoloured eyes, and dark circles beneath the eyes.

Diagnosed with Hypothyroidism

When I was young, my mother had a huge scar on her neck and when I asked her where it came from, she told me she'd had her thyroid taken out. That was all she ever said.

Now, I wish that I'd asked her more questions, because I ended up inheriting a thyroid condition from her.

At first, I didn't know I had a thyroid problem because it began acting up right when I was going through menopause. The symptoms are so similar that I just thought it was menopause.

At this time I decided to go to a doctor who uses natural products to help treat the symptoms. I told him I was feeling tired and fatigued, and that I was getting regular bouts of depression and just feeling sad. I had a feeling I was going through menopause, but I had no idea I was experiencing a thyroid problem, too.

Luckily for me, the doctor picked up on it and sent me for testing. Not all doctors are as good as him and not all connect the dots, so you have to ask to be tested. Also, symptoms of a thyroid problem are hard to detect and a lot of the time, go unnoticed.

I now take T3 triiodothyronine for my hypothyroidism. In the USA, this medication is called Cytomel. Since I have been taking these tablets, I feel so much better.

What the Thyroid Does

The thyroid gland regulates the rate of metabolism of the body. It is also known as the hormone factory of the body, as it manufactures a number of hormones for the body. T3 and T4 are the major hormones amongst them. Among various other things, these hormones control the body's metabolism and energy levels. If there is a lack of, or excess, of these hormones, the body fails to function properly.

While lack of these hormones makes the body sluggish and slow, an excess of them makes the person hyperactive, sending the body into overdrive.

The thyroid has to be taken care of properly, as damage to the thyroid ends up affecting the entire body over a period of time. Your brain might be affected in terms of memory loss and moodiness. Reproductive health, heart and body weight challenges are some of the issues that can occur with thyroid disorders. Often a factor of autoimmune problems, thyroid malfunction can go hand in hand with cholesterol problems. Your body may experience arthritis type pain, which diminishes as soon as the hormone levels are back to normal.

Hyperthyroidism is the result of an overactive thyroid and is less common than an underactive thyroid or hypothyroidism.

Hypothyroidism is referred to as a low thyroid or underactive thyroid. This is when the thyroid function is too sluggish, and one effect of this is that the metabolism of the body slows down. This is the condition that I have, which means I am hypothyroid. If you are having trouble losing weight no matter what you do, this could be the reason.

With this condition, the thyroid gland, a small butterfly shaped organ located at the base of the neck, does not produce enough hormone to function properly.

What happens is that the thyroid gland takes in iodine, combines it with tyrosine (an amino acid) and converts it into the hormones T4 and T3. If your thyroid is normal, 80% will be T4 and 20% T3. These hormones travel through the bloodstream, converting oxygen and calories into energy. If this process doesn't work properly, then the calories and oxygen cannot convert the energy properly and you may gain weight or be incapable of losing weight.

The following are other symptoms of as underactive thyroid, and next to them are the symptoms I had. These symptoms began when I first started to go through menopause.

- Hoarseness (*Yes, and this still occurs when I get tired or stressed.*)
- Depression (*Yes*)
- Dry and coarse skin
- Fatigue and weakness (*Yup, this one too.*)
- Weight gain (*Yes*)
- Low basal temperature, cold intolerance, cold hands and feet (*Yes*)

- High cholesterol
- Insomnia *(Yes)*
- Heavy menstrual periods
- Poor memory, forgetfulness, dementia *(Yes to all but dementia)*
- Immune system problems
- Nervousness and tremors
- Hair loss
- Sluggish bowels, constipation
- Low sex drive
- Tingling hands or feet
- Infertility
- You may even experience recurrent pregnancy loss
- Carpal tunnel syndrome
- Difficult menopause *(Yes)*
- Brittle nails

In the best-seller *What Your Doctor May NOT Tell You About Menopause*, Harvard-trained family physician Dr. John R. Lee explains his results in treating women with symptoms of thyroid problems. In a broad sense, estrogen makes calories from food to be stored as fat. Thyroid hormone makes calories from food to be converted into energy. Excess estrogen interferes with normal thyroid hormone function. Progesterone helps "oppose" and keep undesirable side effects of excess estrogen from happening.

Progesterone helps the body use fat for energy, and when progesterone is present in healthy levels, the thyroid functions more as it is supposed to. Dr. Lee found a clear pattern in his patients with a progesterone deficiency; their underactive thyroid symptoms lessened when natural progesterone supplementation was introduced and hormone balance was achieved.

When you are trying to lose weight, a lot comes down to your metabolism, and if you have untreated hypothyroidism, you will find no amount of dieting or exercise will take the weight off. You may, in fact, put on weight.

I have always had a weight problem, as you know, and I have only just begun to understand what my body needs.

To help myself lose weight, I've found that a low-calorie diet, spread over the day, is necessary to keep my metabolism up. With hypothyroidism patients, a combination of low calories and lower metabolism can send the body into "hoard" mode.

Now, I break up calories into 4-5 meals a day, eating every 2 ½ to 4 hours. You have to focus on low glycaemic foods and those with high fibre, and of course, low calories. (Check out my previous chapter on diet.) I have found that by doing this, plus taking my T3 tablets and regular exercise, the weight comes off.

If you have a thyroid disorder, don't be discouraged. The symptoms can be painful and drag you down. It is important to get the help you need.

You can live with a thyroid disorder; just try and avoid stress, rest, eat a healthy diet, exercise, enjoy life and enjoy every moment.

> *(Disclaimer–The information presented here should not be interpreted as medical advice. If you suspect you have a thyroid problem, please consult your physician as early as possible for diagnosis and treatment options.)*

"You were put on this earth to achieve your greatest self, to live out your purpose, and to do it courageously."

—*Steve Maraboli*

Finding Your Purpose

As I near the end of my story, I would like to talk about purpose and the importance it played in my new journey, which began with Nutrimetics.

When you join Nutrimetics, they ask you to find your purpose, write it down, and then set your goals.

But how could I set a goal when I had zero vision of my purpose?

I simply didn't know how to do it. At the time I was bankrupt, and afraid the future didn't look too rosy. When all I was doing was just surviving day to day, I couldn't think of where I wanted to go.

First, I had to learn the difference between a dream and a goal.

Dreams are what you wish for and there is no time frame. Dreams just sit there, and they may or may not happen. You know this, but you dream about them, anyway. I never had 'expensive' dreams like owning a boat or flashy cars, because to me, those things seemed far out of my reach.

On the other hand, there are goals. Goals are an outgrowth of your dreams, but a goal has a specific deadline. So, you dream about something, then by putting a deadline on it, it turns into a goal… Yes, I could do that!

And the difference between a purpose and a goal? Well, a purpose is a dream or a goal that is never-ending. It has no deadline, no beginning, no end. It is a guiding principal.

I was still having trouble with "my purpose," so I started by setting some goals. And what amazed me when I finally set these—and they were only little ones at first—was that after I wrote them down, believed I could achieve them, visualized them, repeated them every day, my goals came true. But I was getting stuck on finding my purpose. I really didn't know why I was on this planet. Yes, I felt I was put here to be more than a wife and mother, friend or grandmother—but what? What could that purpose be?

In search of this, I attended many life-changing seminars and of these, Anthony Robbins is one person who taught me so much. He took me through the process of finding "me," which is a book in and of itself. If you can't get to one of his seminars, you might buy one of Anthony's books, and I highly recommend *Awaken the Giant Within*.

I won't take you through that whole journey, other than to say it's a step-by-step process. And to find your purpose, you must talk about your values and goals, the building blocks of your passion and dreams.

How do you think?

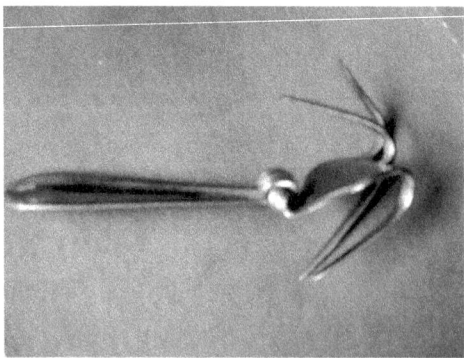

Many of the limitations we face in life are self-imposed. What you believe about yourself can keep you locked behind your fears or push you forward into living your dreams.

I was in a very bad space for a long time, I had no faith in myself, and it is only because I decided to step away from my old beliefs and move forward, that I was able to break the chains. I did this because I didn't want to feel the pain any more; the feeling of failure can destroy you. It takes courage and commitment, but you can do it. I did it, and so can you.

With years of conditioning to undo, moving forward wasn't easy. Actually, it was damn hard, not only getting rid of the beliefs, but the whole process.

What you create through your thoughts is a belief system, and that belief system ultimately determines whether you live a successful and fulfilling life. If your belief system believes you are going to live a life of poverty, then most definitely, you will!

The key to changing your belief system is changing your thoughts. You become whatever you believe you are. So you *need* to think wonderful things about yourself. If you believe you are worthless, you will be worthless.

After a while, I began to believe I was worth more and could do more, even if I had no idea how to get there.

On the internet, I came across Orison Swett Marden, who wrote *How to Get What You Want.* In this book, Marden stresses:

"Stop thinking trouble if you want to attract its opposite; stop thinking poverty if you wish to attract plenty. Refuse to have anything to do with the things you don't want. Instead you must think about those things you want to attract."

Marden writes about how much our thoughts influence the outcome of our life. To paraphrase Marden, how often do we hear people talk about someone, saying, "Everything that person does succeeds!" or "Everything he touches turns to gold"? Why? Because, that person can *visualize* the success of all their work, and they are backing up their vision by their efforts. Marden states that by clinging to your vision, by vigorous resolution and persistent, determined Endeavour, you are continually making yourself a powerful magnet to draw your own to yourself. Consciously or unconsciously, you are using the divine intelligence or force by the use of which every human being may mould himself and his environment according to the pattern in his mind.

Our mind is such a powerful tool! At a seminar I attended, everyone in the audience was asked to hold onto a fork–which wasn't flimsy–and relax their minds. We were told to visualize a big, burning ball above our head and feel its heat go into our body, down our arm, into our hand and then into the fork. It was amazing; I could feel my arm getting hot, and then my fingertips got so hot that I twisted the fork three times, as though it were made of soft metal. Then I took the prongs and bent them back. Once that fork cooled down, there was no way you could change its shape back. Every now and again I pull that fork out to remind myself of just what the mind can do.

How does a purpose make you feel?

When you find your purpose, it's as though a light bulb has been turned on. It pushes you out of bed in the morning, and what might have been drudgery for you just a day before, is now grand opportunity and discovery. You are on fire! Purpose gives meaning to why you're doing what you're doing. It pushes your ambition through the roof. Your purpose will provide your inner drive and can give your life immense fulfillment and certainty, a life full of meaning.

Your purpose taps into passion, inspiration and commitment on a grand scale, and being able to know and communicate your purpose to yourself and others is what sustains it.

Listen to that voice talking to you. Don't listen to the people trying to pull you off track, criticising you! Don't let anyone steal your dream or pull you down. With purpose, there are no negativities; you have now found that passion, you know what you want and you are going to go for it. This is what you live for.

You must recognize the unique gift of "you." You're an individualized, phenomenal expression of life. There is only one of you. You are special, because there is no one on this planet like you.

Everyone on earth has a purpose. When you have the right purpose, you'll easily develop the right vision. When you have the right vision, you'll quickly recognize the right goal. Step-by-step, you will find it. I never thought I would, but I have.

When I was at school, I didn't get good grades in certain subjects, mainly because they bored me, but I did get good grades in others, because I enjoyed–and in some cases, loved–what I was doing.

Life is like this. If you enjoy your "work," for example, that's wonderful; it means you look forward to going to your job. But what if you hate it, and every morning when you wake up, you are filled with dread?

I believe we are all on this planet for a reason, a purpose, a mission, and most people have difficulty getting focused on what it is they're here for, because they are already doing something else, day in, day out.

Working 9-to-5 can often block your progress towards that better and higher use of your time and talents. I have seen it so many times: people who are talented, but they get stuck or afraid and don't move towards what they really want to do, their purpose. They think, "Who is going to pay the bills?" And "it's better to be safe than sorry." They are caught up in the trap of making a living rather than designing a life. I admit that I did it, too.

This is where your "balance" comes in, enabling you to do both.

On the journey of finding your purpose, you have to make sure that your basic needs are met, but you must understand the difference between what you want and what you really need in order to move forward. In other words, if you don't yet have the money to sustain yourself and your family, don't quit your job to follow your purpose. For my whole journey, starting with Nutrimetics, Rob always worked and supported me. He knew it was something I had to do and not once did he stop me. That is one reason I love him so.

Don't listen to the naysayers who complain, "I know what I'm good at and what I love to do, but I can't make money from it." Don't even think about the money side of things. If you think your purpose is drawn towards money, it shouldn't be. You are not here for that.

There are so many people who will focus on you and what you're doing because it distracts them from the disappointment of their own lives. But you are different. You want to be creative; you want to have passion in your life, that fire in your belly that gets you moving.

In order to do this, you have to get rid of all negativity–and especially that "failure mentality."

Your purpose taps into inspiration, passion and commitment on a grand scale. While I am not an especially creative person, when I knew what I wanted, my creativity exploded! I don't know where all the ideas were coming from, but they just kept on coming.

Once I had found my purpose, I started to create in my mind my vision for the future: what it meant to me, how I wanted it to look, what I wanted to achieve and who I wanted to become, and this led me to put a strategy in place and set my goals. Setting goals keeps you on track, and you find you start to move forward.

The process

Let me share with you what worked for me.

I identified a time when I could have a few hours alone and uninterrupted. I found a comfortable spot where I knew nobody could disturb me. I took out a pen and paper, burned some lavender, and allowed myself to think.

I had a lot of "stuff" in my head I needed to thrash out. I wanted to find my purpose, and really, it wasn't so long ago that I didn't even believe there was such a thing.

So the first thing you need to believe is that you are here for a reason, and next, you are going to identify it.

Put aside time when you know you'll be alone. On top of a sheet of paper, write, "What is my true purpose in life?"

Now, close your eyes and think about that question, then let the answers flow. Don't judge yourself or think that anything is too silly.

Just think. The answers that come to you can be anything—words, sentences, or drawings. Just write. You may end up with a lot of rubbish, but eventually, the true answers will start coming through. You may get similar answers. It doesn't matter; just keep asking the question and writing.

Think back to when you were a child. What did you want to be when you grew up? Why? Who was your role model and why? Try to understand why you wanted to be this or that.

Think of a time when you were on a roll and thought, "Life is fantastic!" How did you feel? What did you see? What were you experiencing, what were you doing? Try to smell it, hear it, see it and taste it. Were you writing, singing, dancing? Helping someone?

Now, take yourself back to being a child again, a child that can have anything he or she wants. You only have to express your heart's desire and it will instantly be yours. What is it?

If you think of something, but some little voice says, "You can't do that," write it down, anyway. (I have done things that never, even in my wildest dreams, did I think I could accomplish.)

Or you may hear nothing but dead silence. You may think nothing is coming through, that this process isn't working; you may get impatient and think this is ridiculous. Push this aside and keep listening. If anything you write brings up strong emotions, circle it and keep writing.

You may be looking for something huge. You may think it needs to be massive, but it might not be. A life of significance is a life of growth and contribution. The biggest struggle will be getting out of the old level to the next level. This is the growing process. Stick with it. You may be scared or nervous about getting to the next level, so you procrastinate or don't really push yourself. The worst part is getting started. It's not too hard; just remember why you are doing this.

One thing I will say is: don't get so caught up with planning and charting your future that you never begin living it. Smell the roses.

I have been to quite a few seminars and talked to many people. You often see the same faces, and I like to find out how people are doing. Sometimes people go to all the seminars, read all the books, and do the planning, but they just can't step out of their comfort zone and move forward. They get stuck because, while they are going to the seminars, they do nothing with the knowledge they are acquiring.

What are you willing to sacrifice or endure for your purpose and mission on this planet? What would you sacrifice in order to move into a new life, in order to obtain your dream of doing what you love every day? Your purpose in this lifetime is to do the thing that you love to do. If you don't love it, don't do it. Simple.

Without your purpose identified firmly in your mind, you will wander through life, never quite feeling right.

There is so much change around us, but if you find something deep inside of yourself, it doesn't matter what happens in the outside world; that part of you does not change. You can't change disasters or death, but you can control what you do. If you have your values in place and a purpose, this will pull you through.

When I went through alcoholism, my first bankruptcy and other afflictions, I didn't have these ideals in place because back then, I had never heard of them. This was a whole new world for me, so it took me longer to get to where I am now. If I had known of this world – a world with purpose–earlier, I believe I'd have been successful a lot more quickly.

Of course, discovering your purpose is the easy part. The difficult part is keeping it in mind on a daily basis and working on yourself to the point where you *become* that purpose. I have struggled with this aspect, and felt guilty. Don't get so busy with everyday life that your purpose and goals are forgotten or put on hold.

And whatever you do, don't overanalyze things. It makes life more stressful, and sweating the small stuff gets you nowhere. I tend to be like this and sometimes, it can be a good thing, but you mustn't analyze things so much that you do nothing about anything. Don't suffer from "analysis paralysis."

As many wise souls have said: It's not the destination, it's the journey that counts.

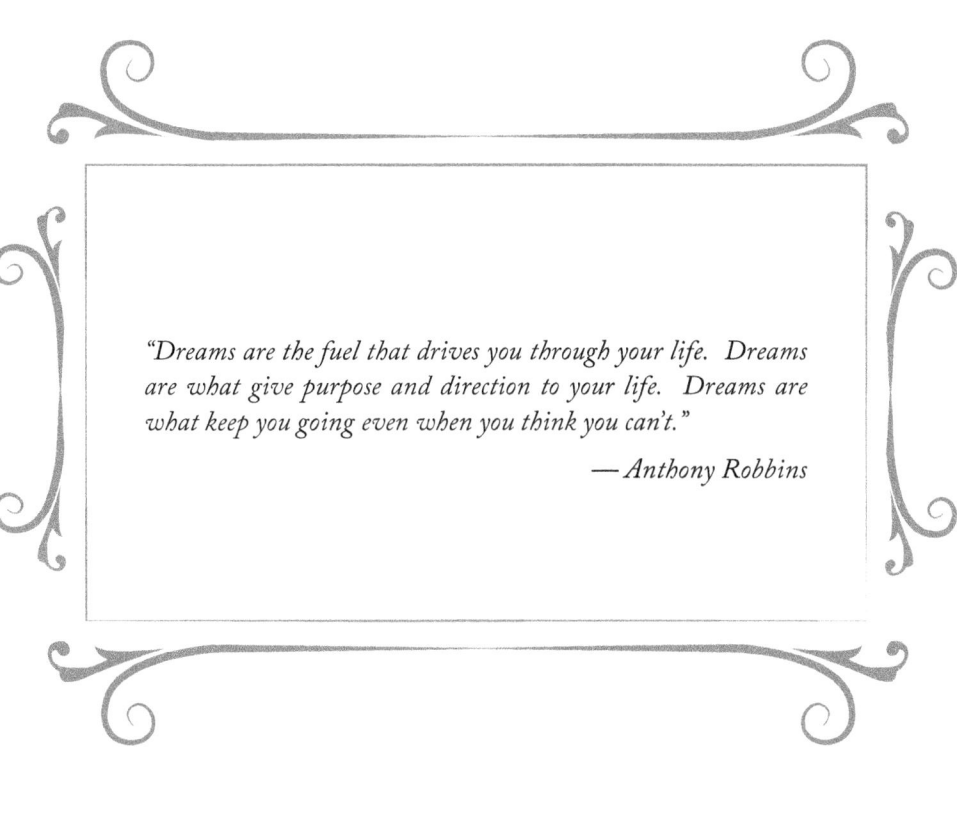

"Dreams are the fuel that drives you through your life. Dreams are what give purpose and direction to your life. Dreams are what keep you going even when you think you can't."

— *Anthony Robbins*

Ingredients for Success

Every great journey begins with a journey of possibilities, and the following is a summary of all I have learned in the hope that it will both inspire and guide you on your way to a healthy, fulfilling and happy life—one where you find your true purpose.

First, as stated, you need to have a purpose, and your passion will drive that purpose. A goal is a purpose in action. Visualise your goals, and this will subconsciously act as a powerful motivator. You can't lose if you know where you are going.

When I was going for my Nutrimetics car, I visited a car yard and had a photo taken in front of the same model of car I was aiming to earn through Nutrimetics. I got into the car to get the feel and smell of it. I took a photo of the car, and pasted a Nutrimetics logo on the door of the car in the photo so it looked just like the real one I wanted so badly. I visualised myself in the car. I could smell the leather and feel the newness of the car. As far as I was concerned, it was already mine.

I believe money itself doesn't amount to success. Love what you do and the money will follow, and along with that will come success. My father was a pioneer of Mandurah and all I wanted was to sit down with him and hear his life story, but it never happened. He was too busy when I was growing up, and when I was a working adult, I was too busy for him. It was a vicious circle, and when we lost him, I was devastated. Hence the old saying: "Most people spend most of their lives earning a living rather than designing a lifestyle." I intend to change this with my children and grandchildren.

Goals, resilience, sense of humour

Goals will give you a purpose and direction. Remind yourself of your infinite power and perfection in order to develop the right attitude for success.

Have your goal–whatever is important to you–written down and embedded in your mind. Push yourself out of that comfort zone and keep pushing.

Have a burning fire in your belly.

Have a desire in your heart and believe it. It can all be yours.

All of this gives you strength and when you have strength, watch out! The sky is the limit.

If you encounter challenges, you need to pick yourself up and start again. Life is like being in a boxing ring; sometimes the punches come from all directions. You have to be able to handle the blows and bounce back.

Over the years, my desire and my goals have been so strong that I've smashed down any brick walls that got in the way of achieving them.

Of course, you will find that when you want something, or you're moving towards your goal, a lot of obstacles will get in your way. How I overcame this was by focusing on the job at hand, and everything around me seemed to sort itself out.

Develop the ability to laugh at yourself and have fun. And when those brick walls get in your way, just say, "The universe is testing me again," and laugh it off.

Setbacks are part of growing and developing. I have learned that as long as you are prepared to learn and grow, you will succeed.

Don't compare yourself with others; compete with yourself. Challenge yourself!

Competition can be a very strong motivator. I have experienced how it becomes most powerful when you compete with yourself and when you learn from your setbacks.

Take responsibility for yourself.

Like any business, it takes consistent time, effort and appreciation to develop. What I am doing now, writing my book and building my website, is still my business. There are no shortcuts, and building something takes and needs considerable hard work and long hours.

Remember: If it's to be, it's up to me.

Motivation, determination, energy

It might be a desire for money, freedom, status, a flexible lifestyle or independence. No matter what you want, you must *want* to be a winner to succeed.

All the right techniques and ingredients won't get you to the winning line without an inner need for achievement.

Self-motivation is key. People can inspire you, but you need to learn to motivate yourself, with books, CDs, whatever, with energy and enthusiasm.

You need to do whatever it takes.

And you need energy to achieve great goals. Energy is a by-product of loving your work, being enthusiastic and having the desire to achieve. If you love what you do, you'll never work another day in your life.

Belief in yourself, enthusiasm and self respect

Believe that you deserve success. Believe that you have the talent and skills to achieve that success.

With the quality of self belief, you will draw people to you. It is a very contagious quality. It attracts like a magnet.

Love yourself; enjoy your own company. Put a value on your time, effort and energy. This is where time management is very important.

Believe in yourself and trust yourself. Act confidently until you feel it inside.

Fake it until you make it.

Commitment and persistence

When you make a commitment to a project, things will start to happen. Stick with an idea to the end, no matter what. Commitment to your goals will always be tested. Almost as soon as the ink is dry on your goal sheet, your commitment will be tested. Someone or something will stand in the way of you achieving your goals. I call these objections "brick walls." Learn to go over the wall, or climb under it, or smash through it. But don't let it stop you. This is just a test, of you and your commitment to your task. If there isn't a brick wall, then maybe you haven't asked enough of yourself. Motivate yourself and get on with it.

You'll notice how quickly an obstacle will dissolve when you are totally committed. Commitment and tenacity are two strong elements in goal setting. They enable you to be empowered and to empower others to succeed with their chosen goals.

Believe me, it can be hard, but it can be done and only you can do it. It's worth it.

Why must life be difficult? Why can't we all just sail on smoothly through the ocean of experience? Well, without a "down," we would never appreciate the true meaning of an "up." Without a challenge, why would we ever bother to bring about chance? Without doubt, how would we ever appreciate certainty?

Have staying power. Never take no for an answer. Always stay with it. Break down those brick walls.

Initiative and risk taking ability

Be proactive. Nothing happens unless you make it happen. Learn to be the captain of your ship, the master of your own destiny.

Without being a gambler, you need to take risks to develop your business. You need to step out of that comfort zone and feel the pain.

You need a sense of adventure and you need to take responsibility for your actions if things don't work out.

It's like when we went bankrupt; if I had taken more responsibility for the way the hotel was run, I believe things would have turned out differently. With risk comes responsibility.

A poor man said, "I work hard for my money." A rich man said, "My money words hard for me."

Planning and preparation

Make sure you plan so that you can acquire the knowledge, skills and assistance you will need to reach your goals. Don't be afraid to ask for help. Plan your work and your time, and you will achieve order and organization in your life. Set to work and enjoy the energising effects of action.

Time-planning teaches you to be effective. It allows you to spend more of your time doing things that are of most value, being a mother/father, wife/husband, lover or friend, or just having time to be yourself.

There is no way you can plan your day-to-day existence without knowing what you want to achieve in your life.

First, work out what you want. List your priorities and then break these down into day-to-day projects.

Plan your time and plan your life

Waste your time, and you waste your life.

Planning cuts out worry, anxiety, tension, and you don't have that pressured feeling that everything is on top of you.

Become aware of how you spend your time, and use those spare ten and fifteen minutes constructively.

Pre-plan everyday and you will experience a tremendous sense of achievement as you cross out each task that has been accomplished, no matter how menial. I even write down things like laundry, shopping, cleaning, and if I do something that isn't on my list, I write that down, too, then cross it off. It means that I have achieved even more!

Do the difficult jobs first.

You will find the more organised you are, the more spare time you will have to spend with the people you love, and the more time you will have for fun.

Pace yourself to reduce stress.

Make sure you give yourself time to plan.

My youngest son lost 30 kilos and he is my mentor. I know I will soon get back to my ideal weight.

Meditate, practice relaxation techniques daily. If nothing else, do some deep breathing.

Balance your life between your needs, your work and your family commitment.

This is a poem by Brian Adams.

- *With discipline*
- *Comes organisation*
- *Strength of purpose*
- *Determination and success*
- *Without discipline*
- *There is disorganisation*
- *Confusion and failure*
- *Carry each job to completion*
- *To do this is to avoid confusion.*
- *Back your organised effort*
- *With enthusiasm*
- *Faith and integrity*
- *Disorganisation means overload*
- *You must learn to say no to certain things*
- *Juggle tasks*
- *Try not to be everything to everyone*
- *Don't blame others for you lack of time*
- *Do it right, do it right now*
- *Do this and you will not only succeed but you will GROW.*

Resourcefulness and discipline

You will need to find creative ways to solve problems and do more with less. You will need to use resources more economically.

Business is a matter of solving problems. When the problems stop, business stops.

You need to exercise common sense to solve problems with minimum time, energy, and expenditure.

You need to be flexible in your approach, because if you become obsessed with one idea, it might block your ability to see another solution.

Living Life does not happen without consistent effort. We need to invest regular time, effort and resources.

Creativity, a desire to learn and knowledge

We are all creative; you just need to dig deep. For every problem, there is a solution. Keep looking until you find it. You will make mistakes, but through trial and error, you will learn and grow. You will discover what works and what doesn't. I sure did!

You need to keep reading, learning new skills and finding better ways to develop your mind. Stay open, aware and receptive.

I've spent many thousands of dollars on seminars, books, DVDs and CDs to feed my mind, and as a bonus, I've met some incredible people along the way. If I hadn't had done all of this, I wouldn't have the knowledge I have now. So don't be afraid to ask the questions, and ask for help when you need it.

In order to succeed, you need knowledge. Once you have mastered how to obtain knowledge, the world is your oyster. And like a parachute, your mind will only work if it's open. If you are close-minded, you are blocking out knowledge.

Knowledge is one of life's greatest gifts. But it means nothing unless you do something with it. Knowledge isn't power – action is power, and applied knowledge is power.

Self-made "Luck" and integrity

I hate it when people say to me, "You are so lucky!" I believe you make your own luck. Through action, effort, and the process of DOING, you get lucky. And integrity ensures you will be in business for a long time. Do business with the idea you will develop honest, ongoing relationships with customers, building a rapport. Look for win-win opportunities in your dealings.

Build your value and the money will follow. **Life is not about waiting for the storm to pass, it's about learning to dance in the rain!**

Good luck with your goals and may your dreams become reality.

INGREDIENTS FOR SUCCESS

- ☐ Vision and loving what you do
- ☐ Goals, resilience and a sense of humour
- ☐ Motivation, determination and energy
- ☐ Belief in yourself, enthusiasm and self-respect
- ☐ Commitment and persistence
- ☐ Initiative and risk-taking ability
- ☐ Planning and preparation
- ☐ Resourcefulness and discipline
- ☐ Creativity, a desire to learn and knowledge
- ☐ Self-made "luck" and integrity

(Check off which ingredients you already have. This will show you what you need to work on.)

"When you want something, all the universe conspires in helping you to achieve it"

— *Paulo Coelho*

TAKING STOCK

Past hurts and past experiences have made me move forward and write this book so that I can inspire as many people as possible, so you don't have to go through what I have. Or, if you have experienced the same hardships, I can let you know that not all is lost and you can move forward and have a wonderful life.

You have read my stories but I am going to share with you just a few points about how it all turned out. It is a bit involved, but you'll get the idea. I want to show you that I am a real person who went through both ups and downs in life and business.

Writing this book involved sitting with my sister, conjuring up all my childhood memories and realizing it wasn't all in my head. Mine wasn't a pleasant childhood, but I made the best of it. Actually, on my own or with my friends, I had a fantastic time–so many adventures and so many 'cubbies'. I don't blame my parents, because they didn't know any different, but it made me aware that I should show much love and support to my own children, freely and unconditionally. In addition, I have a relationship with Rob that is totally satisfying and filled with love and respect. I love my children, grandchildren and Rob with all my heart and soul and believe it is the journey I have been through that has brought me to this place.

Boarding school taught me that I am capable of doing things without any help, I just have to try. And it taught me skills that I needed, such as dressmaking.

When we lost the hotel, it took me on a voyage of finding myself, stepping out of my comfort zone and making a life of my own. By leaving the hotel, I got further away from the world of alcohol that I once inhabited. And I realized that Rob loved me for me, and not what I had.

When I went bankrupt, both times it forced me to acquire knowledge on finances and taught me how to "go without." If it weren't for this, I would never have moved forward financially to acquire the knowledge and education I needed and the motivation to challenge myself. This I had to learn the second time around, because "I hadn't learnt the lesson yet", and that lesson was that I don't need "stuff" to be happy; I am happy with my family and life.

When I gave up drinking, well, what can I say? It changed my life, it cleared my head, I could think straight. Rob and I stopped that vicious cycle of fighting which, in turn, saved our marriage.

Looking back on my life, I believe the alcoholism, bulimia, slimming tablets, the Zoloft (for depression) and sleeping tablets were all connected.

First it was bulimia. I didn't want to be that overweight child any more, so at 15, I started to make myself sick. I wasn't doing it often, but when my marriage fell apart and I joined the party scene, it escalated.

When my first marriage broke down and I was feeling low, a psychologist put me on Zoloft, even though I wasn't diagnosed with depression. I tried to get off the drug, but that made me feel worse, so for years I was on and off anti-depressants.

Next came the drinking, and I became seriously depressed, with no self-esteem. I had feelings of worthlessness, and thought I was a failure.

I was never obese, but took slimming tablets to keep up with the party scene, to give me a buzz and keep going. And I took sleeping tablets regularly, just to get some sleep.

It wasn't until late in my 30s that I set out to stop all of these addictions and was able, step-by-step, to set myself free.

Thinking back to my alcoholic days, depression, and attempted suicide, it was a really bad place, but it built me into who I am today. I can relate to my children, especially Kane, and help them get through hard times. Because I have been in Kane's situation, I can understand his feelings and his pain, give him advice and guide him. I believe if I hadn't been through all of this myself, I wouldn't have been able to help him. Today, he has grown into a positive person whose life passion is to help and inspire people to overcome their difficulties like he has, because he also has been there and done it, can relate to it all, and he, too, wants to share this with others.

I think about my relationships with men: my father, my brother, Bruce and everyone I met until Rob came into my life. By going through all that hurt, I learned to love and respect myself, which I didn't do before. I opened myself up and it is now so easy to give love, and respect others. And through it all, I have come to love, respect and appreciate Rob with my whole soul.

It wasn't until writing this book, and especially the chapter about my hysterectomy, that I realized that once I couldn't rely on my biological ability to create connections, I had to find a new method of creating connections.

That is what I am doing here.

If I have anything I need to work on personally, I now know not to leave it, thinking it will just go away. More than likely it won't—and my stories attest to that! I always go to the doctor and get checked if I have a problem, and I make sure my children and husband do the same. I know that doing this has probably saved our lives, and in other cases, explained what we were going through, which made it more manageable. Health issues don't take over my life and make me miserable. I deal with them.

When I began working with Nutrimetics, it changed my whole way of thinking. It put me on a path of self-discovery, of wanting to grow, of wanting more out of life, and not just in a money or material sense. I want a full, rich life in a spiritual way.

It also introduced me to the world of Anthony Robbins, the teachings of such greats as Napoleon Hill and many other great people. Going to seminars and reading books changed my direction.

Real estate took me to a whole new level of finance, a world I never thought I would love. It really took me to the next level, a level I tried, thought I enjoyed and loved. Eventually, however, I found this wasn't the path I was meant to be on.

When we were forced to sell our home, it made me realize I should not be complacent. Once again, it pushed me to search for more knowledge so that I could grow.

My backpacking adventure with my son Ryan–well, what can I say? If you ever have a chance to do something like this with your children, grab it with both hands and go for it; it was the best! We bonded, had fun and really got to know each other–and overcame the fear of terrorism.

Being there for the birth of my grandchildren is something so beautiful and wonderful. To share this experience with my daughter, Sharon…well, words will never explain the deep love I have for them all.

My daughter's stroke, Kane's problems, Ryan losing his job–I have been there for them all and it has made me appreciate and love my children even more. All these things brought us closer.

By writing the chapter on weight and bulimia, I had to go back to a place I wanted to forget. Actually, this is true for most of the book! And, yes, a lot of stories resurfaced that I am not proud of. For me to write what I did, I had to do a little bit of research on exercise and eating, along with other areas. I have learned a huge amount about nutrition, menopause, and so on. It has been one really exciting journey and I've found that I want to keep on learning, especially about eating healthy and fitness. You are capable of achieving anything with a strong, healthy body.

Once I made up my mind and got rid of those 'excuses,' I wanted to change. First, it was all about fitness, weight, and healthy eating (we were eating healthy food, just a bit too much of it!), then my total existence was raised to a level of fulfilment and freedom that I never thought possible.

I am not quite where I want to be yet with my weight and level of fitness; it's a slow journey, but that is the way I like it. I am comfortable with my 'new mind' and I'll never think about dieting again. No longer will the scales rule me, nor will I ever try to lose a huge amount of weight in a week. It's now about lifestyle for me. I truly believe a strong healthy mind resides in a strong healthy body.

Life is so short and that is why I have taken steps to become fit and healthy, so I can have not just a longer life, but a life of fun, loving and enjoyment, with energy right up to the day I die. Just to restate, I don't want to be an 'old nanna.'

Kane called me last night. He said, "I'm just ringing to tell you how much I love you." His mate's mother had just died. Rob and I and the children always tell each other, "I love you" at the end of every phone call. Those three little words mean so much. Life is so short.

Learning how to set up a website, social media, the internet, still overwhelms me. It is my passion, and yes it is hard, and yes I have to outsource quite a lot, as I don't understand it, but it is a win win situation. Not only am I learning, but I am also helping other people make a living. And with the feedback they give me, I know I am making a difference in their lives.

You are never too old to try new things. Rob and I are living proof of this. Keep moving and you will keep living.

When I hit a brick wall, I think about why I have hit it. Is it stopping me so that I will think about the direction I am going? Or is it so that when I break through, I will move forward? Or is it both?

I believe it is both, and when it happens to me, I look at both scenarios.

I now take time to think, change my attitude, refuel and put a plan into action.

I have learned to think before I leap. If you are about to jump, but you're not sure if it is right, take a deep breath and think.

To get to where I am now, I have taken little steps. When you have huge goals that seem too far to reach, if you don't take little steps to get there, it becomes such a huge task that you are just setting yourself up for failure.

I needed to find my purpose and I did, and now I am on a journey that I truly love. Before, I was floundering and going nowhere. Finding my purpose has given me energy and excitement.

We spend thousands of dollars attending workshops and courses, and reflecting on our lives to understand ourselves. Who would have thought that as a result of writing this book, I would also be purging past experiences? Perhaps the best way to solve a problem is by writing a journal or just working things through on paper. I have just done that with my life, and the insights and perspective I have gained by taking the time to actually do this have been therapeutic.

They say life's a journey, not a destination, and mine has been just that. I discovered that the reason for this journey was to discover who I am and my life's purpose.

It was interesting putting my life on paper and seeing where I was and where I am now. I now believe quite strongly that if I could come through all of this, *anyone can*, and if I can make the journey less difficult for someone, that will be the ultimate. I have the power to help and inspire others because I have been there and done that, and that is the journey I truly want to take.

Don't try to do it all at once. It has taken me years and years. Remember, step-by-step and you will achieve anything your heart desires.

The wonderful people I have met on this journey have been exceptional! When you step into the world of self-discovery, it opens up a whole new world of exceptional, helpful people.

Being there for my children, grandchildren and Rob is my priority. If they need me, I am there, and nothing gets in the way! Words can only say so much, but hugs, kisses and support mean so much more.

My husband and children have always believed in me, and over the years, they have helped me so much. Now, as a family, we can reap the rewards, our precious time together. Over the years I had robbed myself of this simple pleasure. I have had to go through years of reconditioning in all areas of my life, weight, finances, health, self esteem and more.

But now, I have found 'me' again, and I am in control of my life.

> "There is no scarcity of opportunity to make a living at what you love; there's only scarcity of resolve to make it happen".
>
> —Wayne Dyer

You have come to the end of my book, but not the end of my journey. There is a lot more to learn and do at 63! We are still young, with a lot of life left in us yet.

I would like to thank you for taking this journey with me. I hope I have inspired you in some way and if I have, I would love to hear from you.

If I can help in any way, I am here.

> You can contact me through my website: http://www.inspirational-quotes-and-thoughts.com/
>
> Facebook page: www.facebook.com/inspirationalquotesandthoughts
>
> Twitter: www.twitter.com/moyamulvay
>
> Pinterest: https://au.pinterest.com/moyamulvay/
>
> You Tube https://www.youtube.com/TheQuotesandthoughts,
>
> Instagram https://www.instagram.com/moya_mulvay/
>
> or send me an email: moya@inspirational-quotes-and-thoughts.com

GO OUT AND MAKE IT HAPPEN FOR YOU, TOO! AND LIVE WITH PASSION!

Wishing you the best of Success, Love and Laughter

—Moya

Life begins when you open your true nature.

Epilogue

I wrote this book and created my colouring books to inspire and guide people, to help.

At first, the word "help" scared me, as helping is a huge job. I felt as though I would be taking on the world and worried that I might fail doing it. It has taken me years to get out of failure, and I don't want to go back there. I knew this task would take all my focus and energy, and worried that my "balance" would be gone.

But looking at and tapping into my desire to inspire people has given it a whole new meaning.

The past few years have been one hell of an emotional roller coaster ride for us and I've worked so hard to get to where I am now. But it has been and is a pleasurable journey. The ultimate pleasure in life sometimes requires short term pain to reach it, and that ultimate pleasure is who you become.

I have learned along the journey that self esteem comes from facing challenges. I've learned to ask the question: How can I use that pain to move forward? By learning from it. I don't look back and dwell on the past.

I am here now, but I live in the future. I am always one step ahead of myself. I need challenges in my life and by looking for them, I am always growing, always creating, modifying and improving my vision of the future.

The moral of this story is you can do whatever you want—you just have to want to do it.

And there is the inspirational story about my husband Rob:

Rob's worked most of his life as a bricklayer and is now 63. He has had a knee reconstruction and his body is full of aches and pains. He was getting too old for the job that he had been doing all his life.

Unfortunately, both of us still had to work. Our son-in-law was a ranger in our area and Rob talked to Andrew quite often about becoming a ranger himself.

I never really thought he was serious. But yes, my man was serious and he was going to do it!

Do you remember how hard it was when you first learned to drive a car, and how it became second nature to you once you got used to it? Well for 40 years, Rob was like that with his bricklaying job. Even though he had to read plans and set out the job and use his brains, it was simply second nature.

Now, because of the physical limitations that his age had brought upon him, he decided it was time for him to go easy on his bricklaying job and get started on becoming a ranger. He put a plan in action, booking into a two-week course for the rangers. He had to study, read, write and take exams, which he aced–and here is a man who hadn't studied for 48 years!

He worked all week. From Monday to Friday, he would do bricklaying and then, on weekends, work experience with Andrew. Saturday was a 12-hour work day and Sunday an 8-hour shift. And he loved it!

He has now started as a full time casual ranger. Even though he is used to physical work and now has more mentally demanding work, he is determined to make it work, and I know he will. The only thing that is holding him back is not being able to use the computer, but I am teaching him that, and typing, too–the right way, so he will have an edge over everyone else. I am so proud of him for taking this step, for stepping out of his comfort zone. He loves the work, and so does his body. A whole new adventure and career at 63!

Remember, you are never too old to move forward.

I can't deny that the future scares me. Just like having your first child, you are not always sure you are doing the right thing, but all you can do is try. I do things in baby steps, and that is how I've arrived here. Just like raising your child, it is a learning process along the way.

Through this book, I have shared my journey and how I overcame the obstacles along the way. My next journey is just another chapter for me, and I will conquer it, step-by-step. I am now going to take a deep breath, look at the whole picture and put some action in place.

After all, it's not about the destination. It's about the journey. That is what excites me now.

Appendix I

"It's not about getting what you want, it's about experiencing what you really need by becoming more."

—*Anthony Robbins*

The Men in My Life

I decided to include this chapter at the back of my book, because I will be talking about some of the men who have come in and out of my life. I won't go into too much detail, but I want it to be known that the events described in this book happened. It is safe to say I have had challenging relationships with some of the men listed here, but even so, they helped make me the person I am today and for that I am thankful.

Harold Blakeley, Sr., my father

My father was born in 1907 and was old school. His mother, who wasn't married to his father, left him when he was two years old, so he never enjoyed the warmth of a mother or his father.

My father worked really hard all his life and when he bought the hotel, it became his world. I really think he didn't know how to show affection, as he had never had it himself. I loved and respected my father. I just wish I'd had more time with him.

Harold, my brother

My brother is seven years older than me and for some reason, Harold and I have never got on. Even as a child he seemed to dislike me. When we lost the hotel, a bad situation became even worse. But even though we do not get along, I feel for him; he is not married, he doesn't have any children and is very bitter. I would love to bring him into our family, but he doesn't want to be involved. When I do see him, I just want to give him a big hug, but he is so aloof that I can't.

My brother seemed to be forced into a life he did not want or choose. Dad had the hotel, so of course, the son is expected to take over the family business. However, I believe that Harold's talents lay elsewhere. He is very artistic, and musical, he can play the drums, and is a beautiful painter. I believe he is a soul who should have been free to pursue his passion for the arts; this is where he shines the brightest. When it came to running the hotel, he was hamstrung from the start, since he is not a people-person or a hard worker like my father. The hotel wasn't where his future should have been.

But this does say something: let your children follow their passion and purpose in life. Don't make decisions for them or force them to do things that they don't want to do. Let them make their own mistakes, so they can learn from them.

Bruce, my first husband

It may look like Bruce was awful to me—and back then I thought he was—but our relationship was doomed from the start. He eventually met someone more like him and he fell in love with her. Why should I take that away from him? He only did what he had to do, even though the children and I got hurt in the process. I went right off the rails when we broke up, but it is all about life's lessons, and as with all difficult experiences, I just had to go through it to get me to where I am now. The children were young and adapted well. The children of divorce do fine as long as there is no nastiness between the "ex's."

Bruce took the children every weekend, which was good because I was going through difficult times and with him, they had some stability. The major thing Bruce and I never did was bad-mouth each other to the children and I find this is crucial. Even if you can't get on as partners, the other person is still your child's mother or father and you must respect that.

When I look back on my relationship with Bruce, I can say for certain that I loved him. He was my first love, but I really think I went into the relationship for the wrong reasons. The main reason I wanted to get married was to get out of my parents' house. The other reason was I just wanted to be loved. Looking back, Bruce and I had very little in common and it was for the best that we went our separate ways.

Bruce remarried and I couldn't wish for a better stepmother for my children than Anne. Certainly, I didn't like her in the beginning, but she did the right thing by my children and she made Bruce happy, which I couldn't do. It was a lot for her to take on a partner with two children—not very many people can do that sort of thing. You have to be special, and I truly thank her for everything she has done.

What I am trying to stress here is that if your relationship breaks down, don't take the name calling and finger pointing path; it only makes matters worse and hurts people. Most of all, it will hurt your children. Just understand that although it is painful, it happened for a reason, and move on with your life.

If that hadn't happened to me, I would never have met Rob, my wonderful husband of 35 years, and we wouldn't have had our son, Kane.

Now I am going say something here that I am not proud of, but that is what this book is about, isn't it?

Writing this book has been an amazing journey for me. I have gone back and re-examined my life and many of the decisions I have made. And to tell you the truth, looking back on where I was and the things I have done, I was shocked. Sometimes, when you put it all together, it doesn't look good.

As I mentioned, Bruce left when Ryan was six weeks old; Sharon wasn't quite one year and I didn't meet my husband, Rob, for another five years. But, in that five years before Rob, I lived with six different guys and in between them, I dated other men. Luckily, my children were young and don't remember most of them, only the two that were more involved in their lives. Looking back on it, I should have held back and respected myself more.

Rob Mulvay, my husband

Today when Rob and I see people from our past, they are amazed we are still together. To the outside observer, it would appear that our relationship was doomed from the beginning, with all the fighting and breaking up and making up. We have been through some turbulent times together, but it has made us stronger. Now we both realize just how much we love, respect and need each other.

As I look back on all my past relationships I can tell you that I have NEVER experienced from anyone else the love that I receive from Rob and the love I have for Rob. If Bruce hadn't left me, I would never have found this and, of course, Rob and I would never have had Kane.

When I decided to write this chapter, I thought it would be good for Rob and I to discuss it, so one day we went out for lunch. To my surprise, it turns out he feels the exact same way I do. I wanted to share this with you.

So many times we have said that that when we're together we just want to "crawl into each other," but Rob has a better way of putting it. He said it is the moulding of each of our personalities to become one. How true this is; over the years, you get so in tune with each other, that sometimes you don't even need to speak. It feels wonderful.

When Rob goes to work, every now and then, I will still put a little note in his smoko box, just to let him know how I feel and what he means to me.

We express our love all the time and don't take it for granted. The little sweet touches we exchange as we walk past each other, or the hug in the kitchen for no reason. The kisses, not just one, but at least two kisses, when we wake up, go to work, get home, go to bed. And all the sneaky ones in between.

When we are both home during the middle of the day, and if we feel like a bit of loving, well we can and we do, just because we can.

Going to bed at night, we always touch in some way, whether it is touching the other one with our foot or holding hands.

If we are away from each other, we will ring just to say, "I love you," and we never hang up without saying I love you. Even the kids and I say this to each other.

One day recently, Rob got a bit flustered before he went to work. After he left, he called me at 6.30 a.m. and asked, "Did I give you a kiss before I left the house?" and I told him that he did. He replied, "I couldn't remember if I did or not, and I want to tell you that I love you." It was the perfect start to the day, and that is what love does; it makes you happy and content.

I could go on and on about what love is to us, but I think you get the picture. Yes, we are both 63 years old and have been together for 35 years, and we have gone through some terrible times, but look where we are now. Even though my life has been tough sometimes, I wouldn't have wished for it to be any different, as I have learned and grown from all of it.

Appendix II

I love this timeless poem, and I also have the music for it. It was written around 1920 by lawyer Max Ehrmann, who was based in Indiana. The wisdom of many of the old writings is inspiring and that is why I have gathered many Public Domain books on my website. Some of these books were written hundreds of years ago, but they are still inspiring and relevant in today's society.

DESIDERATA

Go placidly amid the noise and haste, and remember what peace there may be in silence. As far as possible, without surrender, be on good terms with all persons.

Speak your truth quietly and clearly, and listen to others, even the dull and ignorant; they too have their story. Avoid loud and aggressive persons; they are vexations to the spirit.

If you compare yourself with others, you may become vain and bitter, for always there will be greater and lesser persons than yourself. Enjoy your achievements as well as your plans.

Keep interested in your own career, however humble, it is a real possession in the changing fortunes of time. Exercise caution in your business affairs, for the world is full of trickery.

But let this not blind you to what virtue there is; many persons strive for high ideals, and everywhere life is full of heroism. Be yourself. Especially, do not feign affection.

Neither be cynical about love, for in the face of all aridity and disenchantment, it is as perennial as the grass. Take kindly the counsel of the years, gracefully surrendering the things of youth.

Nurture strength of spirit to shield you in sudden misfortune. But do not distress yourself with dark imaginings. Many fears are born of fatigue and loneliness.

Beyond a wholesome discipline, be gentle with yourself. You are a child of the universe, no less than the trees and the stars; you have a right to be here. And whether or not it is clear to you, no doubt the universe is unfolding as it should.

Therefore, be at peace with God, whatever you conceive him to be, and whatever your labours and aspirations, in the noisy confusion of life, keep peace with your soul. With all its sham, drudgery and broken dreams, it is still a beautiful world. Be cheerful. Strive to be happy.

Appendix III

Books I have read and seminars I've attended

I have been to a lot of seminars and read a lot of books. Some were better than others.

I am enclosing a list of those that were most memorable to me, the ones that started my journey of self discovery. There have been many and I don't want to overwhelm you, so I am sticking with my favourites.

The most vibrating, power-radiating books that will shape your destiny, enrich your future, and turn your hopes and dreams into solid success-realities are the books I have found in the public domain, books like *Think and Grow Rich* and the *Law of Success in 16 Lessons*, *Acres of Diamonds*. And the list goes on. Once I found these books and tapped into what they were saying, it changed my life forever.

I have them all (if not now, then in the future, as I will keep adding to this list) on my website for you to download. Some have been around a hundred years, but they are extremely inspirational and we can still use the advice they contain in this day and age.

Robert Kiyosaki, <u>Rich Dad Poor Dad</u>

This was the first book I read of Robert's, and it is absolutely brilliant. Give it to your kids; I did. School teaches us nothing about money, and the result is that people learn to work for money, but never learn to have money work for them.

Also check out:

Robert Kiyosaki, **Rich Dad Poor Dad for Teens**

Robert T. Kiyosaki and Sharon L. Lechter, **Rich Dad's Guide to Becoming Rich… Without Cutting Up Your Credit Cards**

Robert T. Kiyosaki and Sharon L. Lechter, **Rich Dad's Who Took My Money?: Why Slow Investors Lose and Fast Money Wins!**

I picked up one of Jan Summer's books when I was in Nutrimetics and this was when I realized that I needed to get into property to get ahead. All her book are fantastic:

Jan Somers, **Building Wealth Through Investment Property**

Jan Somers, **Building wealth in Changing Times**

Jan Somers, **More Wealth from Residential Property**

Jan Somers, **Building Wealth Story by Story**

Anthony Robbins

Tony is an extraordinarily successful entrepreneur; he has been a consultant to businesses and governments all over the world. He shows you his most effective strategies and techniques for mastering your emotions, body, relationships, finances, and life. He has been a huge influence on my life.

Some of Anthony's seminars I have attended:

Unleash the Power Within (Both my sons and Rob attended, as well.)

Date with Destiny

Wealth Mastery

Real Estate Mastery

Life Mastery (Rob also came with me)

Anthony Robbins also has a huge range of DVDs, which I highly recommend.

Awaken the Giant Within

Giant Steps

Inner Strength

Notes from a Friend

On the Tropic of Time

Unlimited Power

Unlimited Power, A Black Choice

Energy for Life

Andrew Matthews

I have read all of Andrews's books and I gave my son Kane *Follow Your Heart*, which helped turn him around. When Ryan was going through a hard time just recently, I recommended Andrew's books to him and they helped him, as well. They are easy to read and powerful:

Andrew Matthews, Follow Your Heart

This is about doing what you love, dealing with problems, finding your power, and peace of mind. Finding Purpose in Your Life and Work.

Andrew Matthews, Making friends

About the people we love, who help and depend on us. People who we want to see and don't want to see. It's about enjoying the company of other people, dealing with "doom," how to say no. It's about understanding that if you want friendship, you must first be a friend.

Andrew Matthews, Happiness Now

A book for busy people! It is about balancing relationships, finding career success, prosperity and peace of mind.

Andrew Matthews, Being a Happy Teen

Do you ever wish **you were older? Had more money? Looked different? Had different parents?** Do you ever feel, **"No one understands me!"** Do you ever wonder, **"Will I fall in love?"** Do you ever ask, **"Am I normal?"** If you answered "yes" to half of the above, you sound perfectly normal.

Andrew Matthews, Happiness in a Nutshell

A hugely popular, pocket-sized book of Andrew Matthews' favourite sayings.

Andrew Matthews, Happiness and Hard Times

This one will feature my story! A fantastic book on survival.

Tony Melvin, <u>From Red To Black: How To Get Out Of Debt</u>

How to make and control money. This shows you how to communicate with creditors, avoid going bankrupt, minimise stress, achieve financial goals, and lots more.

Tony Melvin Ed Chad <u>Wealth for Life</u>

This also includes my story. A wealth creation strategy on how to acquire wealth.

Dale Beaumont, <u>Secrets of Male Entrepreneurs Exposed</u>

I started to read Dale's books and needed an answer to a question, so I emailed him. He didn't e-mail me back. He rang me! I was so impressed that I made a point of learning more about him.

He has a course on how to write and publish a book, so I bought it and that was the start of my journey of writing my memoirs. He was the person who suggested I call the book "overcoming." We weren't sure about the rest, but that beginning was the structure of the whole book and future books that I will write. What I love about his books is that he interviews people from all walks of life, so you are presented with a whole range of different people's outlooks on things.

Dale's other books include:

<u>Secrets of Property Millionaires Exposed</u>
<u>Secrets of Female Entrepreneurs Exposed</u>
<u>Secrets of Young Achievers Exposed</u>
<u>Secrets of Small business Owners Exposed</u>
<u>Secrets of Great Public Speakers Exposed</u>
<u>Secrets of Inspiring Women Exposed</u>
<u>Secrets of Great Success Coaches Exposed</u>
<u>Secrets of Entrepreneurs Under 40 Exposed</u>
<u>Secrets of Top business Builders Exposed</u>
<u>Secrets of Top Sales Professionals Exposed</u>
<u>Secrets of Marketing Experts Exposed</u>
<u>Secrets of Stock Market Traders Exposed</u>
<u>Secrets of Inspiring Leaders Exposed</u>
<u>Secrets of Internet Entrepreneurs Exposed</u>

T. Harv Eker, Secrets of the Millionaire Mind: Mastering the Inner Game of Wealth

Fantastic book! It changed my mindset about money. Then I gave it to Rob, and he couldn't put it down. Because we have been bankrupt, we needed to get that out of our head.

Jack Canfield, Mark Victor Hansen and Peter Vegso, Chicken Soup for the Soul

They have written a huge amount of books and tell inspiring stories of people from all different walks of life and all different circumstances.

John Gray, Men Are from Mars, Women Are from Venus: The Classic Guide to Understanding the Opposite Sex

A practical guide for improving communication and getting what you want in your relationships. I have seen John Gray at seminars a few times and he is a crack up!

Tom Venuto, The Body Fat Solution: Five Principles for Burning Fat, Building Lean Muscles, Ending Emotional Eating, and Maintaining Your Perfect Weight

This book is amazing! It contains a lot of good, quality information, but it is also easy to understand. It has become a constant reference guide for me in my battle to keep fit and healthy. This book was a big turning point in my life and it helped me understand what exactly happens in the "eat, exercise and lose weight" cycle. I would recommend this book to anyone.

Bill Phillips, Body for Life: 12 Weeks to Mental and Physical Strength

This is an excellent book if you're a fitness beginner who's trying to figure out how to get in shape and stay in shape. It's also good if you've been working out and/or dieting for a while and don't seem to be making much headway towards losing weight and getting in shape. Phillips does a good job of explaining the basic building blocks of fitness and debunks a lot of the more prevalent fitness myths. He covers the proper way to exercise, both aerobic and weight training, the proper way to eat (not some fad diet but rather, how to eat real food in a healthy way), and how to motivate yourself and keep yourself motivated to stick to your goals.

Stephen R. Covey, The 7 Habits of Highly Effective People

Applied knowledge is the quickest and safest path to success in any area of life. Stephen Covey has encapsulated the strategies used by all those who are highly effective. Success can be learned and this book is an excellent way to learn how to do that.

Stephen R. Covey, First Things First

This is a must-read for professionals in any walk of life. Covey and the Merrills (the co-authors) promote a principle-centred leadership style focusing on personal leadership. Their philosophy is that you can't lead others unless you can lead your own life first. The authors promote that when a person aligns his or her life with internal principles, then that person is able to focus on what's important, not what's urgent.

Stephen R. Covey, Principle Centered Leadership

We learn Covey's philosophy for creating more meaningful relationships and successes in the workplace—something we should be striving to implement throughout business and industry. He shows us how to implement these techniques in the home and elsewhere, and the result is that we will be rewarded with happiness and a fulfilling future.

Graeme Alford, Never Give Up: the Power of Mental Toughness

I gave this book to my son Kane and it helped him immensely. This book tells it all! Graeme destroyed his family and his career and even went to jail. His comeback from, and triumph over, adversity is a clear message to us all.

A final message from a great artist:

"What would life be if we had no courage to attempt anything?"

—*Vincent Van Gogh*

www.ingramcontent.com/pod-product-compliance
Lightning Source LLC
Chambersburg PA
CBHW050527300426
44113CB00012B/1985